About Jim Haynes

Before becoming a professional entertainer in 1988 Jim Haynes, who has master's degrees in literature from the University of New England and the University of Wales, taught in schools and universities from outback New South Wales to Britain and back again. Since then he has toured extensively here and overseas, appeared regularly on television and worked in radio. He has released many albums of his own songs, verse and humour and has produced volumes of verse for the ABC.

Jim is four times winner of the Comedy Song of the Year Award at the Tamworth Festival, his biggest hits being 'Don't Call Wagga Wagga Wagga' and 'Since Cheryl Went Feral'. He won the Bush Laureate Book of the Year Award in 1996 for his collection of verse *I'll Have Chips* and again in 2001 for his compilation *An Australian Heritage of Verse*. He is also the author of a volume of stories *Memories of Weelabarabak: Stories of a Bush Town*, and the very successful *Great Australian Book of Limericks*.

AN AUSTRALIAN
TREASURY OF
POPULAR VERSE

JIM HAYNES

ABC
BOOKS

For Robyn

Published by ABC Books for the
AUSTRALIAN BROADCASTING CORPORATION
GPO Box 9994 Sydney NSW 2001

Copyright © this collection Jim Haynes 2002
Copyright © in individual poems remains with the authors

First published October 2002
Reprinted December 2002

National Library of Australia
Cataloguing-in-Publication entry
    An Australian treasury of popular verse.
    ISBN 0 7333 1022 2.
    1. Australian poetry. I. Haynes, Jim. II. Australian
    Broadcasting Corporation.
A821.008

Cover design by Jane Cameron/Fisheye
Set in 11.5/14 pt Bembo by
Midland Typesetters, Maryborough, Victoria
Colour files by Colorwize, Adelaide
Printed and bound in Australia by
Griffin Press, Adelaide

5 4 3 2

Contents

Thanks

I would like to thank The Mitchell Library, State Library of New South Wales; The National War Memorial; the compilers of previous verse anthologies, including Nancy Keesing and Douglas Stewart, AB 'Banjo' Paterson, Bill Scott, Bill Wannan and David Mulhallen; Jacqueline Kent for her advice and quality control; Sally Cohen who did the typing; John Derum and Margaret Weissman for their help with CJ Dennis; Stuart Neal of ABC Books for once again allowing me to indulge my passion for Australiana; Russell Hannah; Frank Daniel; Grahame Watt; and everybody who bought my previous collection, *An Australian Heritage of Verse*. I should also like to acknowledge Patricia Rolfe's history of the *Bulletin*, *The Journalistic Javelin*. The poems by Blue the Shearer are from his forthcoming collection, and appear here courtesy of Col Wilson.

Editor's Note

This selection is designed as an old-fashioned 'treasury' of Australian rhymed verse for modern times, a cross between an Australian version of Palgrave's famous treasury of British verse and the collections of amusing and entertaining short verses that were popular when I was a child. It is restricted to rhymed verse and I have attempted to include verse which is of interest to the general population.

It is not a literary collection. Included are ditties, folk poetry, doggerel, 'bush' verse and also some beautifully crafted reflective, humorous and thought-provoking 'poetry'. It is verse that I hope will appeal to all kinds of readers.

The poets represented are a mixture of past and present writers and the style of the verse varies from rather archaic to modern. While some of the older verse requires a little effort to read, this collection is easily accessible to anyone with a basic education and a layman's understanding of Australian culture, history and lifestyle.

The verse here is meant to be read for pleasure. I am very mindful of the huge resurgence in recitation of popular verse and the use of verse as public entertainment in recent times. With so many festivals and competitions based on verse these days I have attempted to make this collection a compendium of verse for reciters. Here are poems for all occasions and all types of audiences.

One reason I have called the collection a treasury is that many of the poems are either discovered or rediscovered treasures. One of the most satisfying things about *An Australian Heritage of Verse*, the last collection of verse I compiled, was that I received so many similar responses from readers. Many were thrilled to rediscover verse for which they had long been searching, others were just as happy to be exposed to verse never previously anthologised (hidden in long out-of-print books and magazines) and still others enjoyed finding the work of many new writers of rhymed verse. There are many verses in this collection which also fit into these three categories. Rather than listing the verse by author or chronology I have arranged it under broad-based categories where a subject or theme gives each section some cohesion.

I have attempted to spread the humorous verse around and to separate it into several categories. Thus, there is a general section of humorous verse, 'Lies and Laughter', and the more acerbic comic verse will be found in the sections titled 'Comments and Curses' and 'Satires and Sarcasms', but humorous verse also occurs in every section of the book, as you might expect.

If any readers wonder why certain classic verses are not included in this collection of over 500 Australian poems, it is almost certainly because they are included in *An Australian Heritage of Verse*, my previous collection for ABC Books. None of the poems in that collection of almost 400 are included in this anthology of over 500. The two collections are entirely different and therefore complementary.

Some fine verse has been omitted simply because I had many examples covering a particular topic, theme, opinion or attitude. Many are here because they fitted the bill when I needed a particular viewpoint or mood. While I haven't been able to include all the verse covering particular topics, I have attempted to give readers a wide range and experience of Australian popular verse to enjoy.

INTRODUCTION

Digging for Treasure

My idea in assembling this collection was to present a treasure trove of various kinds of rhyming Australian verse, written over the last two hundred years, purely for enjoyment. I have attempted to include old favourites, half-forgotten poems, long-forgotten poems, completely undiscovered verse and new work by contemporary writers. The whole lot number more than five hundred. They vary greatly in subject material and literary quality but have two things in common – they all rhyme and they are all, with one notable exception, Australian.

The exception is 'The Anzacs' by Edgar Wallace, a wonderful tribute to the Australian and New Zealand Army Corps written within months of the landing at Gallipoli. I decided to 'borrow' the poem for the collection on the grounds that, although it is the work of an Englishman, it expresses a clear sense of Australian patriotism. Perhaps its English origins are not surprising; after all, many so-called Australian poets such as Charles Thatcher, Harry 'The Breaker' Morant and Will Ogilvie were born in Britain and never became Australian citizens. (It was not possible to be naturalised in their day, of course: Britons choosing to reside here were considered Australian.)

So, where does all this Australian verse come from? I wish I could say with 'Banjo' Paterson:

I have gathered these stories afar, in the wind and the rain,
In the land where the cattle camps are, on the edge of the plain.

While I am sure some of the verse by Harry Morant, EJ Brady and Bruce Simpson was written in cattle camps, I have gathered it from just about everywhere *except* a cattle camp on the edge of a plain. I found these poems in many obvious places and in some quite unexpected places too.

Some verse comes from colonial times, the period from the earliest

1

years of European settlement through to the gold rushes and expansion of the 1860s. Then come many poems from the golden period of the *Bulletin*, which developed and articulated the popular version of the Australian national character from the 1880s to the 1930s. Finally there is quite a large representation from the last sixty years, from World War II through to the 'bush verse' resurgence of the present day.

The colonial period is represented by some notable early poets such as Charles Thatcher, who wrote delightful satirical and humorous doggerel for the general public, and Charles Harpur, whose more lyrical descriptive verse heralds that of Henry Kendall, another pre-*Bulletin* poet and our finest descriptive verse writer of the nineteenth century.

Such poets as John Dumore Lang, Marcus Clarke and Ernest Favenc are also represented from this period. Much of their work has often been anthologised and is not too difficult to find in print, although some of their verse included here, particularly the more light-hearted examples, took some tracking down.

Most of the 'buried treasures' dug up for this volume actually come from the *Bulletin* period. Hundreds of poets and verse writers were discovered and published by *Bulletin* editors AG Stephens, James Edmond and SH Pryor from the 1880s through to the 1920s. Ironically, then, in this age of plenty many treasures became 'lost'.

However, certain poets became very famous indeed. Paterson, Lawson, CJ Dennis, and to a lesser extent Will Ogilvie and Mary Gilmore became the great names of Australian verse. Their most popular verses were much anthologised and recited, studied, learned and, indeed loved by ordinary Australians. Much of their work has remained popular long after their deaths.

But the passing of time has robbed new generations of some of their best verse. Mary Gilmore's classic popular poem of 1940, 'No Foe Shall Gather Our Harvest' (featured at the time as a lead article in the *Australian Women's Weekly*, no less) had long been out of print when I included it in *An Australian Heritage of Verse*. Similarly, many of the most amusing and appealing works by Paterson, Lawson and CJ Dennis are totally unknown to today's readers and reciters. All three wrote prolifically, Dennis alone more than 3000 poems, from which I've yet to find a 'dud'. Many less well-known poems from these famous poets are included here.

Another group of *Bulletin* poets have fared much worse. Dorothea Mackellar, WT Goodge, Barcroft Boake, Harry Morant and Thomas E Spencer are mostly remembered for one or two well-anthologised poems. These 'one-hit wonders' were all writers of excellent, entertaining and moving verse. I have spent many wonderful hours with long-forgotten volumes in the literary Aladdin's Cave that is the Mitchell Library of the State Library of New South Wales, in an attempt to redress the balance.

Morant is a particularly interesting case. I find his best verses most appealing and refreshingly honest, though perhaps politically incorrect by today's revisionist standards. 'The Breaker' is well known as an historic figure due to a number of successful books and a popular film. He has become a symbol of Australian independence and his story is a rallying point for republican sentiment. Yet his verse is little known today; indeed, many people feel strongly about what he represents but are unaware that he was a poet too.

The real forgotten poets of our Australian verse heritage include *Bulletin* poets Charles Souter from South Australia and Lawson's mates and contemporaries EJ Brady, Victor Daley and Jim Grahame. Their poetry has virtually disappeared over recent decades with the odd exception such as Jim Grahame's 'Whalan of Waitin'-a-While'.

And what jewels are among the lost works of these neglected poets! Grahame's wonderfully wry reflective verses about ageing, Daley's biting satires and Souter's touching visions of bush life and sailing days still glitter with the lustre of recognition, compassion and relevance. I think they are timeless verses. Written in an era when people had more time to read and ponder the human condition, these verses are still vibrant today and have, for today's readers, a lovely patina of nostalgia.

Kenneth Slessor, a well-known poet much studied in schools and universities, wrote a great deal that needs rediscovery. Slessor's epic poem, 'Five Bells', recently won a radio poll as Sydney's best-loved poem, but his delightfully ironic and wistful rhymed verse is virtually unknown today, even though his collections *Darlinghurst Nights* and *Backless Betty from Bondi* were republished in the 1980s. I have included my favourites from those collections here.

3

Like Slessor, Leon Gellert, also a Sydney journalist and editor, is remembered for one section of his work. The poetry Gellert wrote as an Anzac has been well anthologised, but his delightfully silly animal rhymes are seldom seen today. In this collection they are well represented, along with some of the poetry he wrote on Anzac Cove, which you will find in the section 'Deployments and Despatches'.

Some of the poetry in that section comes from the archives of the Australian War Memorial. The time I spent researching there I found not only rewarding but very moving. The number of soldiers who wrote verse in both world wars is staggering. From young privates to top-ranking officers, bush lads and farmers to city boys, their handwriting was mostly copperplate and their English expression exemplary. They obviously had a very different basic education to the one offered today, perhaps not as comprehensive, but effective.

The poetry uncovered in the War Memorial came from several sources: letters home, the many small magazines printed behind the lines during World War I and contributions to the official wartime collections such as *The Anzac Book* and *Khaki and Green*. The verse is filled with beautifully expressed patriotism, resignation, homesickness and questioning, as well as ironic humour and a stoic acceptance of the soldier's lot.

The handwritten poems and letters from Anzac Cove are so poignant to read that I dare the most cynical reader to attempt the task without being moved to tears. We are incredibly fortunate as a nation to have an institution like the Australian War Memorial preserving this part of our heritage. The treasures unearthed there for this collection are merely a small sample of the wealth of published, unpublished and personal material preserved there.

Not all the war poetry collected here was found in the War Memorial, however. My discovery of Tip Kelaher's verse was one of those strange synchronistic coincidences. I happened to purchase at auction part of the library of the estate of a distinguished scholar, Professor HJ Oliver. Consequently I discovered that he and I had attended the same school and that he had lived just around the corner from my current home for many years, although we never met. A few days later, among a pile of books in a secondhand shop, I found *The Digger Hat*, a collection of verse by Tip Kelaher, with an introduction by Professor Oliver. That connection encouraged me to pick the volume out and open it, only to find that Oliver had written the introduction because Kelaher, killed in action in Egypt in 1942, had been his best friend and schoolmate.

The slim volume of verse was published just three months after Kelaher's death and the verses are honest expressions of humour, patriotism and a deep homesickness for the bush life he knew and the Sydney he loved. Coincidentally I had lived in the same suburbs of Sydney and the same area of north-west New South Wales as Tip Kelaher, and I happen to share his enthusiasm for Randwick racecourse and Coogee beach. His verse moved me deeply and I have included quite a bit of it in this book.

After World War II rhymed verse was rather unfashionable. From this period I have included some short, well-crafted lyrical verse by poets like Ernest G Moll, Roland Robinson and Ronald McCuaig. At this time, the champions of popular rhymed verse were apt to be the anthologists such as Nancy Keesing and Douglas Stewart, Bill Scott and Bill Wannan, who edited collections of work by earlier and anonymous poets.

For many years Bill Wannan presided over the verse and Australiana columns of the popular magazine *Australasian Post*, publishing much topical verse submitted by readers. In the final two years of the magazine's life, 2000 and 2001, I became the last person to hold that position. Poor old *Aussie Post* was on its last legs, but the magazine's last editor, Gil Chalmers, allowed me to solicit rhymed verse from its devoted readers right to the bitter end. The massive amounts of verse that arrived each week belied the magazine's falling circulation and convinced me that there is still a strong love of rhymed verse among ordinary Australians.

Many of the verses that appeared in my column before the magazine's end, and some that I never had the chance to use, are part of this collection. None of the writers of those verses has ever been published or anthologised, with the notable exception of Wilbur Howcroft, so more buried treasure was added to the hoard.

Wilbur Howcroft, from the Mallee district of Victoria, a regular contributor to that *Aussie Post* column, is one representative of another kind of poet: the writer of quality rhymed verse who is little known outside their local area. Verse like his often becomes popular with 'bush verse' performers and is passed around until it becomes wrongly credited as anonymous. This has happened to other writers such as Bruce Simpson and Col 'Blue the Shearer' Wilson. Some of Bruce Simpson's early poems became so much part of the general repertoire of reciters that their authorship was mistakenly credited to people who had regularly used them to entertain.

When I was 'doing the poetry' on the popular ABC radio program 'Australian All Over' in the late 1980s I came to realise how many local poets were out there, writers like Grahame Watt in northern Victoria, the late Charlie Marshall in central Queensland and Neil Carroll in the central west of New South Wales. Most of these poets' work was known only through the local press and radio but the revival of 'bush verse' as entertainment has brought their work to a wider audience.

So the final category of hidden verse treasures are the poems that until now have been available only in the self-published volumes sold at folk festivals, country music events and bush verse gatherings. Poets such as Janine Haigh, Glenny Palmer, Bobby Miller and Frank Daniel are stars in the 'bush verse' performance arena and, while aficionados are well aware of their verse, readers unfamiliar with the folk and country music scene may never have encountered their work until now.

These works are somewhat easier to track down now that an established set of recognised national awards exists for published and recorded verse. The Australian Bush Laureate Awards attract most of the self-published books and albums of verse to compete for recognition with books and CDs produced by publishers and record companies. The number of good-quality publications and albums entered for these awards increases annually.

Occasionally someone simply walks up and presents a treasure from their attic or basement. The woman who presented Frank Daniel with a rare signed volume of Jim Grahame's collected verse after a performance one day at Tamworth certainly saved me many hours of research, as did Frank who allowed me to borrow the precious book in order to plunder its treasures for this volume.

People like Frank Daniel and my good mate Grahame Watt are always 'putting me wise' to good contemporary writers of rhymed

6

verse as well as helping me track down half-remembered fragments. I thank them for being crewmates on my voyage of discovery and treasure-hunting.

So not all the gems were found in the Mitchell Library or the Australian War Memorial. They have come from many times and many places: some quite well-known to particular audiences or at particular times, others very well hidden. Some were unearthed by my habit of haunting secondhand book shops across Australia. Luckily I have been able to indulge this part of the search while pursuing my 'day job' as a touring performer.

My 'day job' also comes in handy when I get to spend time travelling and sharing ideas with people knowledgeable in the area of our verse heritage. Slim Dusty, Joy McKean, Ted Egan and the friends who write for them and share that heritage, such as Kelly Dixon and Bruce Simpson, have all contributed to this volume and my previous collection in different ways.

A selection of verse as wide as this, ranging as it does from the jokey jingles of Anon through acerbic though ephemeral social comment and observation to some beautiful poetry by the likes of Lawson and Kendall at their best, can risk becoming a collection that is too diffuse. I hope the treasure chest accommodates and displays the range of gems, from precious diamonds and well-worked gold to baubles and trinkets, to your satisfaction. I conclude with A.B. 'Banjo' Paterson's apology for the less literary verses:

> They are just the rude stories one hears in sadness and mirth,
> The records of wandering years, and scant is their worth.
> Though their merits indeed are but slight, I shall not repine,
> If they give you one moment's delight, old comrades of mine.

Lies and Laughter

Secular Speculations

Rhymed verse and humour go hand in hand. Ditties, doggerel, limericks, kids' rhymes and games and insults – all these have long been part of the Anglo-Celtic verse tradition.

In the Australian 'bush' verse tradition this tendency is, if anything, even stronger. The very first identifiable published example of a 'bush ballad' is usually accepted to be 'Sam Holt' by GH Gibson (Ironbark) in the *Bulletin* in March 1881. It was a good example of humorous doggerel, sarcastic, unoriginal, parodying a popular song of the time, and using 'broad' humour. The humour in 'Sam Holt' is a higher priority than literary merit – a tendency in 'bush' verse which has continued.

But many examples of humour, satire and sarcasm can be found in colonial rhymed verse long before 'Sam Holt'. Charles Thatcher and Marcus Clarke regularly used this type of rhymed verse as a vehicle for humour and satire long before the *Bulletin*.

In this section I have included the more light-hearted verse. Some examples are silly and nonsensical in the tradition of British nonsense verse, some are whimsical and serendipitous, some use broad humour, some are fine examples of the tall tale tradition of comedy narrative. There are also a few examples of children's playground ditties and rhymes.

Secular Speculations
Wilbur G Howcroft

Do daughters of vicars
Wear calico knickers
Or do they wear panties quite brief;
Or like Eve before 'em,
With lack of decorum,
Make do with a rather slight leaf?

Do daughters of deacons
Wear sweaters like beacons
To fill all male viewers with lust;
Or were they taught early
A well-brought-up girlie
Possessed no such thing as a bust?

Do daughters of wowsers
Parade in tight trousers
That show off their shape to a T;
Or do they wear dresses
(The idea oppresses)
That reach from the neck to the knee?

Do daughters of preachers
Appear on our beaches
In bathing gear scanty but cute;
Or are they forbidden,
And made to keep hidden
What killjoys would have us refute?

Cousin Robert
Russell Hannah

We've got a cousin Robert who can talk you half to death,
He'll talk for days and weeks and months and never stop for
    breath,
When he enters talking contests he puts on quite a show,
He makes all the other entrants look like Marcel Marceau.

They say that talking as a sport may soon be recognised
Like Tae Kwon Do and swimming, the kind that's synchronised.
For talking's universal and it's done in every nation
And the world controlling body is the Talking Federation.

There'll be specialist divisions, like talking through your hat,
And talking through your pocket, and when you chew the fat.
There'll be talking under water, there'll be talking to a crowd
There'll be talking very softly, and talking very loud.

And at the next Olympics will talking be the sport,
That everybody talks about? If not, it bloody ought!
We'll let politicians enter but I reckon we should try,
A system where they score more points if they don't tell a lie.

With all this talk of talking I think that I've digressed,
For what this poem was all about was Robert, he's the best.
He'll be the medal favourite, he's sure to win the gold,
All the other talkers will be left out in the cold.

He is so good that he would be impossible to beat.
So far in front would Robert be the judges couldn't cheat.
What motivates this man of words? Ask him if you dare,
As long as you're on holidays and have a week to spare.

Does he talk for fame and fortune? Does it give him a great high?
Or does he talk to compensate for being a bit shy?
Is it the cheering of the throng? Is it the victor's crown?
(Though the crowd are wearing hearing aids and have 'em all
    turned down?)

Those of us who know him well (his deafened kith and kin)
Know what it is that gives him his amazing will to win.
The thing that drives him on, you see, with victory in reach,
Is the knowledge that the winner gets to make a victory speech.

Prunes

Anon

Prunes, prunes, the musical fruit,
The more you eat the more you toot.
What are prunes? There's some dissension.
But I think they're plums gone on the pension!

The Traveller

CJ Dennis

As I rode in to Burrumbeet,
I met a man with funny feet;
And, when I paused to ask him why
His feet were strange, he rolled his eye
And said the rain would spoil the wheat;
So I rode on to Burrumbeet.

As I rode in to Beetaloo,
I met a man whose nose was blue;
And when I asked him how he got
A nose like that, he answered, 'What
Do bullocks mean when they say 'Moo'?'
So I rode on to Beetaloo.

As I rode in to Ballarat,
I met a man who wore no hat;
And, when I said he might take cold,
He cried, 'The hills are quite as old
As yonder plains, but not so flat.'
So I rode on to Ballarat.

As I rode in to Gundagai,
I met a man and passed him by
Without a nod, without a word.
He turned, and said he'd never heard
Or seen a man so wise as I.
But I rode on to Gundagai.

As I rode homeward, full of doubt,
I met a stranger riding out:
A foolish man he seemed to me;
But, 'Nay, I am yourself,' said he,
'Just as you were when you rode out.'
So I rode homeward, free of doubt.

I Met a Man

Anon

As I was going up the stair
I met a man who wasn't there.
He wasn't there again today.
Gee, I wish he'd go away.

Who?

Ross Noble

Who gets to cut the barber's hair
Or pull a dentist's teeth?
Who makes a banker's personal loan?
Who makes the florist's wreath?

Who fixes up mechanics' cars
Or neurosurgeons' brains?
What if tow-trucks have a prang
Or physios get strains?

Who judges what the judges do
Or nurses nurse when ill?
Who sits the babysitter's kids?
Prescribes the doctor's pill?

When the undertaker dies
Who plants him in the ground?
And when the searchers all get lost
Who's left to look around?

What if fire trucks catch fire?
Who saves a lifeguard's life?
What if umpires can't agree
Or police get into strife?

I guess I'm really lucky,
My job's not on that list.
So I can go on loafing
'Cos I know I won't be missed.

The Night We Shot the Pig

Neil Carroll ('Hipshot')

I've shot a few foxes and 'roos in my time
And ducks. Mate, I'm really a corker.
But one shooting incident sticks in my mind
It's the night that we got the big porker.

We were having some trouble with foxes, for sure
They were pinching the eggs and the fowls,
And you should have heard them the evening before
With the yaps and the squawks and the growls.

Next morning we missed a few chicks from the run
And the old broody leghorn was fretting.
We saw where a pig had been having some fun;
He'd pushed a great hole in the netting.

So we worked out a way to give him a pay
'Twas too cold to sit up all night.
We loaded the gun, ran a string round the run,
Hooked it up to the trigger . . . just right.

It was well after dark when we heard a dog bark
Then a squeal, with a high note of warning,
A grunt and a cough and both barrels went off.
We had fifteen dead chooks in the morning.

But all jokes aside, it worked and he died
In the lignum and didn't Mum rouse;
Imagine the smell when he started to swell!
Nearly drove us all out of the house.

So we dragged him away, and we burnt him one day
And I've still got the tusks from his jowls.
But from then evermore we bought eggs from the store . . .
'Cause the dogs ate the rest of the fowls.

A Salesman Named Phipps

Anon

They've buried a salesman named Phipps.
Who married, on one of his trips,
A widow named Block
And then died of shock,
When he found there were five little chips.

My Homeland

Wilbur G Howcroft

In the Mallee swamps where the crayfish romps
And the mugwump howls to the moon,
Where the mopoke hoots at the bandicoots
And the sunburnt bullfrogs croon.

Where the bunyips play at the break of day
And the blowflies start to sing,
Where the maggots prance in a stately dance
And you hear the dingbats ring.

In the Mallee heat where the mud-eyes bleat
And the hoop-snake builds its nest,
Where the bull-ant roars at the cuspidors
And the titmouse rubs its chest.

When the day is done with the rising sun
And the moon shines when it's sunny,
There's a bumble bee with a busted knee
Through falling off its honey.

Where the earwigs run in the midnight sun
And the morning peewee thrives,
Where the botfly darts at your underparts
As the tawny frogmouth jives.

In the Mallee sky where the emus fly
And the wild bull tomtits call,
'Cross the sandhills damp see the white ants tramp
While the kangaroosters brawl.

The Parable of the Two Bulls
Ron Ball

On a hillside out in Arnhem Land,
Two scrub bulls scouted out the land,
An old one, wise and fat and strong,
And his yearling son who tagged along.
They chanced upon this valley green;
The young one gasped to see the scene,
Cows and heifers, rolling fat,
Spread out for miles upon the flat.
The young bull yelled, 'I'm going mad!
Can I race down and do one, Dad?'
But father said, 'Hang on, my boy,
We'll stroll down slowly, just enjoy
The scenery and don't get hot,
And then . . . we'll do the bloody lot.'

My Family Tree
Val Read

My grandad was the local drunk and grandma was a tart,
'Twas she who posed for 'Chloe', Melbourne's famous work of art.
She hangs up there immodestly, as bare as she was born,
Still causing consternation for upholders of reform.

Dad was an SP bookie, as sharp as you could get,
The punters called him 'Shonky' for he rarely paid a bet.
Mother was a barmaid renowned in northern pubs,
My sister's still a stripper in those sleazy Sydney clubs.

My brother is in prison in a constant state of bliss,
He had a big plantation of high-grade cannabis.
My cousin owns a tow-truck and a suspect factory,
Where cars are 'renovated' then transported secretly.

We claim we're law-abiding, just larrikins at heart,
We're descended from Ned Kelly, so we have to play the part.
I'm regarded as a traitor, called the black sheep of my tribe,
'Cause I'm the local copper! (But I'm not above a bribe.)

Cutlery

Jim Haynes

When Asian children learn 'pianner'
In the regimented Asian manner.
Conscientiously they play,
At least an hour every day
(As soon as they can walk and talk!)
A little tune called 'Knife and Fork'.

A Bush Christening

AB Paterson ('The Banjo')

On the outer Barcoo where the churches are few,
And men of religion are scanty,
On a road never cross'd 'cept by folk that are lost,
One Michael Magee had a shanty.

Now this Mike was the dad of a ten-year-old lad,
Plump, healthy, and stoutly conditioned;
He was strong as the best, but poor Mike had no rest
For the youngster had never been christened.

And his wife used to cry, 'If the darlin' should die
Saint Peter would not recognise him.'
But by luck he survived till a preacher arrived,
Who agreed straightaway to baptise him.

Now the artful young rogue, while they held their collogue,
With his ear to the keyhole was listenin',
And he muttered in fright while his features turned white,
'What the divil and all is this christenin'?'

He was none of your dolts, he had seen them brand colts,
And it seemed to his small understanding,
If the man in the frock made him one of the flock,
It must mean something very like branding.

So away with a rush he set off for the bush,
While the tears in his eyelids they glistened –
''Tis outrageous,' says he, 'to brand youngsters like me,
I'll be dashed if I'll stop to be christened!'

Like a young native dog he ran into a log,
And his father with language uncivil,
Never heeding the 'praste' cried aloud in his haste,
'Come out and be christened, you divil!'

But he lay there as snug as a bug in a rug,
And his parents in vain might reprove him,
Till his reverence spoke (he was fond of a joke)
'I've a notion,' says he, 'that'll move him.'

'Poke a stick up the log, give the spalpeen a prog;
Poke him aisy – don't hurt him or maim him,
'Tis not long that he'll stand, I've the water at hand,
As he rushes out this end I'll name him.

'Here he comes, and for shame! ye've forgotten the name –
Is it Patsy or Michael or Dinnis?'
Here the youngster ran out, and the priest gave a shout –
'Take your chance, anyhow, wid "Maginnis"!'

As the howling young cub ran away to the scrub
Where he knew that pursuit would be risky,
The priest, as he fled, flung a flask at his head
That was labelled 'Maginnis's Whisky!'

Now Maginnis Magee has been made a J.P.,
And one thing he hates more than sin is
To be asked by the folk who have heard of the joke,
How he came to be christened 'Maginnis'!

The Man from Blackheath

Anon

There once was a man from Blackheath,
Who sat on a pair of false teeth.
He rose with a start,
And said, 'Bless my heart,
I've bitten myself underneath!'

The Day the Spaceship Took Aunt Meg

Wilbur G Howcroft

The day the spaceship took Aunt Meg
Was funny in a way –
We still recall her wails of woe
Like it was yesterday.

Aunt Meg was letting loose the dog
Beside the chicken coop
When downwards dived a UFO
And took her in one swoop.

They vanished into outer space
As quick as one could wink.
Grandfather got an awful fright
And almost dropped his drink.

'What's Meg a-doin' now?' he growled,
'She's allus been too flighty –
A-gallivantin' round like that
And her still in her nightie!'

But Uncle sadly shook his head
And said, 'Alas, alack,
I can't help feeling worried they
Might bring the old girl back.'

And sure enough that very night
They dumped her off, then fled,
But left a note pinned to the coop:
'Have taken dog instead.'

Quay!

WT Goodge ('The Colonel')

A man wandered down to the Circular Quay,
And over the beautiful harbour looked huay
Exclaiming, 'My heart, I am longing to fluay
Far over the waves of the emerald suay,
The suay, the suay, the emerald suay
Far over the waves of the emerald suay!'

'The love of my heart is unfaithful to muay,
I dreamed that no mortals were happy as wuay!
Oh, cruel, tyrannical, merciless shuay!
More cruel than the waves of the pitiless suay!
The suay, the suay, the thundering suay
The hissing, the foaming, tempestuous suay!'

'And now that my fortunes are all up a truay,
The barque of my life drifting onto the luay,
My bosom still swells with the thought that I'm fruay,
As fruay as the open and rippling suay,
The suay, the suay, the beautiful suay
The leaping, the laughing, the rollicking suay!'
(Then he went to North Shore from the Circular Quay!)

While Shepherds

Anon

While shepherds washed their socks by night
All seated round the tub
A bar of Sunlight soap came down
So they could rub rub rub.

McArthur's Fart

Ron Bath/Andrew Bleby

Back in Donga country there's a tale the old folks tell
Of a man whose name is famous in the town of Bungadell.
And, if you like, I'll tell you all about this little town.
It's a dry and dusty place until the rains come down.

Back in nineteen twenty-seven, when it hadn't rained for weeks.
There was bull-dust in the billabongs and dead sheep in the creeks,
But the hero of our story was soon to help them out –
On the day McArthur farted and saved the town from drought.

Now no one knew too much about this joker from the scrub,
We'd heard some yarns about him from the drovers in the pub,
Some said he came from Bunker's Run and some from Buela's Park
But the one thing that they all agreed – he sure knew how to fart.

Now Bungadell was dry and hard like a three-week-stale old crust,
The sheep were drinking whisky but were only pissing dust,
They had a dam up in the hills, a mile or so from town
That should have filled the water tanks, but not a drop come down.

They sent a deputation up to see what could be wrong
And found they had a problem that they hadn't counted on,
Old Bert's dead horse was blocking up the channel from the dam,
You'd reckon they could shift it but the bloody thing was jammed.

Fifty blokes with crowbars struggled fifty days and nights
But couldn't shift the bastard, it was stuck there good and tight.
The dam was full of water but they couldn't get it out,
Till the day McArthur farted and saved the town from drought.

They blasted it with dynamite and couldn't get it loose
And even Murphy's bullock team just wasn't any use.
'There's only one last chance!' said Clancy's brother Blue
'We'll have to get McArthur and see what he can do!'

Well, the cry went up, 'McArthur!! He's the one who knows the art
He'll send that dead horse flying with a well-constructed fart!'
And so the townsfolk waited for the day to come about
The day McArthur farted and saved the town from drought.

At last McArthur came and all the people gathered 'round
To see the man whose fart was gonna send the waters down.
He came on two big horses, with half his bum on each,
A bum so wide a man could drive a tram between the cheeks.

McArthur was a quiet bloke but thorough, through and through
He said, 'I'll need some food and drink, so see what youse can do.'
They started preparations and laid out a mighty spread,
With forty tons of onions and a pile of prunes and bread.

They had fifty tons of blue-vein cheese and fifty kegs of stout,
The day McArthur farted and saved the town from drought.
He sat back with a knife and fork and really knocked it back,
He finished off those kegs of stout in thirty seconds flat.

McArthur got up slowly and he turned his bum around
And the people all took cover as they heard a dreadful sound,
Like the roaring of a lion, and a chill ran through each heart
As McArthur's body trembled and let go a mighty fart!

He farted and he farted till the earth began to shake,
The hills began to tremble and the dam began to break,
And still McArthur farted till he made the thunder crack.
The winds they howled, the lightning flared, the sky was turning
    black.

They heard it up in China where the up-side-downers dwell,
They heard it up in Heaven and they heard it down in hell.
I hardly need to tell ya, it was really on the snout
The day McArthur farted and saved the town from drought.

That was how McArthur saved the town of Bungadell
And still his memory lingers on (and so too does the smell)
And even down in Adelaide they've heard about his arts
And every other year they hold a Festival of Farts!

The Cocky from Henty
Jim Haynes

Said a very rich cocky from Henty,
'I'll spoil the family now I have plenty.'
And how did he spoil it?
With a new indoor toilet,
And a lifetime supply of Glen 20.

A Walgett Episode
AB Paterson ('The Banjo')

The sun strikes down with a blinding glare,
The skies are blue and the plains are wide,
The saltbush plains that are burnt and bare
By Walgett out on the Barwon side –
The Barwon River that wanders down
In a leisurely manner by Walgett Town.

There came a stranger – a 'cockatoo' –
The word means farmer, as all men know
Who dwell in the land where the kangaroo
Barks loud at dawn, and the white-eyed crow
Uplifts his song on the stockyard fence
As he watches the lambkins passing hence.

The sunburnt stranger was gaunt and brown,
But it soon appeared that he meant to flout
The iron law of the country town,
Which is – that the stranger has got to shout:
'If he will not shout we must take him down,'
Remarked the yokels of Walgett Town.

They baited a trap with a crafty bait,
With a crafty bait, for they held discourse
Concerning a new chum who of late
Had bought such a thoroughly lazy horse;
They would wager that no one could ride him down
The length of the city of Walgett Town.

The stranger was born on a horse's hide;
So he took the wagers, and made them good
With his hard-earned cash – but his hopes they died,
For the horse was a clothes-horse, made of wood!
'Twas a well-known horse that had taken down
Full many a stranger in Walgett Town.

The stranger smiled with a sickly smile –
'Tis a sickly smile that the loser grins –
And he said he had travelled for quite a while
In trying to sell some marsupial skins.
'And I thought that perhaps, as you've took me down,
You would buy them from me, in Walgett Town!'

He said that his home was at Wingadee,
At Wingadee where he had for sale
Some fifty skins and would guarantee
They were full-sized skins, with the ears and tail
Complete, and he sold them for money down
To a venturesome buyer in Walgett Town.

Then he smiled a smile as he pouched the pelf,
'I'm glad that I'm quit of them, win or lose:
You can fetch them in when it suits yourself,
And you'll find the skins – on the kangaroos!'
Then he left – and the silence settled down
Like a tangible thing upon Walgett Town.

2B or not 2B

Anon

Said Hamlet to Ophelia, 'A sketch I'll do of thee,
What kind of pencil shall I use? 2B or not 2B?'

The Confession

Jim Haynes

Father Connolly, our local
Long-suffering Catholic priest,
Ministered mostly to the new born,
Due to wed, or just deceased.
And his life was uneventful
If you didn't count the days
He taught scripture in the schoolroom,
To a room full of O'Sheas.

A small and loyal group
Came to mass each week.
And an even smaller group
Had confessions they must speak.
So he was surprised and puzzled,
When confession time came round,
To hear a voice beyond the grille
With an unfamiliar sound.

'Father,' said a gruff old voice,
'I'm nearly eighty-two,
But lately something's happened
That I've got to tell to you.
This beautiful blonde teenage girl
Has got a crush on me!
And since she led me to temptation
We make love constantly.

'I thought that I was past it
But I find out now I'm not,
So we make love once or twice a day
Which for me is quite a lot.'
Said the father, 'This is dreadful,
You must stop – you have no choice!'
'I can't stop, we both enjoy it,'
Replied the gruff old voice.

'But you must,' the priest insisted,
'And you must do penance too!'
'Oh I couldn't,' said the voice,
'I'm not a Catholic like you.'
'Not Catholic?' gasped the cleric,
'Then why tell me what you've done?'
'Are you kiddin'? I am eighty-two,
I'm telling everyone!'

It's Something in Me Genes

Charlee Marshall

I wuz down in Brisbane Frid'y week, an' went ter see the quack –
I reckoned it wuz time ter take it easy;
I don't want you people thinkin' I'm a hy-pro-chon-driac,
But jus' lately I bin feelin' kinda queasy;
Me 'ead aches somefin' orful, an' me lips are dry an' blue,
I gets giddy sometimes ridin' round the fences,
An' I reckoned 'e c'd fix me up (I'm only twenty-two)
Wiv a bottle o' the dope that 'e dispenses.
Well, 'e fiddles in me singlet – I refused ter take it orf –
Wiv a stealthy-scope an' similar machines;
An' then 'e puts 'is finger – well . . . I turns me 'ead ter corff,
An' 'e ups an' says, 'There's somethin' in y'r genes!'

What the 'eck's 'e think I am – some kind o' bloomin' flower?
I may be slow an' sorta stumble-witted,
But ever since me mother smacked me fingers in the shower
I've known that I wuz properly outfitted.
'There's somethin' in y'r genes,' 'e says. 'It's caused y'r glands ter
    swell;
Jus' sit 'ere while I go an' fetch a nurse.'
Then she comes in, blonde an' beautiful, an' straight orf I could tell
The swelling 'ad quite suddenly got worse!
But they 'eld me jaws wide open an' they leaned across me chair,
They used me tongue fer playin' trampolines;
An' 'ow the 'ell they saw a thing by lookin' down from there,
But they both agree, 'There's somethin' in y'r genes!'

'The only cure,' the Doctor says, 'is ton-sil-ect-om-y!'
The nurse jus' nods 'er 'ead, 'There's little doubt
They'll be no use at all ter 'im like that, don't you agree?'
An 'e peeks again, an' says, 'They must come out!'
'*Come out!*' . . . my Gawd, two little words: they 'it me like a rock!
At twenty-two I'd 'ardly started livin',
But I'd done me share o' markin' calves an' couldn't stand the
    shock
If they tried ter take away what I wuz given.
I'd seen 'em use an iron on colts what burned the 'and that 'eld it;
We'd cleaned up lots o' tom-cats in our teens –
An' I'm damned if I'll crawl in a sack an' wait there ter be gelded
Jus' because I'm blessed wiv somethin' in me jeans.

So I tol' the Doc politely that I'd think about it later;
I grabbed me 'at an' sidled out the door;
An' threw the scrip 'e gave me in the first incinerator
'Cos I won't be needin' doctors any more.
There's a pub in Augathella where they keep the bar-maid busy
Servin' medicine ter cure a 'usky throat,
An' a double scotch will fix ya anytime yo're feelin' dizzy –
Ev'ry illness 'as its simple antidote.
Ter them fancy Brisbane doctors I 'ave said me last good-bye,
They c'n sit an' read their glossy magazines;
An' I'll keep this solem' promise till the very day I die –
I'm gonna die wiv somethin' in me jeans.

A Macadamia Mademoiselle

Grahame Watt

A macadamia mademoiselle,
For a Kingaroy peanut once fell,
No ifs and no buts,
She just went quite nuts,
Yes, she really came out of her shell.

Chopsticks

Col Wilson ('Blue the Shearer')

There's a little Chinese cafe, down the road in my home town,
Where they serve the most exquisite Chinese food.
And I used to watch in envy as the patrons scoffed it down,
Using chopsticks, in the way I wished I could.

So I joined the 'Chopstick Users Club' to see if I could gain
The kind of chopstick expertise I'd need
To eat Chinese with chopsticks and brother, how I trained,
To use those sticks with grace, and style, and speed.

I learned the upward looping scoop, the backhand twist and lunge.
The plain, the purl, the thrust, the follow-through.
'Til I could manage anything, from rice to crumbs of sponge,
Then I knew the time was right for my debut.

There's a little Chinese Cafe, down the road in my home town.
That's where I went to demonstrate my skill.
I ordered prawns and almonds and some wine to wash it down,
Quite determined not a single drop to spill.

Over-confidence perhaps, luck wasn't on my side.
I admit, what happened wasn't nice.
About to take a mouthful, the 'sticks began their slide,
And 'spang' – the air was filled with prawns and rice.

A lady right across the room fell flat upon her back.
When asked if she was hurt, began to cry,
Accused me of delivering a cowardly attack,
For I'd hit her with an almond in the eye.

I helped her up, apologised, and then she screamed again.
And when I found out why I wished to die.
I looked where she was looking and there I saw, quite plain,
A braised king prawn stuck firmly in my fly.

Of course, she got the wrong idea and worked up to a state,
And, from the Chinese cafe, out she stormed,
Came back with a policeman and screamed in tones of hate,
'There's a maniac in there – and he's deformed.'

When I proved that I was normal things soon settled down,
And home I went, food-stained and battle-scarred.
There's a little Chinese cafe down the road in my home town.
But I don't go there anymore, I'm barred.

Mary Had a Lot
Anon

Mary had a little lamb; she also had some steak,
Then ice-cream with some topping and a slice of chocolate cake,
A lamington, a piece of pie and then some liverwurst;
Now Mary's in the hospital because her tummy burst.

A Nautical Yarn
Keighly Goodchild

I sing of a captain who's well known to fame;
A naval commander, Bill Jinks is his name.
Who sailed where the Murray's clear waters do flow,
Did this freshwater shellback, with his 'Yo heave a yo'.

To the port of Wahgunyah his vessel was bound,
When night came upon him and darkness around;
Not a star on the waters its clear light did throw;
But the vessel sped onward, with a 'Yo heave a yo'.

'Oh captain! Oh captain! Let's make for the shore,
For the winds they do rage and the waves they do roar!'
'Nay, nay!' said the captain, 'though the fierce winds may blow,
I will stick to my vessel, with a "Yo heave a yo".'

'Oh captain! Oh captain! The waves sweep the deck;
Oh captain! Oh captain! We'll soon be a wreck –
To the river's deep bosom each seaman will go!'
But the captain laughed loudly, with his 'Yo heave a yo'.

'Farewell to the maiden – the girl I adore;
Farewell to my friends – I shall see them no more!'
The crew shrieked with terror, the captain he swore –
They had stuck on a sandbank, so they all walked ashore.

Pillmania
Glenny Palmer

I've got pills for arthritis, bursitis, colitis,
And pills for an itis that's yet to be named.
I've got sleepers and weepers and drops for me peepers
And tablets to keep us emotionally tamed.

I've got ointments for healing the skin that is peeling
Off knees that went feeling 'round gardening beds.
I've got lotions and potions to deal with emotions
That cause silly notions in most of our heads.

When I'm feeling sardonic I reach for the tonic
That deals with my chronic demonic disdain,
And I can't get enough of this wonderful stuff
So I huff and I puff 'til it's topped up again.

If I get a psychosis from bad halitosis
The doc gives me doses of peppermint drops,
And they come in quite handy when Constable Randy
Says, 'Blow in the bag!' 'cause they help fool the cops.

Yes, the muck I ingest at the doctor's request
Would be put to the test if he gave it a try.
What he makes me inhale, it could land me in gaol
And it works without fail, 'cause I think I can fly!

I've got transplanted parts, brand new kidneys and hearts
With a pacer that starts them up just as they choose,
But that little blue pill that turns 'won't' into 'will'
(For those over the hill) tends to blow out me fuse.

Still, me bones are all creakin', the future looks bleak 'n
I'm freakin' from leakin' each time that I sneeze;
I've got two metal hips; I want collagen lips,
And some tucks and some nips, and me boobs double Ds.

But they say I'm too old, that I'm losing my hold,
That I'm growing blue mould where my attributes lied,
It's a bit hard to check, 'cause I can't stretch me neck
And me old man got decked, 'cause he reckons they died!

He's a fine one to talk! He can hardly still walk,
And to him a good stalk is a mythical bird.
If I talk slap and tickle the silly old hick'll
Just break out in hives, so it's always deferred.

Well it looks like I'm done for; I can't make a run for
One more bit of fun 'fore I curl up and die.
I might swallow the lot, that should clean out the rot,
And the worst that can happen? I'll leave on a high!

Kevin from Kongwak
Jim Haynes

My ex-friend Kevin from Kongwak,
Came to stay with me once, not so long back,
And took stuff from my house,
The miserable louse.
He still hasn't given one thong back!

Script for Old-Time Sequence Dance
Harry Bowers

I have seen some old time dancers do some fancy stepping out,
They say Ogilvie from Queensland is as good as most about;
But I saw a bloke from Melbourne who could beat Col Ogilvie,
Tho' where he got his script from is a mystery to me.

He put his left foot forward, swivelled right foot to the side,
Then did a kind of forward square, as in the Palais Glide.
Side together, side and close, with angles to the wall,
Some quick steps like a Chassis – yet, not quite that at all.

Then he did a reverse pivot, stepped across to fall away,
Four more quickies going forward – promenade and rondelay.
Then three more quicks together like some Tango-style Cha-cha,
Then he stopped and smiled – he'd made it . . . to the toilet from
    the bar.

A Bad Break!

WT Goodge ('The Colonel')

The preacher quoted and the cranks
Among his congregation smiled,
'How sharper than a serpent's thanks
It is to have a toothless child.'

He saw he erred, his eyes grew wild,
He frowned upon the mirthful ranks:
'How toothless than a serpent's child
It is to have a sharper's thanks!'

Tall Timber

CJ Dennis

A snake that fastened on a man's leg in Burnie, Tasmania, was much disgusted to find that the leg was a wooden one.

That sort o' reminds me of the old days (said Bill)
In the bush at Toolangi, at Switherton's mill –
A sor-mill, you know – an' the sawyer we 'ad
Was old 'Oppy McClintock, a wooden-legged lad.
'E was walkin' one day for to tighten a peg,
When a tiger snake grabs at 'is old timber leg;
An' there it 'angs on, till I fetched it a crack,
But old 'Oppy jist grins as 'e starts to walk back.

An' then somethink 'appens. We seen 'Oppy stop,
As 'e stumbles a bit, an' looks down at 'is prop
With a dead funny look. Then 'e lets out a yell:
'Ere, boys! Take it off me! It's startin' to swell!
Well, we unstraps 'is leg, an' it swole an' it swole.
Snake pisen? Too right! 'Twas a twenny-foot pole
In less than five minutes! Believe it or not.
An' as thick – it's as true as I stand on this spot!

We was 'eavin it out, when the boss starts to roar:
'Ere! Why waste good wood? Shove it on to the sor!
So we sors it in two, down the middle, an' then,
Them there slabs swole an' swole; so we sors 'em agen.

An' we sors, an' we sors; an' it swole, an' it swole
Till the end of the day, when the tally, all tole,
Was two thousan' foot super. You doubt it? (said Bill)
You ask any ole 'and up at Switherton's mill!

Hark

Anon

Hark the herald angels sing
Beecham's Pills are just the thing.
Peace on earth and mercy mild,
Two for an adult one for a child.

My Wise Old Grandpapa

Wilbur G Howcroft

When I was but a little chap
My Grandpapa said to me,
You'll need to know your manners, son,
When you go out to tea.

Remove the shells from hard-boiled eggs,
Make sure your hat's on straight,
Pour lots of honey on your peas
To keep them on your plate.

Blow daintily upon your tea
To cool it to your taste,
And always pick bones thoroughly,
With due regard for waste.

Be heedful of your partners' needs,
Attend their every wish;
When passing jelly, cream or jam,
Make sure they're in the dish.

When eating figs or coconuts,
To show you are refined,
Genteelly gnaw the centres out
And throw away the rind.

If you should accidentally gulp
Some coffee while it's hot,
Just raise the lid politely and
Replace it in the pot.

Don't butter ice-cream when it's warm,
Or drink soup through a straw.
Thus spoke my wise old Grandpapa
When I was only four.

The Crim from Long Bay

Russell Hannah

A cunning old crim from Long Bay
Studied grammar by night and by day.
Then changed all the functions
Of verbs and conjunctions,
And shortened his sentence that way.

Mulga Bill's Bicycle

AB Paterson ('The Banjo')

'Twas Mulga Bill, from Eaglehawk, that caught the cycling craze;
He turned away the good old horse that served him many days;
He dressed himself in cycling clothes, resplendent to be seen;
He hurried off to town and bought a shining new machine;
And as he wheeled it through the door, with air of lordly pride,
The grinning shop assistant said, 'Excuse me, can you ride?'

'See here, young man,' said Mulga Bill, 'from Walgett to the sea,
From Conroy's Gap to Castlereagh, there's none can ride like me.
I'm good all round at everything, as everybody knows,
Although I'm not the one to talk – I hate a man that blows.
But riding is my special gift, my chiefest, sole delight;
Just ask a wild duck can it swim, a wildcat can it fight.
There's nothing clothed in hair or hide, or built of flesh or steel,
There's nothing walks or jumps, or runs, on axle, hoof, or wheel,

But what I'll sit, while hide will hold and girths and straps are
    tight:
I'll ride this here two-wheeled concern right straight away at
    sight.'

'Twas Mulga Bill, from Eaglehawk, that sought his own abode,
That perched beside the Dead Man's Creek, beside the mountain
    road.
He turned the cycle down the hill and mounted for the fray,
But ere he'd gone a hundred yards it bolted clean away.
It left the track, and through the trees, just like a silver streak,
It whistled down the awful slope towards the Dead Man's Creek.

It shaved a stump by half an inch, it dodged a big white box:
The very wallaroos in fright went scrambling up the rocks,
The wombats hiding in their caves dug deeper underground,
As Mulga Bill, as white as chalk, sat tight to every bound.
It struck a stone and gave a spring that cleared a fallen tree,
It raced beside a precipice as close as close could be;
And then, as Mulga Bill let out one last despairing shriek,
It made a leap of twenty feet into the Dead Man's Creek.

'Twas Mulga Bill, from Eaglehawk, that slowly swam ashore:
He said, 'I've had some narrer shaves and lively rides before;
I've rode a wild bull round the yard to win a five pound bet,
But this was the most awful ride that I've encountered yet.
I'll give that two-wheeled outlaw best; it's shaken all my nerve
To feel it whistle through the air and plunge and buck and swerve.
It's safe at rest in Dead Man's Creek, we'll leave it lying still;
A horse's back is good enough henceforth for Mulga Bill.'

The Six-Stitcher
Frank Daniel

A brand new six stitcher, shiny, red and hard.
Dad saw us playing with it as he walked across the yard.
'Where'd ya get that, fellas?' was his curious remark.
'It's alright Dad, we found it in the long grass at the park.'
'You sure that it was lost?' Dad's voice was turning sour.
'Bloody oath!' my brother said, 'They were searching for an hour!'

Tangmalangaloo

PJ Hartigan (John O'Brien)

The bishop sat in lordly state and purple cap sublime,
And galvanised the old bush church at confirmation time;
And all the kids were mustered up from fifty miles around,
With Sunday clothes, and staring eyes, and ignorance profound.
Now was it fate, or was it grace, whereby they yarded too
An overgrown two-storey lad from Tangmalangaloo?

A hefty son of virgin soil, where nature has her fling,
And grows the trefoil three feet high and mats it in the spring;
Where mighty hills uplift their heads to pierce the welkin's rim,
And trees sprout up a hundred feet before they shoot a limb;
There everything is big and grand, and men are giants too –
But Christian knowledge wilts, alas, at Tangmalangaloo.

The bishop summed the youngsters up, as bishops only can;
He cast a searching glance around, then fixed upon his man.
But glum and dumb and undismayed through every bout he sat;
He seemed to think that he was there, but wasn't sure of that.
The bishop gave a scornful look, as bishops sometimes do,
And glared right through the pagan in from Tangmalangaloo.

'Come, tell me, boy,' his lordship said in crushing tones severe,
'Come, tell me why is Christmas Day the greatest of the year?
'How is it that around the world we celebrate that day
'And send a name upon a card to those who're far away?
'Why is it wandering ones return with smiles and greetings, too?'
A squall of knowledge hit the lad from Tangmalangaloo.

He gave a lurch which set a-shake the vases on the shelf,
He knocked the benches all askew, up-ending of himself.
And oh, how pleased his lordship was, and how he smiled to say,
'That's good, my boy. Come, tell me now; and what is Christmas
    Day?'
The ready answer bared a fact no bishop ever knew –
'It's the day before the races out at Tangmalangaloo.'

Arthritis

Jim Haynes

Dipso Dan was wandering slowly up the street
From the Tatt's to the Royal one day.
When he met Father Connolly, local Catholic priest,
'G'day father, going my way?'

The priest gave Dipso a long and rueful look
And smiled at the drunkard's little joke.
'Sure I'll walk with you, Dan, you're not looking well
And it's been quite a while since we spoke.'

So they walked together, quite an odd pair,
The priest stepping purposeful and sprightly,
Serious expression, hands behind his back,
Dipso Dan meandering slightly.

'I'm not feeling too bad,' confided Dipso Dan,
'Last week I had a touch of laryngitis,
But I'm glad I met you, Father, I've been meaning to ask,
What is it that causes that arthritis?'

'Here's a chance,' thought Father Connolly,
'To subtly reform this fellow I've been praying for for ages.'
'Arthritis, Dan,' he said, 'well now I believe
It develops through a series of stages,

'The first of these is physical – alcohol abuse
May be a major factor I suppose,
And then of course there's hygiene, not washing regularly,
And sleeping in the open in your clothes.

'And some of it is spiritual – arthritis takes a hold
When a person loses self-respect.
So it's caused by a combination of drinking, poor hygiene,
Sinful living and neglect.'

'Well, blow me down,' gasped Dipso Dan, 'so that's arthritis, eh?
I simply wondered how a bloke would spot it,
And I only asked you, father, 'cos I read the other day,
In the paper, that Pope John Paul has got it!'

Astronomy
Bartlett Adamson

Twinkle, twinkle, little star, I don't wonder what you are.
You are just a whirling planet or a hunk of molten granite.

A Tale of Termites
Bruce Simpson ('Lancewood')

Stranger, please pause by this old bungalow,
For it hides a grim battle that ebbs to and fro,
A primitive struggle devoid of romance,
'Twixt the Camooweal drunks and the giant white ants.
No quarter is given, no mercy displayed,
In this fight to the death with the termite brigade,
But if their rampaging is not soon reduced,
You can all say goodbye to the old Ringer's Roost.

There are termites to the left and termites to the right,
And their molars are grinding by day and by night,
They raid and they ravage and plunder unchecked,
And they're larger, much larger than one would expect.
By wall plate and rafter they stealthily creep,
And God help our hides if they catch us asleep,
And if we can't turn their attack mighty soon,
We'll be under the stars by the change of the moon.

There are white ants below and white ants above,
In the floorboards and battens and rafters they love,
They deploy to the left and attack from the right,
And their molars are grinding by day and by night.
They break up our parties and ruin our rest,
And they are, in a nutshell, a damnable pest,
And if we can't deal them a kick in the slats,
I fear it's the end of these bachelor flats.

We've tried every method to stop their advance,
We've fought them with poison and baton and lance,
But it does little good, for in thousands they breed,
And they sharpen their fangs as they look for a feed.
An expert was called in to give us a quote,
But as soon as he entered they sprang at his throat;
He fought himself free with the leg from the bed,
And one flick and 'I'm going,' he screamed as he fled.

They've ravaged our larder, our furniture too,
And one night they punctured a carton of brew,
Then the word got around to the whole of their tribe,
And they bunged on an orgy I couldn't describe.
They've cleaned up our wood heap, our outhouse as well,
The 'Man who comes round' said he'd see us in Hell;
They've eaten our moleskins and eaten our Bex,
Two novels by Thwaites and a pamphlet on sex,
And if very soon we don't stop their advance,
Then I'll transfer the deeds to the flamin' white ants.

Crawliwigs

Anon

Reginald Cadwallider, scientifically inclined,
Always had taxidermy firmly on his mind.
Crawliwigs and crows and creepers, gathered far and wide,
Reggie stuffed and mounted 'em, and others too beside.
Far afield he found fine fishes, finches, frogs and fleas,
And killed and skinned and stuffed and mounted birds and bugs
    and bees.

One day afield he met a swaggie, trudging down the track,
His old black billy swinging and his swag upon his back.
'Pardon me,' said Reggie, 'If you live round about
Can you help me find the kind of fauna I am seeking out?
See I'm a taxidermist and I'm seeking creatures rare,
Reptiles, creepicrawlies, have you seen some anywhere?'

'I have,' replied the swaggie, 'reptiles, snakes and lizards too!
I can tell you where there's heaps of 'em! A squirming bloomin' zoo!
'Pink and blue and spotted ones, I've seen thousands, mate!
Crimson rats and yeller frogs, I'll give it to you straight!
'Red-haired beetles chasin' spotted spiders all about,
And blue-nosed toads with purple stripes and waistcoats inside-out!'

'Heavens, man!' cried Reggie, 'Where are they? In the scrub?'
'No!' the swaggie told him, 'Down the track, at Casey's Pub!
Underneath the v'randah, sometimes crawling through the floor!
And if you can spare a bloke two-bob . . . I'll go and see some more!'
Reginald Cadwallider, scientifically inclined,
Sadly headed home and left the 'specimens' behind!

None So Deaf
Heather Hastings

I said to him, 'You're deaf, you know!'
Said he, 'I'm not, you mumble so.'
I spoke to him about the news,
Shouted to him all my views
About the Lebanese hostages.
'No thanks,' he said, 'Not sausages!'

I told him, in a louder shout,
'I've made your lunch, I'm going out.
Ham and tomato, hot on toast.'
He said, 'Rotten tomato? On a post?'
I yelled, 'Your deafness is a pest,
I'll arrange for us a hearing test!'

Well, I've no hearing aid it's true –
But he, poor bloke, came home with two!

Grandkids

Col Wilson ('Blue the Shearer')

The grandkids are coming. They are? They are?
Quick. Hide the computer, and lock up the car.
Lift all the breakables onto the shelves.
Teach grandfolk the art of defending themselves.
Take plenty of vitamins A, B and C,
For strong and resilient, you'll need to be.

Say Goodbye to harmony, Goodbye to quiet.
Your home will resemble an out-of-hand riot.
Make sure that you check out your washing machine,
(Those washing nappies will know what I mean)
And don't let the two-year-old near the TV,
There might be a programme you're wanting to see.

Hang on to your patience with both of your hands,
The dear little darling will not understand
If you shout: 'Will you stop it. You must not touch that.'
Or: 'Don't kick the dog,' and: 'Put down the cat.'
'Don't wake the baby by yelling and screaming.'
And: 'Isn't it time you were in bed and dreaming?'

There's Erin. Two months, and queen of the castle,
Food in one end, and waste out the other.
How can one baby, so tiny and frail,
Be so possessed of such ear-splitting wail?
And how does she know, when she's starting to squeal,
That the rest of the household are having their meal?

But how can you even pretend to be cross,
With the Queen of the castle. The Princess. The Boss.
When she looks up and smiles, gurgling and gooing.
You don't have a choice. You just stop what you're doing.
And pay her homage of which she's deserving.
She makes the demands, and you do the serving.

Now Matthew. He's one of the terrible twos,
No wonder some grandfathers get on the booze.
They christened him Matthew, but I have a notion,
He should have been christened Perpetual Motion.
They say that it's cruel to keep them in cages,
And that they grow out of it, slowly, in stages.

But the question that hovers on everyone's tongue,
Is: 'How long does it take to stop being that young?'
And tell me, wise counsellor, what guarantee
Can you give to grandparents they're better at three?
If it wasn't for Play School on the TV,
We'd be in a rest home, Grandmother and me.

He is ever so charming, ever so sweet.
His capture of grandmother's heart is complete.
But I am his grandfather. I am much sterner,
Or is it, perhaps, that I'm just a slow learner?
When he looks up at me and says: 'Gamfarver. Cuddle?'
All thoughts of discipline melt into muddle.

I have to survive, or turn into a rover,
If the grandchildren's holiday, isn't soon over.
And it's true, they are going, I'm sad to relate,
But we'll sleep for three days, when they go out the gate.
And following that, we must build our physique,
For the other three grandkids are coming next week.

The Person from Perth

Anon

There once was a person from Perth
Who was born on the day of his birth.
He was married, they say,
On his wife's wedding day,
And died when he quitted this earth.

Calling All Cars

Max Fatchen

All areas were notified.
It seemed a puzzling case.
The raspberry ripple ice cream tub
Had vanished without trace.

A tub of most exquisite brand
And only newly bought,
Identikits were quickly scanned
And witnesses were sought.

The motive? It was surely greed
And those who probe and pry
Can be a shrewd and dogged breed
Who test each alibi.

For suddenly the breakthrough came
But only just in time.
Within an ear, a whispered name
Connected with the crime.

And so we happily report
That, by informers branded,
The criminal has now been caught
Red-raspberry-ripple-handed.

The Weelabarabak Bugle

Jim Haynes

The *Weelabarabak Bugle*,
That's the paper in our town,
It's the method by which
All the news is spread around.
Each Monday and each Thursday
The *Bugle* hits the street
And if you've never read it
Then you've missed out on a treat.

The editor, Old Jonesy,
Puts most of it together.
He does the features and the photos,
The farm news and the weather.
But as it's only twice a week
The weather's yesterday's.
Mrs Phillips does fashion news
And reviews the local plays.

On Thursday it'll tell you
The weekend netball draw
And you read it on a Monday
If you want to know the score.
How did footy go on Sunday?
What's news down at the school?
Call it 'two minutes silence'
And you're only being cruel!

Sure Jonesy sometimes rushes
And small mistakes occur.
The CWA President's mad
At what he did to her!
It was underneath a photo
Of her with a champion scone.
Well, a name like Mrs Tucker,
Is a bad one to get wrong!

Even headline spelling errors
Are not difficult to find,
'*Members Active In The Loins Club*',
Is one that comes to mind.
There was, '*Councillors Pass Motions
On Brand New Town Hall Roof*',
And '*Surveyor Leaks On Subdivision
Our Photo Shows The Truth!*'

Though the news that's in the *Bugle*
Is always *based* on fact,
The prejudice of editors
Must remain intact.
And Jonesy was a decent,
Well-meaning country bloke
Who hated unions, migrants,
And all them 'city folk'.

One day he had a message,
O'Shea's pig dog had gone wild!
Broke its chain and tried to maul
The O'Sheas' youngest child,
Who no doubt had been tormenting it
As he was wont to do,
But the child had been saved
By a stranger passing through.

He'd pulled up, grabbed a tyre lever,
Dashed into the fray,
Took the brunt of the attack,
Killed the dog and saved the day!
Jonesy soon was on the scene
And the bloke was interviewed,
(While waiting for the ambulance,
'Cos he was badly chewed.)

He said he lived in Sydney,
But was born in the UK.
He was a trade union organiser
Visiting branches up our way.
And the headline for our hero?
Jonesy's best one yet,
'City-Based Pommy Communist
Kills Local Kiddy's Pet!'

Frustration

Anon

His ship came in
But sad to state
He's now too old
To navigate.

Just A Note

Anon

Just a note to say I'm still alive and haven't passed on yet,
Though these days I remember a lot less than I forget.
I've got used to my arthritis and I guess I'm now resigned
To my dentures and bifocals, but gee, I miss me mind!

I often can't remember, when I'm standing on the stair,
If I'm going up for something or I've just come down from there.
And I hold the fridge door open and I stand there, full of doubt;
Did I just put some food away or come to get some out?

Or I rush into the spare room and I hesitate because
I needed something urgently, but can't think what it was.
Now, if it's not my turn to write, you'll pardon me I'm sure.
Sometimes I think I've written to you just the day before.

Well, I guess it's time to mail this, think that's all I have to say,
Except, of course, I wish you didn't live so far away,
And I'm standing by the mail-box and boy, is my face red!
Instead of posting this to you, I've opened it instead!

SECTION TWO

Havens and Heartlands
Over the Ranges and Into the West

Here is a collection of mostly descriptive and reflective verse relying heavily on the Australian landscape for its subject material. These poems are about the emotional responses of Australians to that varying landscape.

Many of the poems in this section are contemplations on the lives lived in certain settings, reflecting the impact the natural or rural environment has on those who inhabit or visit these regions.

Our greatest reflective writer of rhymed verse, Henry Lawson, is well represented here along with his contemporaries Paterson, Jim Grahame and Jack Moses. Poets of a previous era, such as Harpur and Kendall, and those of modern times, like Archie Bigg and Graham Fredriksen, are included here. The prevailing themes and attitudes are timeless.

I think this common desire to relate landscape to self-perception over two centuries of verse writing shows just how powerful a force is Australia's natural and rural landscape in our attempts to define ourselves in verse and literature.

Over the Ranges and into the West

Henry Lawson

Let others sing praise of their sea-girted isles,
But give me the bush with its limitless miles;
Then it's over the ranges and into the West,
To the scenes of wild boyhood, we love them the best.

We'll ride and we'll ride from the city afar,
To the plains where the cattle and sheep stations are;
Where stockmen ride hard, and the drover starts forth
On his long, lonely journey 'way up in the North.

When your money is low, and your luck has gone down,
There's no place so lone as the streets of a town;
There's nothing but worry and dread and unrest,
So we'll over the ranges and into the West.

The drought in the West may spread ruin around,
But the dread drought of life in the city is found;
And I'd sooner tread on the long dusty way,
Where each one you meet says, 'Good day, mate, good day.'

The Sanctuary

JW Gordon (Jim Grahame)

By fallen trees and broken gates an old bush track is leading
Along the banks of green lagoons where water-fowl are feeding.
The spoonbill struts amongst the weeds; there's many a crane and
    plover;
The wily birdhawk sits on guard; the wood-duck flies to cover.

The old mud house is crumbling there – the stockyard fence is
    falling –
And from a gum-tree near the dam a love-bird's mate is calling.
Across the flat where once grew wheat a dog-leg fence is reaching
To where the yellow box-trees bloom and cockatoos are screeching.

Then further on through low pine belts, where plain and range are
    meeting,
The brolgas dance in stately grace, the jackass laughs a greeting.
The 'twelve apostles' hop and skip, the 'happy families' chatter.
From daybreak till the sun goes down is just an endless patter.

Here from a giant kurrajong some young galahs are peeping,
And underneath where shades are deep the kangaroos are sleeping.
There are no campfires burning here, no bushmen's axes ringing,
The trees are green with yellow blooms where parakeets are
    swinging.

Young wattle trees and scented gums and native shrubs are
    sprouting –
There are no sheep to eat them out, there are no drovers shouting.
The bronzewing pigeon calls its mate just as the sun is sinking
And flies to gilgais in the scrub where wallabies are drinking.

Jindalee
Jack Moses

I'm going home to Jindalee,
The sweetest spot on earth to me;
The moon and stars shine brighter there,
Than I have seen them anywhere.

The fleecy clouds float into view,
And roll around the ranges blue,
Then sail away, so soft and free,
Across the lands of Jindalee.

My neddy's tugging at the rein;
He knows he's going back again.
We've been droving, don't you see,
Far, far away from Jindalee –

'Way where the cattle rush at night,
As mad as hornets in their fright.
Oh, I'll be glad, and so will he,
To see the kids at Jindalee.

On his broad back they'll quickly lob
(They use a stump there for that job).
Tho' once it was a big gum-tree,
It's built our house in Jindalee.

My wife is standing at the gate –
No man could have a better mate;
A smile, a kiss, hot scones for tea,
And I am home in Jindalee.

My Choice
Wilbur G Howcroft

You can talk of tropic sunrise,
Waving palms and all of that,
Or the miracle of morning
Mists above the river Platte.

Not for me those far-off places
For I'd far, far rather see
That old Mallee moon a-shining
Through a eucalyptus tree.

Some folk rave of Taiwan temples
And the sands of Suva Bay,
Or a Moslem mosque by moonlight
In some country far away.

Give me tree-lined tracks at sunset
And the sound of rustling wheat,
Plus the peaceful, plodding patter
Of my horse's homebound feet.

Venezuela, Valparaiso,
Vera Cruz and Everest –
Patagonia, Puerto Rico,
All are lauded as the best.

But I'll settle for the magic
Of a magpie's song at dawn
While I watch the furrows turning
In the soil where I was born.

There are those who sing the praises
Of the sands at Waikiki,
Others claim the beach at Bali
Is the only place to be.

Well, I've done me share of tripping
And I'd swap the bloomin' lot
For a wallow in our house dam
When the weather's good and hot!

Madagascar, Magdalada,
Mandalay and Mozambique –
Where unsettled souls go striving
For the happiness they seek.

Yet at hand's a kindly country
Where the mopokes call at night
And devoted sheep dogs greet you
At the morning's early light.

Saunter slowly through the scrublands
With no special aim in view
While you watch the wildlife wonders
In their rural rendezvous.

Here the bush birds build their bowers
And, on aimless afternoons,
You can linger there and listen
As they trill their tranquil tunes.

Samarkand and San Marino
Have attractions I'll agree,
But I'm blowed if they can better
Billabongs and billy tea!

Set your sights on Surakarta,
Take that trip to Trinidad –
Old frequented lanes I'll follow
Where I lingered as a lad . . .

Wheatlands Summer
Audrey McGilp Smith

Bulloaks are rustling, restless and bustling,
While magpies warble a hawk hovers high.
Wavy and shimmering, blurry and glimmering,
Oceans of light ripple over the rye.
From scented gums flowering a noise overpowering
Of garrulous parrots that chatter and fight.
Warm winds are battling, ripe corn heads rattling
And quail whirring upward in spasmodic flight.
Dust clouds are whirling, banners unfurling,
Mirages flickering out on the plain,
Galahs are scene-stealing, screeching and wheeling,
And a plover cries plaintively, waiting for rain.
Where capeweed glows hazily lizards lie lazily,
The sheep pant in huddles, drugged, comatose.
There's contentment developing with warmth so enveloping
This vastness of vistas brings restful repose.

Song of the Wheat
AB Paterson ('The Banjo')

We have sung the song of the droving days,
Of the march of the travelling sheep;
By silent stages and lonely ways
Thin, white battalions creep.
But the man who now by the land would thrive
Must his spurs to a ploughshare beat.
Is there ever a man in the world alive
To sing the song of the Wheat!

It's west by south of the Great Divide
The grim grey plains run out,
Where the old flock masters lived and died
In a ceaseless fight with drought.
Weary with waiting and hope deferred
They were ready to own defeat,
Till at last they heard the master-word
And the master-word was Wheat.

Yarran and myall and box and pine –
'Twas axe and fire for all;
They scarce could tarry to blaze the line
Or wait for the trees to fall,
Ere the team was yoked and the gates flung wide,
And the dust of the horses' feet
Rose up like a pillar of smoke to guide
The wonderful march of Wheat.

Furrow by furrow, and fold by fold,
The soil is turned on the plain;
Better than silver and better than gold
Is the surface-mine of the grain.
Better than cattle and better than sheep
In the fight with the drought and heat.
For a streak of stubbornness wide and deep
Lies hid in a grain of Wheat.

When the stock is swept by the hand of fate,
Deep down in his bed of clay
The brave brown Wheat will lie and wait
For the resurrection day:
Lie hid while the whole world thinks him dead;
But the spring rain, soft and sweet,
Will over the steaming paddocks spread
The first green flush of the Wheat.

Green and amber and gold it grows
When the sun sinks late in the west
And the breeze sweeps over the rippling rows
Where the quail and the skylark nest.
Mountain or river or shining star,
There's never a sight can beat –
Away to the skyline stretching far –
A sea of ripening Wheat.

When the burning harvest sun sinks low,
And the shadows stretch on the plain,
The roaring strippers come and go
Like ships on a sea of grain;

Till the lurching, groaning waggons bear
Their tale of the load complete.
Of the world's great work he has done his share
Who has gathered a crop of Wheat.

Princes and potentates and czars,
They travel in regal state,
But old King Wheat has a thousand cars
For his trip to the water-gate;
And his thousand steamships breast the tide
And plough thro' the wind and sleet
To the land where the teeming millions bide
That say, 'Thank God for Wheat!'

Summertime

Anon

When summertime comes to Australia
Thongs and stubbies are formal regalia.
With sun, surf and beer
For most of the year,
It's the land of the long bacchanalia.

Midsummer Noon in the Australian Forest

Charles Harpur

Not a sound disturbs the air,
There is quiet everywhere;
Over plains and over woods
What a mighty stillness broods!

All the birds and insects keep
Where the coolest shadows sleep;
Even the busy ants are found
Resting in their pebbled mound;
Even the locust clingeth now
Silent to the barky bough:
Over hills and over plains
Quiet, vast and slumbrous, reigns.

Only there's a drowsy humming
From yon warm lagoon slow coming:
'Tis the dragon-hornet — see!
All bedaubed resplendently,
Yellow on a tawny ground —
Each rich spot nor square nor round,
Rudely heart-shaped, as it were
The blurred and hasty impress there
Of a vermeil-crusted seal,
Dusted o'er with golden meal.
Only there's a droning where
Yon bright beetle shines in air,
Tracks it in its gleaming flight,
With a slanting beam of light.
Rising in the sunshine higher,
Till its shards flame out like fire.

Every other thing is still,
Save the ever-wakeful rill,
Whose cool murmur only throws
Cooler comfort round repose;
Or some ripple in the sea
Of leafy boughs, where, lazily,
Tired summer in her bower
Turning with the noontide hour,
Heaves a slumbrous breath ere she
Once more slumbers peacefully.

O, 'tis easeful here to lie
Hidden from noon's scorching eye,
In this grassy cool recess
Musing thus of quietness.

Condamine Bells

Jack Sorensen

By a forge near a hut on the Condamine River
A blacksmith laboured at his ancient trade;
With his hammer swinging and his anvil ringing
He fashioned bells from a crosscut blade.

And while he toiled by the Condamine River
He sang a song for a job well done;
And the song and the clamour of the busy hammer
Merged and mingled in a tempered tone.

And the bells rang clear from the Condamine River
To the Gulf, to the Leeuwin, over soil and sand;
Desert eagles winging heard his stockbells ringing
As a first voice singing in a songless land.

The smith is lost to the Condamine River,
Gone is the humpy where he used to dwell;
But the song and the clamour of his busy hammer
Ring on through the land in the Condamine Bell.

from . . . The Castlereagh

Charles Souter ('Dr Nil')

Give me the backblocks, the backblocks for me!
With mutton chops and damper and an ounce or two of tea;
My water-bag and blanket and my black 'Jack-Shea',
Among the Warrumbungles on the old Castlereagh.

from . . . The Ocean Beach

Wilfred Mailler

I weary of the sun-scorched plain,
Its yellow, sere monotony;
I want the whisper of the rain;
I want the great, blue, surging sea.

Oh just to wash away the stain
Of dust eternal and be fanned
By winds that sing the strong refrain
Of crested wave and cool, wet sand.

The Norfolk Pine

Archie Bigg

For more than a million years they stand
Planted with care by Father Time,
Tended with love by nature's hand
A beautiful tree, the Norfolk pine.

And through their branches the white birds play
As above they soar and twist and climb
While deep below the rich moist clay
Holds fast the roots of the Norfolk pine.

In the year of seventeen seventy-four
Captain Cook, explorer fine,
Walked the untrodden forest floor
And he told his king of the Norfolk pine.

'I have,' claimed he, 'in my travels vast
'Neath a southern sky where bright stars shine
Found a suitable tree for the yards and masts
Of His Majesty's ships, in the Norfolk pine.'

The settlers came from a distant shore
With a strange new sound in a bygone time
The voice of man with his crosscut saw
As he took for his use the Norfolk pine.

And in anguish nature's hands were wrought,
Be patient, friend, said Father Time.
But man took all and he gave back nought
Though it served man well did the Norfolk pine.

Then a new generation of man was born
And he looked to the future beyond his time
Then he planted the hills that before were shorn
And he planted the valleys with Norfolk pine.

Thus he looked at the forest with different eyes,
At the beauty there of a tree so fine
As it speaks to the wind with a gentle sigh,
A beautiful tree is the Norfolk pine.

from . . . The Schoolhouse on the Plain

Joseph Furphy

On the geodetic line, where the parish boundaries join
At a level and interminable lane
You can see it there alone, standing calmly on its own,
Like an iceberg in a solitary main.
It's a topographic base, and each near or distant place
Is located from the Schoolhouse on the Plain.

It requires a lick of paint, to correct the weather-taint,
And its windows should have here and there a pane;
The open-jointed floor swallows pencils by the score,
And the veteran desks are inked with many a stain;
Still it's proof against the wet and there's lots of service yet
In that unpretentious Schoolhouse on the Plain.

And the lady-teacher there, comes from heaven alone knows
    where,
Like some angel they've vouchsafed to entertain.
She controls her motley drove by the gentle power of love,
Emphasising her affection with a cane –
True, she cavils all the while at the rough, untidy style
Of her pupils at the Schoolhouse on the Plain.

And when she is elsewhere gone, that old school will still live on,
Just as she herself was not the first to reign,
Since, for better or for worse, Young Australia comes in force
(As a reference to the year-book will explain)
And he only leaves a place for his duplicate to grace;
In the roll-book in the Schoolhouse on the Plain.

They mature, and off they drop, in an intermittent crop,
Not a single soul desiring to remain;
Many a shearer, tough and strong; many a drover, two yards long;
Many a bullock driver, hairy and profane;
Many a work-girl; many a wife – looking back upon their life,
Cherish memories of the the Schoolhouse on the Plain.

Some important changes gleam o'er the spirit of their dream,
For existence, as they quickly ascertain,
Is a great deal harder row than they thought they had to hoe,
As they blunder through their honourless campaign,
And they wish with all their heart they could make a second start
At the undervalued Schoolhouse on the Plain.

from . . . Song of the Future

AB Paterson ('The Banjo')

We have no tales of other days,
No bygone history to tell;
Our tales are told where campfires blaze
At midnight, when the solemn hush
Of that vast wonderland, the Bush,
Hath laid on every heart its spell.

On the Road to Bangalow

Jack Moses

I've left the stuffy city
Where my nerves have had a jar,
Through the hustle and the bustle,
Till I dunno where I are.
I'm trampin' in the open,
Just for freedom and a blow,
Where no coppers guard the corner,
On the road to Bangalow.

The Richmond hills are bonny,
And are worthy of a boost,
And we ought to crow our loudest,
Like the rooster on his roost.
I've seen them in the dawning,
And at sunset's ruddy glow,
Where the kookaburra chuckles
On the road to Bangalow.

There's the ibis in the rushes,
And the blue cranes at the pool,
And the kiddies on their ponies,
All a-coming home from school.
The corn is getting riper,
While the pigs and poddies grow;
There's money in the milkers,
On the road to Bangalow.

It's not a Jimmy Woodser
'Cause I've got me cobber here,
And we'll have another snifter
Just to toast the pioneer.
We'll drink this with our hats off,
'Cause we wouldn't like to go
And forget the Digger's father,
On the road to Bangalow.

Aussie Beach Christmas

Clare Bebrouth

Splashing through the surf on a sunny Christmas Day
Zinc cream on the nose to keep sunburn away
Kids on boogie boards come riding to the shore
But when we want to take them home they always beg for more.

Slip slop slap, slip slop slap, that's the way it's done
Christmas on an Aussie beach – the kids all play and run.
Slip slop slap, slip slop slap, that's the way it's done
Christmas on an Aussie beach – no snow but lots of sun.

Lifesavers on the shore, standing bronzed and tall,
A rider on a tricky wave is bound to have a fall.
The flags show where it's safe, the sharks all stay away,
The beach is where we park ourselves each lovely Christmas Day.

Some will go to church, it's right on Christmas Day,
They'll sing along with carols and for peace on earth they'll pray,
Then hurry home for lunch of ham and turkey cold
Then down onto the beach once more, green sea and sands of
   gold.

Slip slop slap, slip slop slap, that's the way it's done
Christmas on an Aussie beach – the kids all play and run.
Slip slop slap, slip slop slap, that's the way it's done
Christmas on an Aussie beach is always so much fun.

The Ten-Mile Coming Down

Graham Fredriksen

Remember well in seasons gone, Pacific cyclones dropped upon
the droughted valley north-west on toward the west divide.
The narrow banks of Ten-mile Creek release the waters as they
   peak
and flats become a tide.

The drovers waiting out the job – they've had to bush the white-
   face mob
behind the Pony Paddock knob until the creek goes down.
They slosh across the fox-tail flats in Drizabones and rain-drenched
   hats;
they're riding back to town.

And Conroy's truck bogged in the wet – *Down deep in mud and
   deep in debt*
– old Conroy cursed; I hear him yet below the bunya scrubs
all loaded down with grey gum logs . . . the clay-red pinch . . . he
   missed the cogs
and sank her to the hubs.

From high upon horizon slopes, the muddy water envelopes
the gully beds; the farmer's hopes are rising with the tide.
The torrents east of Gravel Ridge will join the flow at Ten-mile
    Bridge
on fronts a half mile wide.

The scrubs above the Stanton's Lease abandon now their tranquil
    peace
as raging waterfalls release a boiling white and loam.
Lantana gullies veiled in moss are drowned as mountain cascades
    toss
a mass of swirling foam.

From Carter's Block to Tableland, to Randall's Top, the catchment
    spanned,
through vales where huts and stockyards stand and cattle hug the
    hills,
the water like an ocean pours as bush folk smile from lonely doors
and every tank now fills.

Oh! could we see those days again, the days and days of ceaseless
    rain,
'twould ease the drought's relentless strain and bring the bush alive.
Well I recall how Grandma told of heavens raining liquid gold
like floods of 'fifty-five.

She told of distant youthful days – the memories time could not
    erase –
of Grandad rounding up the strays to move to higher ground;
him riding on his draught-horse mare across the swollen channels
    there
and coming home half-drowned.

Oh! could she be with me once more . . . see Grandma smiling at
    the door;
she has been gone since 'Ninety-four, yet her spirit remains
with children happy in the mud, though isolated by the flood,
in years that brought the rains.

Those happy childhood memories: the leaky ceiling . . . cyclone
   breeze . . .
and Grandma praying on her knees . . . while we all played the
   clown,
and missed a blessed week of school . . . and swam in our own
   front yard pool
and no one wore a frown –
just smiled across a sea of brown . . . and watched the Ten-mile
   coming down.

Adelaide

Charles Souter ('Dr Nil')

The agent's off, the anchor's up, the Old Man's come aboard.
By four bells in the dog watch he'll be drunk as any lord!
We've all sail set and drawing well and Paddy Doyle's been paid,
We're full and sound, A1 at Lloyds, and bound for Adelaide!

For Adelaide! For Adelaide! She is the sailor's joy!
She's fresh and fair is Adelaide, and plump, and not too coy!
I've sailed the blessed world around, loved girls of every shade,
But none so fair as can compare with saucy Adelaide.

. . .

The westerly has thrashed us o'er the Great Australian Bight;
The Old Man reckons we'll be off the Semaphore tonight;
Since last I saw the obelisk far round the world I've strayed,
But always kept my heart's best love for little Adelaide!

For Adelaide! For Adelaide! So sweet and sound and rare!
So trim and tight, with eyes so bright, and gently waving hair!
I've just about been everywhere and many games I've played,
But now I'm singing 'Home Sweet Home', hurrah for Adelaide!

Glenelg
Jim Haynes

Glenelg puts a smile on my face,
With the sea and the sun and the space.
Wish it was my home,
It's a fine palindrome.
Spelled backward it's still the same place.

from . . . The Wind that Buries the Dead
JW Gordon (Jim Grahame)

I spring from the land of the drifting sand,
The wind that buries the dead;
I cover the roads like a rippled beach
Where the feet of the lost men tread;
Old is the night when I take my rest;
I sleep till the flaming noon.
I ride to the height of the clouds at night
As they're scurrying past the moon.

Famine and drought are my henchmen stout,
My lover the wild bush-fire;
I will never shirk full share of work,
And my lover he will not tire,
As he's soaring high where the grass is dry,
With his wings, like a vulture's, spread,
The great trees fall at the crashing call
Of the wind that buries the dead.

He will strip the limbs of the tallest pine
And gnaw through the knotted bole;
Then he bites at the brush like a monster starved
And snarls at a fallen pole.
But the bones of the perished birds and beasts,
When the grassless plains are red,
Will be hidden deep by the restless sweep
Of the wind that buries the dead.

Half crazed with fears a woman peers
For the sight of a child that strayed;
The father has tramped and called all night
While she cared for the rest and prayed.
Two crusted furrows are on her cheeks –
Dry salt of the tears she shed.
Her tears may flow as the seasons go
For the wind will bury the dead.

The bushmen come in a mounted troop
And they scatter on hill and plain;
They follow the gullies and mulga ridge,
But their search will be in vain.
(There's a creeping army of small black ants
That twist like a winding thread
Round and round and across the mound
Where the wind has buried the dead.)

When the rivers rise to the red soil's edge
And the billabongs overflow,
The land turns green in a single night
Where the creeping waters go;
The wild swamp lilies bedeck the ground,
Like a golden mantle spread –
By the rich spring dress may the bush-birds guess
Where the wind has buried the dead.

The Stockman's Last Bed

George Moran

Whether stockman or not for a moment give ear,
For Jack's breathed his last and no more shall we hear
The crack of his whip and his jingling quart pot,
His clear 'go ahead' and his nag's lively trot.

While drafting some cattle down came his good horse,
'Alas,' cried poor Jack, 'I have run my last course!
I'll never more sit in the saddle again,
And bound like a kangaroo over the plain!'

So, stockmen, if ever at some future day
In search of a mob you should happen to stray,
And you come to the spot where Jack's bones are laid,
Far away from the home where in childhood he played,
Tread lightly where wattles their sweet fragrance spread
And the tall gum trees shadow the stockman's last bed.

The Bush Speaks

Ernest G Moll

I will be your lover
If you keep my ways.
All delights I'll give you;
Gum-tree scented days,
Skies where kestrels hover,
Nights with stars ablaze.

But, if you diminish
Care and think me won,
Other gifts I'll give you
Edged with thorn and sun,
And the crows will finish
What I have begun.

At the Melting of the Snow

AB Paterson ('The Banjo')

There's a sunny southern land,
And it's there that I would be
Where the big hills stand,
In the south countrie!
When the wattles bloom again,
Then it's time for us to go
To the old Monaro country
At the melting of the snow.

To the east or to the west,
Or wherever you may be,
You will find no place
Like the south countrie.
For the skies are blue above,
And the grass is green below,
In the old Monaro country
At the melting of the snow.

Now the team is in the plough,
And the thrushes start to sing,
And the pigeons on the bough
Are rejoicing at the spring.
So come my comrades all,
Let us saddle up and go
To the old Monaro country
At the melting of the snow.

'Irish Lords'

Charles Souter ('Dr Nil')

The clover-burr was two foot high and the billabongs were full,
The brolgas danced a minuet and the world seemed made of wool!
The nights were never wearisome and the days were never slow,
When first we came to 'Irish Lords', on the road to Ivanhoe.

The rime was on the barley-grass as we passed the homestead rails,
A 'Darling Jackass' piped us in with trills and turns and scales,
And youth and health and carelessness sat on the saddle-bow,
And . . . Mary lived at 'Irish Lords', on the road to Ivanhoe.

On every hand was loveliness, the fates were fair and kind;
We drank the very wine of life and never looked behind;
And Mary! Mary everywhere went flitting to and fro,
When first we came to 'Irish Lords', on the road to Ivanhoe.

The window of her dainty bower, where the golden banksia grew,
Stared like a dead man's glaring eye, and the roof had fallen
   through.
No violets in her garden bed, and her voice . . . hushed long ago . . .
When last we camped at 'Irish Lords', on the road to Ivanhoe.

Mount Bukaroo

Henry Lawson

Only one old post is standing –
Solid yet, but only one –
Where the milking, and the branding,
And the slaughtering were done.
Later years have brought dejection,
Care, and sorrow; but we knew
Happy days on that selection
Underneath old Bukaroo.

Then the light of day commencing
Found us at the gully's head,
Splitting timber for the fencing,
Stripping bark to roof the shed.
Hands and hearts the labour strengthened;
Weariness we never knew,
Even when the shadows lengthened
Round the base of Bukaroo.

There for days below the paddock
How the wilderness would yield
To the spade, and pick, and mattock,
While we toiled to win the field.
Bronzed hands we used to sully
Till they were of darkest hue,
'Burning off' down in the gully
At the back of Bukaroo.

When we came the baby brother
Left in haste his broken toys,
Shouted to the busy mother:
'Here is dadda and the boys!'
Strange it seems that she was able
For the work that she would do;
How she'd bustle round the table
In the hut 'neath Bukaroo!

When the cows were safely yarded,
And the calves were in the pen,
All the cares of day discarded,
Closed we round the hut-fire then.
Rang the roof with boyish laughter
While the flames o'er-topped the flue;
Happy days remembered after –
Far away from Bukaroo.

But the years were full of changes,
And a sorrow found us there;
For our home amid the ranges
Was not safe from searching Care.
On he came, a silent creeper;
And another mountain threw
O'er our lives a shadow deeper
Than the shade of Bukaroo.

All the farm is disappearing;
For the home has vanished now,
Mountain scrub has choked the clearing,
Hid the furrows of the plough.
Nearer still the scrub is creeping
Where the little garden grew;
And the old folks now are sleeping
At the foot of Bukaroo.

from . . . Where the Saltbush Grows
EJ Brady

I am sitting in a garden, by a harbour prospect fair,
And a green world glows around me into distance everywhere;
And the petals fall in showers
Like a snowstorm of dead flowers,
Where a young wind trips the orchard with the south wind in her
   hair.

We can never rest in cities, as our wise bush-mother knows;
Let the merchant to his market where the golden current flows;
But the bushman's feet must wander
In the open over yonder,
Where old myall droops his branches and the silver saltbush grows.

Song of the Wattle
Veronica Mason

The bush was grey a week today,
Olive green, and brown and grey,
But now the Spring has come this way
With blossom for the Wattle.

It seems to be a fairy tree,
That dances to a melody,
And sings a little song to me,
The graceful swaying Wattle.

Before the wind a maze it weaves,
Golden down in feathery sheaves!
A misty whirl of powdery leaves
The dainty bowing Wattle.

Its boughs up-lift their golden gift,
Sprays of yellow, downy drift
Through which the sunbeams shine, and sift
Their gold dust o'er the Wattle.

The bush was grey a week today,
Olive green and brown and grey,
But now it's sunny all the way,
For Oh! the Spring has come to stay
With blossom for the Wattle.

Spring Song
Roderic Quinn

Sing out and be happy!
The Spring is at hand,
The grass green, and sappy
The trees o' the land.

Sing! For the breeze is
Rustling and silky,
And toys with and teases
Long blossoms and milky.

The root in the juices
Unfrosted drinks deep;
The loving wave sluices
The weeds as they sleep.

Sing out! For the bees in
Their quest of wild honey
Are haunting the trees in
Green places and sunny.

Distant blue reaches
And green hills invite,
Green hills and long beaches
And roads red and white.

Locked waters are calling
With many gold voices,
Where tides gently falling
Make soft liquid noises.

Broad-spreading sun-glamour
Wraps blossom and stream,
Gold-tinting the armour
Of beetles that dream.

Full-sunned on lit ledges
The bronze lizard dozes,
And painting proud ridges
Grow tiny pink roses.

Sing out! and let trouble
Another pursue:
It will burst like a bubble
And vanish for you.

Out, out on old Sorrow,
Who skulks in her sable!
Laugh gaily, and borrow
Gay laughs while you're able.

If any care rankles –
Away! and behold
Pink feet and white ankles
On beaches of gold,

And surf that runs after
To kiss clinging dresses,
And white teeth and laughter,
And wild clinging tresses!

Camped by the Creek

Henry Kendall

'All day the strong sun has been drinking
The ponds in the Wattletree Glen;
And now, as they're puddles, I'm thinking
We were wise to head hitherwards, men!
The country is heavy to nor'ard,
But Lord, how you rattled along!
Jack's chestnut's best leg was put for'ard,

And the bay from the start galloped strong;
But for bottom, I'd stake my existence,
There's none of the lot like the mare;
For look! she has come the whole distance
With never the turn of a hair.

'But now let us stop, for the super
Will want us tomorrow by noon;
And as he can swear like a trooper,
We can't be a minute too soon.
Here, Dick, you can hobble the filly
And chestnut, but don't take a week;
And Jack, hurry off with the billy
And fill it. We'll camp by the creek.'

So spoke the old stockman, and quickly
We made ourselves snug for the night;
The smoke-wreaths above us curled thickly,
For our pipes were the first thing alight!
As we sat round a fire that only
A well-seasoned bushman can make,
Far forests grew silent and lonely,
Though the paw was astir in the brake.
But not till our supper was ended,
And not till old Bill was asleep,
Did wild things, by wonder attended,
In shot of our camping ground creep.
Scared eyes from thick tuft and tree-hollow
Gleamed out through the forest boles stark;
And ever a hurry would follow
Of fugitive feet in the dark.

While Dick and I yarned and talked over
Old times that had gone like the sun,
The wail of the desolate plover
Came up from the swamps on the run.
And sniffing our supper, elated,
From his den the red dingo crawled out;
But skulked in the darkness and waited,
Like a cunning but cowardly scout.
Thereafter came sleep that soon falls on

A man who has ridden all day;
And when midnight had deepened the palls on
The hills, we were snoring away.

But ere we dozed off, the wild noises
Of forest, of fen, and of stream,
Grew strange, and were one with the voices
That died with a sweet semi-dream.
And the tones of the waterfall, blended
With the song of the wind on the shore,
Became a soft psalm that ascended,
Grew far, and we heard it no more.

The Social Centre

Col Wilson ('Blue the Shearer')

The social centre of our town,
Where friends and neighbours meet,
Is not the Civic Centre,
Or the Plaza, down the street.
It's not the pub, the park, the pool,
The busy business strip.
The social centre of our town's
The local council tip.

Every Sunday afternoon,
We go up to the dump,
Loaded up with rubbish,
And we never fail to bump
Into folk we chance to know,
Tipping weeds, and flowers,
And other bits of rubbish,
More interesting than ours.

Our trailer-load of rubbish,
Looks quite mundane to us.
But look at all those people,
They're making quite a fuss

About our busted kettle,
Our iron that works no more,
And those bits of broken fibro –
God only knows what for.

But hang on. There's a bloke arrived.
Look at all his junk.
I'll just hang around, and scavenge through,
When he's done a bunk.
I can see some real good stuff.
I need some sheets of iron.
No need to wait. That other bloke,
Is scavenging through mine.

My wife and I look forward to
Our weekly social outing.
It's very interesting to see
The people up there, scouting
For all those bits and pieces
That other people shun.
In our town's social centre,
There's a place for everyone.

Come-By-Chance

AB Paterson ('The Banjo')

As I pondered very weary o'er a volume long and dreary –
For the plot was void of interest – 'twas the Postal Guide, in fact,
There I learnt the true location, distance, size and population
Of each township, town and village in the radius of the Act.

And I learnt that Puckawidgee stands beside the Murrumbidgee,
And that Booleroi and Bumble get their letters twice a year,
Also that the post inspector, when he visited Collector,
Closed the office up instanter, and re-opened Dungalear.

But my languid mood forsook me, when I found a name that took
    me,
Quite by chance I came across it – 'Come-by-Chance' was what I
    read;
No location was assigned it, not a thing to help one find it,
Just an 'N' which stood for northward, and the rest was all unsaid.

I shall leave my home, and forthward wander stoutly to the
    northward
Till I come by chance across it, and I'll straightway settle down,
For there can't be any hurry, nor the slightest cause for worry
Where the telegraph don't reach you nor the railways run to town.

And one's letters and exchanges come by chance across the ranges,
Where a wiry young Australian leads a pack horse once a week,
And the good news grows by keeping, and you're spared the pain
    of weeping
Over bad news when the mailman drops the letters in the creek.

But I fear, and more's the pity, that there's really no such city,
For there's not a man can find it of the shrewdest folk I know,
'Come-by-Chance', be sure it never means the land of fierce
    endeavour,
It is just the careless country where the dreamers only go.

Though we work and toil and hustle in our life of haste and bustle,
All that makes our life worth living comes unstriven for and free;
Man may weary and importune, but the fickle goddess Fortune
Deals him out his pain or pleasure careless what his worth may be.

All the happy times entrancing, days of sport and nights of
    dancing,
Moonlit rides and stolen kisses, pouting lips and loving glance:
When you think of these be certain you have looked behind the
    curtain,
You have had the luck to linger just a while in 'Come-by-Chance'.

The Old Tin Shed

Archie Bigg

In our back yard is an old tin shed
When I've mowed the lawn and the chooks are fed
I can't disappear but it must be said
I can hide away in the old tin shed.

Out in the shed where I like to be
There are wonderful things for all to see
Some say it's junk but it's treasure to me
Out there in the old tin shed.

There's a bench and a vice and an old wood stove
And a vintage car that my Grandad drove
There's a fishing basket a friend of mine wove
On a nail in the old tin shed.

Up in the loft there are things galore
An old iron bed and a cross cut saw
If I moved them about I'd fit much more
In the loft of the old tin shed.

There's a harness I used on the old brown mare
And a collar too, that ought to be there,
There's a handy box of chains somewhere
On a shelf in the old tin shed.

There's an old piano that's out of tune
And I know that it takes up too much room
And I promise myself I'll move it soon
Out of the old tin shed.

A garage sale would be the shot
I'd write down everything I've got
Trouble is I'd buy the lot
Put it back in the old tin shed.

There's a concrete floor and a light to boot
It's my very own place and I reckon it's beaut
Where I keep my tools and I park my ute
Out in the old tin shed.

When I'm too old to jump and shout
As long as I can still get about
There's one place to find me and there's no doubt
I'll be out in the old tin shed.

'Mullum'

Jack Moses

I am going back to 'Mullum',
To Mullumbimby I must go,
To Chincogan and the cattle,
Where the Brunswick's waters flow.

To the mountain range and valley
Where the mellow thrushes sing
Oh, what memories of mateship,
Oh, what merry thoughts they bring!

Oh, those happy days of boyhood
Splashing in the silvery pool
With the kookaburras laughing
In the gum-trees round the school,

I am going back to 'Mullum'.
And I needs must hurry so,
For somebody's waiting for me
By the sliprails lying low.

I must hasten; I must hurry;
For the sweetest girl in life
Keeps a vigil while I'm coming
She who'll be my Aussie wife.

If God gives us little kiddies,
They will go to our old school;
And they will dive as we did
In the shady swimming-pool.

And they'll love those hills and valleys
Where we'll work and till and sow,
Down by dear old Mullumbimby
Where the Brunswick's waters flow.

The Rush to London

Henry Lawson

You're off away to London now,
Where no one dare ignore you,
With Southern laurels on your brow,
And all the world before you.
But if you should return again,
Forgotten and unknowing,
Then one shall wait in wind and rain,
Where forty cheered you going.

You're off away to London, proved,
Where fair girls shall adore you;
The poor, plain face of one that loved
May never rise before you.
But if you should return again,
When young blood ceases flowing,
Then one shall wait in wind and rain,
Where forty cheered you going.

It may be carelessly you spoke
Of never more returning,
But sometimes in the London smoke,
You'll smell the gum leaves burning;
And think of how the grassy plain
Beyond the fog is flowing,
And one that waits in shine or rain,
Where forty cheered you going.

The Joys of Coming Home

'Badge'

When the sulky wheels are turning with a gravel crunching sound,
And the horse's shoes are firing on the rocky sunburnt ground,
And the shadows ride before me, through the horse's legs that pass
The sulky lamplight, shining on the dried-up brittle grass.

When the ghost-gums in the moonlight gleam against the shadows
    cast,
Where I drive down to the crossing, I'll know I'm home at last.
And the sandy bottomed shallows drag the horse's belly low,
And a blue dog barks a welcome, running with me as I go.

When the moonlight shows the slip-rails and a bread-box on a
    stump,
When the horse's stride grows longer and my heart begins to
thump . . .
When the kitchen door is opened I can end this little poem,
For the night will ring with laughter and the joys of coming home.

from . . . The Old Bush Track

Gertrude Hart

There's a swaying bough that beckons where a magpie flits and
    sings,
There is golden sunshine-laughter that the babbling river brings,
It will lead you, if you follow, to a grey-green twilight land,
Where the spirit of the bush-world waits to take you by the hand,
Roads a-many, eastward, westward, luring forward, stretching back,
You may find your long-lost childhood on the old bush track.

Where the bleached, white trunks are sentries, standing tall and
    thick and straight;
And, ere you know her purpose, you are through the magic gate;
Violet haze on distant ranges, seen through openings in the trees;
As you go the way that wanders with the fitful mountain breeze
Roads a-many, northward, southward, beck'ning forward, luring
    back,
Still the witching dream-spell lingers on the old bush track.

I Wish

Grahame Watt

I wish that I was wealthy, I wish that I could fly
Away to far-off places, to mountain tops so high.
I wish, I wish, that I could go where life is ever free,
Where everyone can build a home and raise a family.

I wish that I could travel to places that I know,
No border guards, no curfew, free to come and go.
I wish that I could live in peace forever and a day,
Where I'm allowed to speak my thoughts, stand and have my say.

I wish for richness in my life, the right to kneel in prayer,
I wish that I could always live without a fear or care.
Where is this land in all the world, this dream I hold so dear?
I tell you friend it's not so far, it's where we are – right here.

The Western Stars

Henry Lawson

On my blankets I was lyin',
Too tired to lift my head,
An' the long hot day was dyin',
An' I wished that I was dead.

From the West the gold was driven.
I watched the death of day,
An' the distant stars in Heaven
Seemed to draw my heart away.

from . . . Sea Fear

Charles Souter ('Dr Nil')

I can't go down to the sea again
For I am old and ailing;
My ears are deaf to the mermaid's call,
And my stiff limbs are failing
The white sails and the tall masts
Are no longer to be seen
On the dainty clipper ships that sailed
For Hull, and Aberdeen!

I can't go down to the sea again:
My eyes are weak and bleared,
And they search again for the gallant poop
Where once I stood and steered,
There's nought but wire and boiler-plate
To meet my wand'ring gaze.
Never a sign of the graceful spars
Of the good old sailing days!

So I will sit in the little room
That all old sailors know,
And smoke, and sing, and yarn about
The ships of long ago,
'The Flying Cloud', 'The Cutty Sark',
'The Hotspur' and 'The Dart' . . .
But I won't go down to the sea again,
For fear it breaks my heart!

Lost

AB Paterson ('The Banjo')

'He ought to be home,' said the old man, 'without there's
    something amiss.
He only went to the Two-mile – he ought to be back by this.
He *would* ride the Reckless filly, he *would* have his wilful way;
And, here, he's not back at sundown – and what will his mother
    say?

'He was always his mother's idol, since ever his father died;
And there isn't a horse on the station that he isn't game to ride.
But that Reckless mare is vicious, and if once she gets away
He hasn't got strength to hold her – and what will his mother say?'

The old man walked to the sliprail, and peered up the dark'ning
    track,
And looked and longed for the rider that would never more come
    back;
And the mother came and clutched him, with sudden, spasmodic
    fright:
'What has become of my Willie? Why isn't he home tonight?'

Away in the gloomy ranges, at the foot of an ironbark,
The bonnie, winsome laddie was lying stiff and stark;
For the Reckless mare had smashed him against a leaning limb,
And his comely face was battered, and his merry eyes were dim.

And the thoroughbred chestnut filly, the saddle beneath her flanks,
Was away like fire through the ranges to join the wild mob's ranks;
And a broken-hearted woman and an old man worn and grey
Were searching all night in the ranges till the sunrise brought the
    day.

And the mother kept feebly calling, with a hope that would not
    die,
'Willie! Where are you, Willie?' But how can the dead reply;
And hope died out with the daylight, and the darkness brought
    despair,
God pity the stricken mother, and answer the widow's prayer!

Though far and wide they sought him, they found not where he
    fell;
For the ranges held him precious, and guarded their treasure well.
The wattle blooms above him, and the bluebells blow close by,
And the brown bees buzz the secret, and the wild birds sing reply.

But the mother pined and faded, and cried, and took no rest,
And rode each day to the ranges on her hopeless, weary quest.
Seeking her loved one ever, she faded and pined away,
But with strength of her great affection she still sought every day.

'I know that sooner or later I shall find my boy,' she said.
But she came not home one evening, and they found her lying
    dead,
And stamped on the poor pale features, as the spirit homeward
    pass'd,
Was an angel smile of gladness – she had found the boy at last.

The Duty of Australians

Henry Lawson

'Tis the duty of Australians, in the bush and in the town,
To forever praise their country, but to run no other down;
Not to start at every nothing with the boast that bluffs and halts,
But to love their young Australia and explain away her faults.

Not to lose their heads in triumph, nor be bitter in defeat,
Not to rave about the coming of a fighting man – or fleet.
When a man or nation visits, in the key-day of its pride,
'Tis the duty of Australians to be kind, but dignified.

We can worship foreign talent – give our money, hearts and hands,
While we send our own, embittered, to win bread in foreign lands.
We are great to men who pedal, men who kick or bat the ball,
While our duty to the stranger is Australia's over all.

'Tis our place, when asked directions by a stranger in the land,
Not to jerk our thumb and mutter, for he may not understand.
We are free and we're enlightened, but at times we may forget
That the grand old-world politeness hasn't ruined England yet.

'Tis our duty to the stranger – landed, maybe, but an hour –
To give all the information and assistance in our power.
To give audience to the new chum and to let the old chums wait,
Lest his memory be embittered by his first days in the State.

'Tis our duty, when he's foreign, and his English very young,
To find out and take him somewhere where he'll hear his native
    tongue.
To give him our last spare moment, and our pleasure to defer –
He'll be father of Australians, as our foreign fathers were!

Spring Song of Sydney
Dorothea Mackellar

Spring has come back to this Sydney of ours;
All the deep gardens brim over with flowers;
All the steep gardens climb down to the harbour
Frothing with blossoms on trellis and arbour.
Clematis, jasmine, wisteria, rose,
Who can keep tale of the pageant that goes,
Scented and hued like the suite of a bride,
Toward the delphinium-blue of the tide?

Hark to the magpie, and in the hush
Now the sun's riding high – listen, a thrush!
Soon, soon the locust will silence their song,
Spring is swift-footed but Summer broods long.

from . . . The Call of London
EJ Brady

I have heard the call of London,
Yea, the savour rising sweet
Of its fleshpots, down in Fleet Street
When success is at your feet.

Now the mail hath brought a missive,
And its writer's pen of grace
Bids me hasten to the struggle
Ere I'm 'distanced in the race'.

'There's a wider field in Britain,
Or in Boston or New York;
Better chances for your effort,
Better payment for your work.

'Sell your socks and sling Australia;
There is nothing in the game.
I am doing well in London,
You can surely do the same.

'Raise the money for a passage,
Let Australia go to . . . Hay.'
So he puts the matter to me
From his fleshpot far away.

As I wrestle with temptation
On this clear October morn,
I can hear the bell-birds chiming
Through the bush, where I was born.

I can see the old gums waving
To the pressure of the wild
Warm winds of golden summer
That I longed for as a child.

So . . . I fling his missive fire-ward,
And I make reply in verse:
'I am married . . . to Australia,
Friend, for better or for worse.

'You may hunt your golden guineas
In the gloom of London town . . .
I am staying in the sunlight.'
And I turn temptation down.

SECTION THREE

Satires and Sarcasms
Any Other Time

All the poems here have a target. Some targets are specific, like bush shanties, politicians, self-assembly instructions, the monarchy, even Australian rhymed verse itself. Other verses are simply cynical reflections on life and its unavoidable and inevitable 'truths'.

The tone of the poetry here ranges from accepting, through gently deprecating to acerbic and insulting. Most of the verse in this section takes an oblique approach to the subject under attack. Many poems use a tongue-in-cheek approach, or even parody other styles to heighten their humour and make their point. The more outright complaining and whingeing verse has a section all to itself further on in the collection.

For me, the master of this style of verse in Australia has to be the almost-forgotten Victor Daley. Born in Ireland in 1858, Daley wrote under the nom de plume of 'Creeve Roe' and died from tuberculosis in 1905. His wonderful poem, 'Vision Splendid' manages to humorously attack various targets such as the proposed new federal bureaucracy, states-versus-commonwealth issues, parochial attitudes to Australian literature, Australian verse, contemporary poets and friends; he even turns the humour on himself.

I have also included examples of verse ranging from the simple jokey doggerel of writers like Jack Moses, Anon and myself through to some very cleverly crafted, wonderfully witty verse, like John Clarke's parody in 'Myer's Whopper'. There is also a lovely example of CJ Dennis's ability to understand and reveal the human foibles of small town life, capturing the attitudes and vernacular of his day to perfection in 'Pitcher Show'.

It is interesting to find that even the older poems here that make fun of colonial issues and affairs, such as 'Captain Bumble's Letter', are still quite accessible and humorous today. While it is true that satire, sarcasm and parody do require a knowledge of the target to be fully appreciated, it seems that, when these forms are done well, the verse is timeless.

Any Other Time

AB Paterson ('The Banjo')

All of us play our very best game –
Any other time.
Golf or billiards, it's all the same –
Any other time.
Lose a match and you always say,
'Just my luck! I was "off" to-day!
I could have beaten him quite halfway –
Any other time!'

After a fiver you ought to go –
Any other time.
Every man that you ask says, 'Oh,
Any other time.
Lend you a fiver! I'd lend you two,
But I'm overdrawn and my bills are due,
Wish you'd ask me – now, mind you do –
Any other time!'

Fellows will ask you out to dine –
Any other time.
'Not tonight, for we're twenty-nine –
Any other time.
Not tomorrow, for cook's on strike –
Not next day, I'll be out on the bike –
Just drop in whenever you like –
Any other time!'

Seasick passengers like the sea –
Any other time.
'Something . . . I ate . . . disagreed . . . with me!
Any other time
Ocean-travelling is . . . simply bliss,
Must be my . . . liver has gone amiss . . .
Why, I would laugh . . . at a sea . . . like this –
Any other time.'

Most of us mean to be better men –
Any other time:
Regular upright characters then –
Any other time.
Yet somehow as the years go by
Still we gamble and drink and lie,
When it comes to the last we'll want to die –
Any other time!

I Wonder

Wilbur G Howcroft

See the silly nitwit,
As witless as a lamb;
I'm glad I'm not a nitwit –
Good grief! Perhaps I am!

See the wicked sinner,
He's sure to go to hell –
A dreadful thought just struck me –
Perchance I might, as well!

See the horrid monster,
So sad to see, but say –
Is there a possibility
That I too look that way?

See the awful singer
Croaking out of key –
I wonder if by any chance
He sounds the same as me?

See the vulgar show-off
Taking up the floor –
Oh Lord, could it be possible
That I am such a bore?

See the hollow humbug
Talking through his hat –
I'd better make an end to this
Before I get like that!

Captain Cook
Jim Haynes

There once was a captain named Cook,
Sailed south just to have a quick look,
There he found a land,
Stuck a flag in the sand . . .
That's how native title got took.

Friendship
Anon

Two old ladies, we sit down to tea,
I'm eighty-four and she's eighty-three,
I hate her and she hates me,
But we're the only ones left, you see.

We meet every Wednesday at half-past three,
I go to her, then she comes to me.
I bore her and she bores me,
But we're the only ones left, you see.

She talks of Harry, and I of Fred,
And all the things they did and said,
We both tell lies and never agree,
But we're the only ones left, you see.

She boasts of the party at Number Three
When Fred kissed her instead of me.
I still wear his ring, so it's plain to see
Why I hate her and she hates me.

Never trust your best friend, they say,
And I don't trust her, not to this day,
But the rest are gone – so we'll pour some tea
For we're the only ones left, you see . . .

Two Fools

WT Goodge ('The Colonel')

There is the fool that spends his money fast,
Grows old and dies a pauper at the last.
There is the fool that hoards it to the end
And leaves it for some other fool to spend.

You Can't Miss It

Col Wilson ('Blue the Shearer')

The first thing that I noticed, when I moved up to the bush,
Was that when I asked directions from a local,
He'd get enthusiastic at the chance to show the way,
Explaining details fine in manner vocal.

You could bet your bottom dollar, if you had to ask the way,
To find the place that you were going to visit,
He'd end the explanation with those words I've come to hate –
'If you follow my directions, *you can't miss it*'.

Those words, '*you can't miss it*', came to represent
The kiss of death, a doomsday guarantee,
That I'd be lost for hours, roaming round the land,
Missing signs that I'm supposed to see.

'Just take the third fork to the left, the second to the right.
Go about two miles down the lane.
Veer right when you reach the creek, don't go up the hill,
And when you pass the haystack, left again.'

'*You just can't miss it*,' says my guide – I'm totally confused.
I hear those words, and give a mournful sigh.
I *know* I'll bloody miss it, he's said those words again.
I'm doomed to miss, no matter how I try.

He cheers me up before I leave, draws a little map,
And says just as I'm getting in the car:
'She's right, *you just can't miss it*,' and adds this sound advice,
'If you're getting bogged, you've gone a bit too far.'

My wife has ceased to worry if I'm missing for a week.
I'm following directions, quite explicit.
She knows I'm lost and wandering, just because someone
Has said to me those fatal words, *'can't miss it.'*

If you're ever out my way, drop in for a drink,
And if you need the answer to 'Where is it?'
It's that house around the corner, where the big tree used to grow.
It isn't hard to find, *you just can't miss it.*

Life
WT Goodge ('The Colonel')

Infant: teething, thrush and croup.
Schoolboy: marbles, top and hoop.
Youth: sweet picnics, cigarettes,
Cricket, football, sundry bets.

Young man: courtship, lovely she!
Married: youngsters, two or three,
Worry, trouble, smile and frown.
'In memoriam – William Brown!'

Success
Jim Haynes

At the tender age of three, success is not staining your pants with
   pee.
Pretty soon that trauma ends, by ten success is having friends.
By seventeen life's a mess with no driver's licence, that's success.
No prize for guessing what comes next, at twenty success is having
   sex.
From thirty to fifty life ain't funny, and we all know success means
   money.
By sixty life is less complex, and success is . . . having sex.
You're a big success at seventy-five if you still have a licence and
   can drive.
By eighty some of the bullshit ends, you're a success if you have
   friends.
And at eighty-five, believe you me, success is not staining your
   pants with pee.

Let Us Rejoice

Anon

Australians all let us rejoice for we are young and white,
The yellow hordes are on the way but we know we are right.
Though we can see undoubtedly our neighbours all are Asian,
We'll sing and dance and wave the flag because we are Caucasian.

A Vision Splendid

Victor Daley ('Creeve Roe')

Half waking and half dreaming,
While starry lamps hung low,
I saw a vision splendid
Upon the darkness glow.

The Capital Australian,
With waving banners plumed –
A shining flower of marble –
Magnificently bloomed.

Beside a snow-fed river
'Twas built in fashion rare –
Upon a lofty mountain,
All in a valley fair.

And I beheld a building
That made a stately show –
'The National Australian
Head Poetry Bureau'.

I gazed upon that building,
With trembling joy aghast;
The long-felt want of ages
Was filled (I thought) at last.

Now he would lodge right nobly
And sleep serene, secure,
All in a chamber filled with
Adhesive furniture.

For never foot of bailiff
Should pass his threshold o'er,
And never knock of landlord
Sound direful on his door.

The State should also aid him
To build his lofty rhyme
On lordly eggs-and-bacon,
And sausages sublime.

And he should drink no longer
Cheap beer at common bar,
But royal wine of Wunghnu
At two-and-nine a jar.

It was a vision splendid,
And brighter still did grow
When I was made the Chief of
'The Poetry Bureau'.

They clad me all in purple,
They hung me with festoons,
My singing-robes were spangled
With aluminium moons.

They also gave me power to
The grain sift from the chaff,
And choose at my large pleasure
My own poetic staff.

Then straightway I appointed
To chant by day and night,
The brilliant young Australian
Who sang 'The Land of Light'.

I also gave in fashion
Hilariously free
'The Girl and Horse Department'
In charge of Ogilvie.

And on the roof-ridge Brady
Sang salt-junk chanties great
To cheer the stout sea-lawyers
Who sail the Ship of State.

And tender-hearted Lawson
Sang everybody's wrongs;
And Brennan, in the basement,
Crooned weird, symbolic songs.

And on a throne beside me,
Above the common din,
He sang his Songs of Beauty,
My friend, the poet Quinn.

Our own Australian artists
Made beautiful its halls –
The mighty steeds of Mahony
Pranced proudly on the walls.

Tom Roberts, he was there, too,
With painted portraits fine
Of men of light and leading –
Me, and some friends of mine.

And Fischer, Ashton, Lister,
With beetling genius rife –
Pardieu! I was their Patron,
And set them up for life.

And from each dusky corner,
In petrified new birth,
Glared busts of me and Barton,
By Nelson Illingworth.

And nine fair Muses dwelt there,
With board and lodging free;
Six by the states were chosen,
And I selected three.

And there we turned out blithely
Australian poems sound,
To sell in lengths like carpet,
And also by the pound.

For Paddy Quinn, the statesman,
Had made a law which said
That native authors only,
On pain of death be read.

O, brother bards, I grieve that
Good dreams do not come true;
You see how very nobly
I would have done to you!

But, ah! the vision vanished,
And took away in tow
'The National Australian
Head Poetry Bureau'.

Parlez-Vous

Anon

An Aussie bloke once in Paree,
Whose knowledge of French was '*Oui, oui*',
Was asked, '*Parlez-vous?*'
And replied, 'Same to you!'
What a master of fast repartee!

How Dacey Rode the Mule

AB Paterson ('The Banjo')

'Twas to a small, up-country town,
When we were boys at school,
There came a circus with a clown,
Likewise a bucking mule.
The clown announced a scheme they had
Spectators for to bring –
They'd give a crown to any lad
Who'd ride him round the ring.

And, gentle reader, do not scoff
Nor think a man a fool –
To buck a porous-plaster off
Was pastime to that mule.

The boys got on; he bucked like sin;
He threw them in the dirt.
What time the clown would raise a grin
By asking, 'Are you hurt?'
But Johnny Dacey came one night,
The crack of all the school;
Said he, 'I'll win the crown all right;
Bring in your bucking mule.'

The elephant went off his trunk,
The monkey played the fool,
And all the band got blazing drunk
When Dacey rode the mule.

But soon there rose a galling shout
Of laughter, for the clown
From somewhere in his pants drew out
A little paper crown.
He placed the crown on Dacey's head
While Dacey looked a fool;
'Now there's your crown, my lad,' he said,
'For riding of the mule!'

The band struck up with 'Killaloe,'
And 'Rule Britannia, Rule,'
And 'Young Man from the Country,' too,
When Dacey rode the mule.

Then Dacey, in a furious rage,
For vengeance on the show
Ascended to the monkeys' cage
And let the monkeys go;
The blue-tailed ape and chimpanzee
He turned abroad to roam;
Good faith! It was a sight to see
The people step for home.

For big baboons with canine snout
Are spiteful, as a rule –
The people didn't sit it out,
When Dacey rode the mule.

And from the beasts he let escape,
The bushmen all declare,
Were born some creatures partly ape
And partly native-bear.
They're rather few and far between,
The race is nearly spent;
But some of them may still be seen
In Sydney Parliament.

And when those legislators fight,
And drink, and act the fool,
Just blame it on that torrid night
When Dacey rode the mule.

Lousy's Eating House

Anon

The place was built of hessian,
It wasn't bad at all;
The menu it was written
In charcoal on the wall.
The serviettes were bran bags,
The table was of bark –
And you often ate a beetle
Or a lizard in the dark.
And very often in the soup
There'd be an old bush mouse:
But they always bulked their crushings
In Lousy's Eating House.

Pitcher Show

CJ Dennis

The pitcher show it comes to town
Every Friday night.
Pitcher show? Pitcher show!
Oh, it's a show all right.
But I scarce 'ave time to look at the screen
There is so much else to be 'eard an' seen
In the audience, all polished an' clean,
Every Friday night.

Oh, the audience is a sight to see,
Every pitcher night:
Stout an' slim all proper an' prim,
Lookin' a orful sight;
Councillor Kidd all fussy an' fat
An' that wife of 'is in 'er ugly 'at
Sniffin' an' starin'; the nasty cat
Every pitcher night.

Butcher, baker an' all o' the town
Come to the pitcher show
All of 'em dressed in their Sunday best,
Sittin' up there in a row.
An' they snuffle an' snigger an' giggle an' grin,
Watchin' the pitcher an' taking it in,
While the boys at the back make a orful din
Up at our pitcher show.

It's as good as a play at the pitcher show,
Every Friday night,
Watchin' the crowd – the meek an' the proud
Gapin' at left an' right.
The couples draw close when the lights go out,
An' the larrikins stamp an' whistle an' shout,
An' the constable puts ole Doogan out,
Every Friday night.

I love the pitchers; but, goodness me!
'Ow can I watch the screen
When me mind's all took, wherever I look,
With things to be 'eard and seen?
Shoes an' stockin's an' 'at an' gown
That never was bought at our shops in town –
While I'm sizin' 'em up an' notin' 'em down,
'Ow can I watch the screen?

I gather the gossip for all the week
Up at the pitcher show.
'Ow they can spend their money no end
Is wot I should like to know.
As I sez to me friend, dear Mrs 'Awke,
It's worth the price an' it's worth the walk
For to 'ear them snippets of whispered talk
Up at the pitcher show.

There's scandalous doin's in this 'ere town,
An' none of 'em's room to talk;
For kettle an' pot is the same bad lot
As I mentions to Mrs 'Awke.
It's 'ard to believe that them tales is true,
But it's easy by addin' up two an' two
To come at the truth. An' I've always knoo
None of 'em's room to talk.

There's Connie Kidd with 'er nose in the air,
Pert as you please at that.
Puttin' on style with 'er 'aughty smile,
An' there, right nex' to 'er sat
The son of the woman wot washes an' scrubs,
Of ole Polly Dibbs with 'er soap an' 'er tubs;
An' 'im she ogles; but me she snubs;
Pert as you please at that.

Take it from me – an' I ain't fur wrong –
Somethin'll soon come out.
Talkin' away so easy an' gay,
An' flashin' 'er smiles about.
Talkin' the whole of the night, them two,

101

I think it's a scandal, indeed I do.
An' 'er father the 'ead of the Council too!
Somethin'll soon come out.

Somethin'll come. You mark my words,
Connie's a fair young minx
Saucy an' gay as the next, they say;
An' I near caught one of 'er winks.
(The pitcher? My it was simply grand!)
But I can't see Connie unless I stand,
Yet I'm almost sure 'e was 'olding 'er 'and.
Connie's a sly young minx.

Fancy 'er married to that young lout.
There'll be a hullaballoo!
An' 'er pa the squire, you might say, of the shire.
Yes, an' a J.P. too.
They was walkin' together when we come out
With 'arf o' the township 'anging about!
An' 'e seen 'er right to 'er 'ome no doubt,
There'll be a hullaballoo!

An' the parson, 'e said as 'e come to the door,
'E said 'twas a scandalous scene.
An' 'e meant 'im an' 'er, if 'e didn't refer
To the pitcher we'd 'ad on the screen.
Well 'e might 'a' meant that, or 'e might 'a' meant this,
An' I'd not be suprised if Bill give 'er a kiss
Tho' that was a bit that I 'appened to miss
Oh, wot a scandalous scene!

The pitcher? 'Twas great! But I dunno the name,
I was lookin' away at the time.
It was 'ow love is blind an' – you know the kind.
The actin' was simply sublime.
The girl 'ad a lover an' e' 'ad a friend,
An' they fought – O, not nothin' to reely offend!
But I didn't see 'ow it come out at the end,
I was looking away at the time.

The pitcher show comes to our town
Every Friday night.
Pitcher show? Well I know
It's a show all right.
When folks fergit their p's an' q's,
I gather quite a lot of news
An' get a lot of privit views
Every Friday night.

Job Application

Janine Haig

I want to work for the council;
I can lean on a shovel, you know;
And if you find speeding concerns you,
I can do things exceedingly slow.
I can act really dumb if you'd rather,
I can stare quite confused at a page,
I can move at the pace of a turtle,
I can do even less for my wage.
I can change a flat if I need to,
I can do lots of things, but I vow
That, if it's not part of my job,
I'll forget that I ever knew how.
I can get in to work late each morning,
And take extra time during breaks,
I can knock off and go home too early,
I will do just whatever it takes.
I can do only what I am told to:
If you tell me the things you expect;
And then when the end of the week comes
I can race back to town for my cheque.

Myer's Whopper

John Clarke ('Fifteen Bobsworth Longfellow')

Take the pieces from the package,
Lay them out as per the graph,
Gathering the bits you'll need,
Removing what you shouldn't have.
With the implement provided
Ease the bearings to the left,
Push the little angled mullion
Up into the socket 'F'.
This will free the moulded bracket
Holding back the nylon strand,
Draw the slippery hoop and coupling
Through the right-hand rubber-band.
Put the topside brown side outside,
Push the inside upside down,
Underneath the left-hand wingnut,
Press the folding backward crown.
Overlapping lifting side-flaps
Lower in to fit the screws,
Pack up tools, retire to distance,
Don protective hat, light fuse.

Leave Him in the Dog Yard

Keith Garvey

He's a nuisance on the place, hasn't any style or grace,
He's the type of horse can send a feller grey,
A treacherous sort of moke who was never properly broke
So leave him in the dogsmeat yard today.

Not a strong and robust steed, just a poor and bony weed,
Though we fed him bales of Riverina hay,
We bought him corn from Gatton but he simply wouldn't fatten
So leave him in the dogsmeat yard today.

A smart and cunning wretch and an awful rogue to catch,
Last night he kicked his mate the baldy bay.
Just watch him dodge and sidle when he sees you with a bridle,
So leave him in the dogsmeat yard today.

At the shows he wins no prize and he's dumped a lot of guys
Who climbed aboard his back in hopes to stay.
Lance Skuthorpe tried to do him but the bludger up and threw
    him,
So leave him in the dogsmeat yard today.

He knows every devilish trick and he loves to strike and kick,
I'll be more than happy when he's far away,
Where his hooves will clump and clatter down the ramp at
    Parramatta,
So leave him in the dogsmeat yard today.

In a greyhound's stomach dark he will race at Wentworth Park,
And never mind the RSPCA,
And the knackery profiteers for his soul will shed no tears,
So leave him in the dogsmeat yard today.

The Digger's Song
Barcroft Boake

Scrape the bottom of the hole: gather up the stuff!
Fossick in the crannies, lest you leave a grain behind!
Just another shovelful and that'll be enough –
Now we'll take it to the bank and see what we can find . . .
Give the dish a twirl around!
Let the water swirl around!
Gently let it circulate – there's music in the swish
And the tinkle of the gravel,
As the pebbles quickly travel
Around in merry circles on the bottom of the dish.

Ah, if man could wash his life – if he only could!
Panning off the evil deeds, keeping but the good;
What a mighty lot of digger's dishes would be sold!
Though I fear the heap of tailings would be greater than the gold . . .
Give the dish a twirl around!
Let the water swirl around!
Man's the sport of circumstance however he may wish.
Fortune! are you there now?
Answer to my prayer now –
Drop a half-ounce nugget in the bottom of the dish.

Gently let the water lap! Keep the corners dry!
That's about the place the gold will generally stay.
What was that bright particle that just then caught my eye?
I fear me by the look of things 'twas only yellow clay . . .
Just another twirl around!
Let the water swirl around!
That's the way we rob the river of its golden fish . . .
What's that? . . . Can't we snare a one?
Don't say that there's ne'er a one?
Bah! there's not a colour in the bottom of the dish!

Philosophy

Victor Daley ('Creeve Roe')

Life is a web with many broken ends:
Then why, O friend, be sad?
Good is not near so good as it pretends;
Bad is not half so bad.

Australian Born

Anon

Australian-born
Australian-bred
Long in the legs
And short in the head.

The Bankrupt Poet

Ernest Favenc

The wind had died to a gentle sigh,
And the ebbing tide left the smooth beach dry,
Where an Austral poet strolled by the sea,
And, said he, 'I am tired of that wattle tree.'

He looked around on the yellow sand –
'I am also tired of that "small white hand".
For metaphors soft I am at a loss,
And I hate the sight of the "Southern Cross".

'As for writing an ode to the "Waratah",
I'd as soon pen an ode to my grand-mama.
And my indolent muse refuses to rave
Of the bushman's bones and his lonely grave.

'The dingo's howl is an ancient theme,
Like that awful lie of the "digger's dream".
Scrub and mountain and boundless plain
Have been used *ad nauseam* again and again.

'The rattle of hooves and the whip's loud crack,
Sung by men who were ne'er on a horse's back,
Are as old as the hills, and the stockmen bold
Is as big a fraud as Coolgardie gold.

'And the cold white moon! Why I really think
That to sing of her would drive me to drink.
A horrible bore is that brown, bush girl
Who rides bare-backed steeds without getting a purl.

'I'd just as soon rhyme of bushrangers' games –
"Captains" Gaslight and Limelight, or some such names;
Or of grim, grey convicts and odorous blacks,
Who killed the bad squatters with awful whacks.

'No! I'll hie me away to some lonely pub,
Concealed in the depth of a shady scrub,
Take a moneyed friend, and I'll let him shout –
The Australian poet's about played out.'

My Literary Friend

Henry Lawson

Once I wrote a little poem which I thought was very fine,
And I showed the printer's copy to a critic friend of mine,
First he praised the thing a little, then he found a little fault;
'The ideas are good,' he muttered, 'but rhythm seems to halt.'

So I straighten'd up the rhythm where he marked it with his pen,
And I copied it and showed it to my clever friend again.
'You've improved the metre greatly, but the rhymes are bad,' he
    said,
As he read it slowly, scratching surplus wisdom from his head.

So I worked as he suggested (I believe in taking time),
And I burnt the 'midnight taper' while I straightened up the
    rhyme.
'It is better now,' he muttered, 'you go on and you'll succeed,
It has got a ring about it – the ideas are what you need.'

So I worked for hours upon it (I go on when I commence),
And I kept in view the rhythm and the jingle and the sense,
And I copied it and took it to my solemn friend once more –
It reminded him of something he had somewhere read before.

Now the people say I'd never put such horrors into print
If I wasn't too conceited to accept a friendly hint,
And my dearest friends are certain that I'd profit in the end
If I'd always show my copy to a literary friend.

The Singer

Charles Souter ('Dr Nil')

Sadness is in her eyes although they be not sad.
Gladness is in her smile and yet she is not glad.
Happiness is in her voice, though sorrow be her part.
She smiles and sings while Death is knocking at her heart.

The Olympians

Wilbur G Howcroft

In Lady Lamphrey's stately home,
Where blowflies never zoom,
And silent-footed servants slink
Submissive round the room –
In Lady Lamphrey's drawing room,
Mid chandeliers and brass,
The 'polished ones' pontificate
Upon the working class.

In Lady Lamphrey's mansion where
No debtors ever call
And busts from ancient cultures stand
Heraldic in the hall –
At Lady Lamphrey's 'afternoons'
The beau monde sip their tea
And denigrate the doings of
The bumbling bourgeoisie.

At Lady Lamphrey's dinners there
Is courtliness and grace
Where no one ever belches or
Has egg upon his face –
In Lady Lamphrey's dining room
They nibble through each course
And, poor fools, miss the rapture of
A good old pie and sauce!

from . . . A Treat for the London Poor

Victor Daley ('Creeve Roe')
(*Written on the occasion of Queen Victoria's Diamond Jubilee procession through the poorer suburbs of London*)

They are hungry; they are ragged; they are gaunt and hollow-eyed;
But their frowsy bosoms palpitate with fine old British pride;
And they'll belt their rags in tighter and they'll hoarsely cry,
  'Hooray!'
When their good queen's circus passes on sexagenary day.
Oh the thunder of the drums,
And the cry of, 'Here she comes!'
Will be better than a breakfast to the natives of the slums.

Sixty years their gracious Queen has reigned a-holding up the sky,
And a-bringing round the seasons, hot and cold, and wet and dry;
And in all that time she's never done a deed deserving gaol –
So let joy-bells ring out madly and Delirium prevail!
Oh her Poor will blessings pour
On their Queen whom they adore;
When she blinks her puffy eyes at them they'll hunger never more.

She has reigned – aloft, sublime –
Sixty years – let joy-bells chime!
And these God-forgotten wretches were her subjects all that time!

Yobbo Poem

Anon

Of course I love ya, darling, you're a really top-notch bird
When I say you're gorgeous I mean every single word.
So ya bum is on the big side, I don't mind a bit of flab,
It just means that when I'm ready, well, there's somethin' there to
  grab
So your belly isn't flat, I tell you I don't care
As long as when I cuddle ya me arms still fit round there.
No sheila who's the age you are has nice firm perky breasts,
They just gave in to gravity, I know you did your best.
I always tell the truth dear, I'd never tell ya lies

I think it's very sexy to have dimples in ya thighs.
I swear upon me mother's grave the moment that we met
I knew you were as good as I was ever gonna get.
No matter what you look like, I'll always love you, dear –
Now quiet while the footy's on and fetch another beer.

A Quatrain
WT Goodge ('The Colonel')

The humble mind let none despise,
Of wit let none be vain,
The germ of genius dormant lies
In every human brain!

Grounds for Divorce
Anon

There was a young drover named Gorse
Who fell madly in love with his horse.
Said his wife, 'You rapscallion,
That horse is a stallion!
This constitutes grounds for divorce.'

The Rabbit
Anon

The bush has been wrecked by the rabbit
Because of the doe's wanton habit
Of fast populating
By just copulating
When any male rabbit can grab it.

A Mountain Station

AB Paterson ('The Banjo')

I bought a run a while ago,
On country rough and ridgy,
Where wallaroos and wombats grow –
The Upper Murrumbidgee.
The grass is rather scant, it's true,
But this a fair exchange is,
The sheep can see a lovely view
By climbing up the ranges.

And 'She-oak Flat's the station's name,
I'm not surprised at that, sirs:
The oaks were there before I came,
And I supplied the flat, sirs.
A man would wonder how it's done,
The stock so soon decreases –
They sometimes tumble off the run
And break themselves to pieces.

I've tried to make expenses meet,
But wasted all my labours,
The sheep the dingoes didn't eat
Were stolen by the neighbours.
They stole my pears – my native pears –
Those thrice convicted felons,
And ravished from me unawares
My crop of paddymelons.

And sometimes under sunny skies,
Without an explanation,
The Murrumbidgee used to rise
And overflow the station.
But this was caused (as now I know)
When summer sunshine glowing
Had melted all Kiandra's snow
And set the river going.

And in the news, perhaps, you read:
'Stock passings. Puckawidgee,
Fat cattle: Seven hundred head
Swept down the Murrumbidgee;
Their destination's quite obscure,
But, somehow, there's a notion,
Unless the river falls, they're sure
To reach the Southern Ocean.'

So after that I'll give it best;
No more with Fate I'll battle.
I'll let the river take the rest,
For those were all my cattle.
And with one comprehensive curse
I close my brief narration,
And advertise it in my verse –
'For Sale! A Mountain Station'.

Epitaph – Williamtown
Anon

Beneath this stone Sam Bodin lies;
No one laughs and no one cries.
Where he's gone, and how he fares,
No one knows, and no one cares.

The Parson and the Prelate
Victor Daley ('Creeve Roe')

I saw a parson on a bike –
A parody on things –
His coat-tails flapped behind him like
A pair of caudal wings.

His coat was of the shiny green,
His hat was rusty brown;
He was a weird, wild sight, I ween,
Careering through the town.

What perched him on a wheel at all,
And made him race and rip?
Had he, perchance, a sudden call
To some rich rectorship?

He'd no such call; he raced and ran
To kneel and pray beside
The bedside of a dying man,
Who poor as Peter died.

I saw a prelate, plump and fine,
Who gleamed with sanctity;
He was the finest-groomed divine
That you would wish to see.

His smile was bland; his air was grand;
His coat was black, and shone
As did the tents of Kedar and
The robes of Solomon.

And in a carriage fine and fair
He lounged in lordly ease –
It was a carriage and a pair –
And nursed his gaitered knees.

And whither went he, and went for,
With all this pomp and show?
He went to see the governor,
And that is all I know.

But in a vision of the night,
When deep dreams come to men,
I saw a strange and curious sight –
The prelate once again.

He sat ungaitered, and undone,
A picture of dismay –
His carriage was too broad to run
Along the Narrow Way!

But, with his coat-tails flapping like
Black caudal wings in wrath,
I saw the parson on the bike
Sprint up the Shining Path.

Faith
Victor Daley ('Creeve Roe')

Faith shuts her eyes, poor self-deceiver!
The last god dies with the last believer.

God and Poets
Jack Sorensen

I think God values spinifex as highly as the rose,
He even may like poetry that reads like rancid prose
The reason I suppose
Is that He feels responsible for all He sows and grows
And so gives equal marks for song to nightingales and crows,
Though why, God only knows.

Captain Bumble's Letter
Charles Thatcher

Don't talk about Sebastopol,
The Russian War is flat now.
Just listen to despatches
Just come from Ballarat now.
Our noble Governor, Sir Charles,
And where is there a better,
Has permitted us to publish
Captain Bumble's private letter.

He writes thus to His Excellency,
'Myself and Major Stiggins
Got our brave fellows all equipped
And started for the diggin's.
Our band struck up "God Save the Queen",
Into cheers our men were bursting,
And every gallant soldier was
For glorious action thirsting.

'Our first attack was on two drays
Which we saw in the distance,
But the enemy surrendered
After just a slight resistance.
We were disappointed in our search
Of these two wretched traitors,
For instead of seizing powder
It was loaded with potatoes.

'We marched but were obliged to halt
On behalf of Sergeant Trunnions,
Who was unable to proceed
On account of having bunions.
We stationed pickets all around
To give us timely warning
And there we bivouacked and slept
Till nine the following morning.

'At length into the diggin's,
Footsore our men did tramp there,
And we took up our position
Within the Gov'ment camp there:
Provisions were served out to all
And my very soul it tickles
To contemplate their ravages
On the cold boiled beef and pickles.

'We watched at night, but all was still:
For glory we were yearning,
And we fired upon a tent in which
A candle was seen burning.
We killed a woman and a child
Though 'twas not our intention;
But that slight mistakes occur
Of course I needn't mention.

'At length in earnest was the strife:
While buried in their slumbers,
We made a bold and desperate charge
And cut them down in numbers.
Our gallant fellows fought like bricks,
The rebels were defeated,
And then by hundreds off they ran
And to the bush retreated.

'Thus all is quiet and I now
Subscribe myself your humble
Devoted servant of the Crown,
Frederick Augustus Bumble.'

Postscript
'Pray send us up some good cheroots
And anything that's handy
And by all means, pray don't forget
We're nearly out of brandy.'

When the Police Force Couldn't Spell
Jack Moses

Years ago when our land was new,
Scholars then were very few,
A poor old cabbie's horse dropped dead
In Castlereagh Street, it was said.

Policeman '9' was standing by
And saw the neddy fall and die.
'On this I must at once report –
Can I spell Castlereagh?' he thought.

God bless the force! They are never beat.
He dragged the horse into K-I-N-G Street!

from . . . The Comment Ironic

CJ Dennis

In response to cable reports of ironical comments from English cricket spectators

We never say Boo!
As Australians do
With a loud and vociferous bellow.
And vulgar abuse?
Oh, I say, what the deuce!
Would you take a rise out of a fellow?
I mean to say – What?
When our passions wax hot
We may even wax slightly satiric,
But not in the way
That Australians may
When the barracking lifts to the lyric.
I will even admit,
Should the circumstance fit,
We may even grow mildly sardonic;
And you'll hear in the hush
Some loud fellow cry 'Tush!'
Well, that is a comment ironic.

Tho' Australians may,
I am sorry to say,
Grow exceedingly coarse in the outer;
And, in fashion quite crude,
Hurl their epithets rude
At a bowler, or batsman or scouter;
In Britain our style
Is to mark by a smile
Or a frown or some fleeting expression
Our views of the play
In a cultural way;
For we're devilish good at repression.
And if some grave breach
Should impel us to speech
It's mellifluous, mild and euphonic.
Should the play be quite bad
We may mutter 'Egad!'
And that is a comment ironic.

Political Correctness
Anon

Said a joker from old Cunnamulla.
'Now you can't joke about race or colour,
Political correctness,
With all its perfectness,
Is making my life a lot duller!'

To The Impressionist School
WT Goodge ('The Colonel')

I'd love to be an artist, an artist free from guile,
And wear long hair and a great big stare,
And a transcendental smile.

I'd love to paint a picture, a picture full of thrill,
Of a knock-kneed horse on the Randwick Course
And the moon behind a hill.

I'd love to paint a portrait, a portrait full of soul,
Of the cross-eyed girl with her hair in curl
And a neck like a barber's pole

I'd love to paint a landscape, a landscape bold and free,
With a Vandyck cliff and a crimson skiff
On a lilac-tinted sea.

Art
Jim Haynes

When I bought an expensive Brett Whiteley
I asked my grandma, who's still sprightly,
'Tell me what you think, Gran.'
And she said, 'Well, I can,
But I can't really put it politely!'

Australia in Contemporary Literature
RH Croll

Whalers, damper, swag and nosebag,
Johnny-cakes and billy-tea,
Murrumburrah, Meremendicoowoke,
Yoularbudgeree,
Cattle-duffers, bold bushrangers,
Diggers, drovers, bush race-courses
And, on all the other pages,
Horses, horses, horses, horses.

The Great Australian Adjective
WT Goodge ('The Colonel')

A sunburnt bloody stockman stood,
And in a dismal bloody mood,
Apostrophised his bloody cuddy:
'This bloody moke's no bloody good,
He doesn't earn his bloody food.
Bloody! Bloody! Bloody!'

He jumped across his bloody horse
And galloped off of bloody course,
The road was wet and bloody muddy.
He rode up hill, down bloody dale,
The wind, it blew a bloody gale.
Bloody! Bloody! Bloody!

He came up to a bloody creek;
The bloody horse was bloody weak;
The creek was full and bloody floody.
He said, 'This moke must sink or swim
The same for me as bloody him:
Bloody! Bloody! Bloody!'

He plunged into the bloody creek:
The horse it gave a bloody shriek:
The stockman's face a bloody study,
Ejaculating as they sank,
Before they reached the bloody bank:
'Bloody! Bloody! Bloody!'

The Uplift

AB Paterson ('The Banjo')

When the drays are bogged and sinking, then it's no use sitting
    thinking,
You must put the teams together and must double-bank the pull.
When the crop is light and weedy, or the fleece is burred and
    seedy,
Then the next year's crop and fleeces may repay you to the full.

So it's lift her, Johnny, lift her,
Put your back in it and shift her,
While the jabber, jabber, jabber of the politicians flows.
If your nag's too poor to travel
Then get down and scratch the gravel
For you'll get there if you walk it – if you don't, you'll feed the
    crows.

Shall we waste our time debating with a grand young country
    waiting
For the plough and for the harrow and the lucerne and the maize?
For it's work alone will save us in the land that fortune gave us
There's no crop but what we'll grow it; there's no stock but what
    we'll raise.

When the team is bogged and sinking
Then it's no use sitting thinking.
There's a roadway up the mountain that the old black leader
    knows:
So it's lift her, Johnny, lift her,
Put your back in it and shift her,
Take a lesson from the bullock – he goes slowly, but he goes!

Rafferty Rides Again

Thomas V Tierney

There's a road outback that becomes a track
Where the hills dip down to the plain;
And on misty moonlit nights up there
The old inhabitants all declare
On his big black stallion (or was it a mare?)
Rafferty rides again.

A bushranger bold in the days of old,
'Twas an evil name that he bore,
Till they shot him down from behind a tree –
At least that's the yarn they told to me
When I asked who this Rafferty bloke might be,
And what he was riding for.

And now it appears, after all the years
That low in his grave he has lain,
That o'er the hills, in the same old way,
Dashing and debonair, reckless, gay,
On his chestnut charger (or was it a bay?)
Rafferty rides again.

I have waited long the old hills among,
But my vigils have been in vain;
I've perched all night in a towering tree,
But devil a ride he'd pick for me,
Though I would have given the world to see
Rafferty ride again.

But the tale is true that I'm telling you,
Though it's ages since he was slain;
To all the folk in the hills 'tis known
That, awesome and spectral, and all alone,
On his snow-white courser (or was it a roan?)
Rafferty rides again.

His Troubles
Victor Daley ('Creeve Roe')

The parson said: 'Your sinful past
Will make for you a fiery rod.'
I smiled, and thought upon the vast
Amused indifference of God.

A Word to Texas Jack
Henry Lawson

Texas Jack, you are amusin'. By Lord Harry, how I laughed
When I seen yer rig and saddle with its bulwarks fore-and-aft;
Holy smoke! In such a saddle how the dickens can yer fall?
Why, I seen a girl ride bareback with no bridle on at all!

Gosh, so-help-me! Strike me barmy! If a bit o' scenery
Like to you in all your rig-out on the earth I ever see!

How I'd like ter see a bushman use yer fixins, Texas Jack;
On the remnant of a saddle he can ride to hell and back.
Why I heerd a mother screamin' when her kid went tossin' by
Ridin' bareback on a bucker that had murder in his eye.

What? Yer come to learn the natives how to squat on horse's back!
Learn the cornstalk ridin'? Blazes! What yer giv'n us, Texas Jack?
Learn the cornstalk – what the flamin' jumptup! Where's my
    country gone?
Why, the cornstalk's mother often rides the day before he's born!

You may talk about your ridin' in the city, bold an' free,
Talk of ridin' in the city, Texas Jack, but where'd yer be
When the stock horse snorts and bunches all 'is quarters in a hump,
And the saddle climbs a sapling an' the horse-shoes split a stump?

No, before you teach the natives you must ride without a fall
Up a gum or down a gully nigh as steep as any wall –
You must swim the roarin' Darlin' when the flood is at its height
Bearin' down the stock and stations to the Great Australian Bight.

You can't count the bulls an' bisons that yer copped with your lassoo
But a stout old myall bullock p'raps 'ud learn yer somethin' new;
Yer'd better make yer will an' leave yer papers neat an' trim
Before you make arrangments for the lassooin' o' him;
'Ere you 'n' yer horse is catsmeat, fittin' fate for sich galoots,
And yer saddle's turned to laces like we put in blucher boots.

And yer say yer death on Injins! We've got something in yer line –
If yer think yer fitin's ekal to the likes of Tommy Ryan.
Take yer karkass up to Queensland where the allygators chew
And the carpet-snake is handy with his tail for a lassoo.

Ride across the hazy regions where the lonely emus wail
An' ye'll find the black'll track yer while yer lookin' for his trail;
He can track yer without stoppin' for a thousand miles or more –
Come again an' he will show yer where yer spit the year before.

But yer'd best be mighty careful, yer'll be sorry yer come here
When yer skewered to the fakements of yer saddle with a spear –
When the boomerang is sailin' in the air, may heaven help yer!
It'll cut yer head off going', an' come back again and skelp yer.

PS: As poet and as Yankee I will greet you, Texas Jack,
For it isn't no ill-feelin' that is gettin' up me back
But I won't see this land crowded by each Yank and British cuss
Who takes it in his head to come a-civilisin' us.

The Smiths

EG Murphy ('Dryblower')

We had many problems set us when Coolgardie was a camp,
When the journey to the goldfields meant a coach-fare or a tramp;
We had water questions, tucker ditto, also that of gold,
How to clothe ourselves in summer, how to dress to dodge the cold.
We marvelled how the reefs occurred in most unlikely spots,
For the topsy-turvy strata tied geologists in knots;
But though we plumbed the depths of many mysteries and myths,
The worst we had to fathom was the prevalence of Smiths.

To say they swarmed Coolgardie was to say the very least,
For they over-ran the district like the rabbits in the East;
The name predominated in the underlay and drive,
The open-cut and costeen seemed to be with Smiths alive;
Where the dishes tossed the gravel they had gathered from afar,
They clustered at the two-up school and at the shanty bar;
And while Jones and Brown were just as thick as herrings in a frith,
If you threw a stone at random you were sure to hit a Smith.

There were Smiths from every region where the Smiths are known
    to grow,
There were cornstalk Smiths, Victorian Smiths, and Smiths who eat
    the crow,
There were Maori Smiths, Tasmanian Smiths, and parched-up
    Smiths from Cairns;
Bachelor Smiths and widower Smiths and Smiths with wives and
    bairns.
Some assumed the names for reasons that to them were known the
    best
When silently they packed their ports and flitted to the West,
Till every second man you met to yarn or argue with
Was either a legitimate or else a bogus Smith.

It really mattered little till the days the big mails came,
And then began the trouble with that far-too-frequent name;
For the Smiths rolled up in regiments when the letter 'S' was called,
To drive the post-officials mad and prematurely bald.
Shoals of Smiths demanded letters that were never to them sent,
Wrong Smiths got correspondence which for them was never meant;
And many a Smith, whose facial calm shamed Egypt's monolith,
Bought jim-jams with the boodle sent to quite a different Smith.

The climax came one Christmas Eve, the mail was on its way,
And the post-officials yearned to block the Smiths on Christmas
    Day;
So they faked an Eastern telegram by methods justified,
Upon it put no Christian name and tacked it up outside;
It was from a Melbourne lawyer, and addressed to 'Smith, Esquire',
It was stamped 'prepaid and urgent', so 'twould confidence inspire,
And when Coolgardie sighted it and marked its pungent pith,
There was pallid consternation in the habitat of Smith.

'Our client has informed us you are over in the West,'
Ran the message, 'and she threatens your immediate arrest;
She hears you're known as Smith, but says you needn't be afraid
If you'll come and face the music and redeem the promise made.'
The population read it, and before the daylight came
A swarm of Smiths rolled up their swags and took a different name,
They declined to 'face the music' and return to kin and kith,
And the maidens who were promised still await the absent Smith.

Behind the Scenes

AB Paterson ('The Banjo')

The actor struts his little hour,
Between the limelight and the band;
The public feel the actor's power,
Yet nothing do they understand
Of all the touches here and there
That make or mar the actor's part,
They never see, beneath the glare,
The artist striving after art.

To them it seems a labour slight
Where nought of study intervenes;
You see it in another light
When once you've been behind the scenes.

For though the actor at his best
Is, like a poet, born not made,
He still must study with a zest
And practise hard to learn his trade.
So, whether on the actor's form
The stately robes of Hamlet sit,
Or as Macbeth he rave and storm,
Or plays burlesque to please the pit,

'Tis each and all a work of art,
That constant care and practice means –
The actor who creates a part
Has done his work behind the scenes.

Eating By Yourself

Kenneth Slessor

Let aristocratic heroes
Boast the platters of the Guelph,
You can dream of Trocaderos
When you're dining by yourself;
You can hover like a glutton,
You can order what you choose,
Try the fricassee of mutton,
Toy with terrapin ragouts,
All the claret of Lugano,
All the fairy teas-and-toasts,
Brought by Ferdinand Romano
And a staff of lovely ghosts.

First the oysters, round and juicy,
Served by some delightful girl —
Call her Nancy, call her Lucy,
She may fetch perhaps a pearl;
Next the soup of tender turtle
From a nymph with yellow hair —
Call her Mabel, call her Myrtle,
She can spice it with a stare;
Then the fowl on gleaming china
That a pretty creature brings —
Call her Dulcie, call her Dinah,
You may find a pair of wings.

For a moment they will glimmer,
For a twinkle they will gleam —
Then the kettle starts to simmer
And they vanish like a dream;
You can whistle for them vainly,
You may call in tender tones,
But the soup is printed plainly
With the name of Foggitt, Jones;
Then you suddenly awaken —
There's a sausage on the shelf,
And the bacon looks like bacon,
And you're eating by yourself!

Superannuation

Anon

Life can be cruel, there is no doubt,
When you've money to burn – the fire's gone out!

'Incognito'

Anon

Every station in the country keeps a pony that was sent
Late at night to fetch a doctor or a priest,
And has lived the life of Riley since that faraway event;
But the stories don't impress me in the least.

For I once owned Incognito – what a jewel of a horse!
He was vastly better bred than many men,
But they handicapped so savagely on every local course
I was forced to dye him piebald now and then.

For I needed all the money that a sporting life entails,
Having found the cost of living rather dear,
And my wife, the very sweetest little girl in New South Wales,
Was presenting me with children every year.

We were spreading superphosphate one October afternoon
When the missus said she felt a little sick:
We were not expecting Septimus (or Septima) so soon,
But I thought I'd better fetch the doctor quick.

So I started for the homestead with the minimum delay
Where I changed and put pomade on my moustache,
But before I reached the sliprails Incognito was away
And was heading for the township like a flash.

First he swam a flooded river, then he climbed a craggy range,
And they tell me (tho' I haven't any proof)
That he galloped through the township to the telephone exchange
Where he dialled the doctor's number with his hoof.

Yes, he notified the doctor and the midwife and the vet,
And he led them up the mountains to my door,
Where he planted, panting, pondering, in a rivulet of sweat
Till he plainly recollected something more;

Then he stretched his muzzle towards me, he had something in his
    teeth
Which he dropped with circumspection in my hand,
And I recognized his offering as a contraceptive sheath,
So I shot him. It was more than I could stand.

But I've bitterly repented that rash act of injured pride –
It was not the way a sportsman should behave,
So I'm making my arrangements to be buried at his side,
And to share poor Incognito's lonely grave.

What's in a Name? (Or . . . What's in a Pie?)
Jim Haynes

The argument rages on a treat,
Is the meat pie really 'meat'?
Can the bits they put inside
As 'meat' be truly classified?

Pie-makers say it's meat, at least
It comes from somewhere on the beast!
And no one's queuing up to buy
An item called 'bull's penis pie'!

There *Is* an Easter Rabbit
Greg Champion

There is an Easter Rabbit, he lives down in the woods
Where he is manufacturing retail Easter goods.
He's rationalised the industry to make it more competitive,
Retrenching a few furry friends to be more get-ahead-ative.
He has seen his market niche and he's out there to grab it.
He really is a very cluey corporate Easter Rabbit!

The Great Secret
Victor Daley ('Creeve Roe')

I met a ghost, some nights ago,
And we walked down the road together.
The moon was full; the tide at flow;
And very pleasant was the weather.

He was an entertaining sprite,
With manners frank and unaffected;
And anyone could tell at sight
He was, or had been, well-connected.

I said: 'In this world do you pass
Much time?' Said he: ''Tis not forbidden.
We are as thick as blades of grass
Around you – but are mostly hidden.'

'And that strange world beyond the sky,
Is it not wonderful and noble?
I long to see it, and to fly
From this base world of sin and trouble.'

The ghost said: 'Chafe not at your lot,
Nor leave too soon your situation;
Our high authorities do not
Encourage reckless immigration.'

'But say it is a happier sphere –
Just give your word and I will take it!'
He smiled and said – 'Like this world here,
It's mostly what you like to make it.'

How We Look at It
WT Goodge ('The Colonel')

No doubt that there are faults in all
As laid to mankind's charge,
But let's be thankful ours are small
While other folk's are large.

Portraits and Personalities

Old Portraits

Our rhymed verse tradition has not included too many poems in praise of great figures from Australian history. There are quite a few poems and ballads in praise of bushrangers and sporting heroes, both real and fictional, but our bush ballad tradition has been more focused on narrative and landscape than portraiture.

The bulk of the verses I unearthed for this section were pen portraits of 'types' and idealised characters, humorous or poignant caricatures, even archetypes, rather than descriptions of real figures.

A brief look through this section shows that without the prolific pen of CJ Dennis it would be a slim section indeed. Dennis had a natural knack for 'character' and was able to describe a 'typical' character or an archetypal Aussie with an accuracy that few other verse writers ever managed. His feel for the vernacular was honed to a fine art in his daily newspaper column in the 1920s and 1930s. Dennis wrote more than 3000 pieces of verse and I have yet to read a real 'dud'. Many of his poems do seem dated due to their 'current event' subject material and the use of colloquial language. Despite this his pen portraits are as vivid and amusing as the day they were written.

Henry Lawson, who beautifully captured the poignancy of character in verse, is also well represented in this section. Several other of our better-known writers of rhymed verse, who have also taken pen portraits into the realm of great literature, are included. For balance I have included caricature pieces and examples of verse where the subject material, the portrayal of historic and popular figures, is a more important priority than literary quality.

Old Portraits
Henry Lawson

Though you tramp the wide land over,
Though you sail in many climes,
There is nothing half so precious
As the portraits of old times;

Of old Grandfather and Granny
In the clothes that then were worn;
Of the house that knew our boyhood,
Or the hut where we were born.

Of our parents, stiff and staring,
In some portrait-taker's den,
On the morning of their wedding –
God, they've seen some times since then!

O they wake the dead within us,
And they bring us back at last
To the courage of our fathers
And the best part of the past.

The Modest Australian
CJ Dennis

He travelled far in foreign lands
To view the sights beyond the seas;
And, when he spoke of distant strands,
Broke into praiseful ecstasies.
But, when they asked of brighter skies
And nobler sights Australia had,
The glad light faded from his eyes
As he gave answer, 'Not too bad.'

He'd seen the wonder of the moon
Upon white Kosciuszko's heights;
He'd walked upon a tropic noon
'Mid palms; he'd seen the fairy lights

Upon 'Our Harbour'; seen the dawn
Come up o'er Hinchinbrook. Yet, should
They ask him of these things, he'd yawn
And tell them it was 'pretty good'.

He'd seen – oh, old familiar things,
But these were close by his own door –
Things not to give his fancy wings
Or wax enthusiastic o'er.
Yet when he ventures overseas
Can he know pride in Nationhood
Who finds in praise of such as these
But 'not too bad' and 'pretty good'?

Bill

Henry Lawson

He shall live to the end of this mad old world as he's lived since
    the world began;
He never has done any good for himself, but was good to every man.
He never has done any good for himself, and I'm sure that he
    never will;
He drinks, and he swears, and he fights at times, and his name is
    mostly Bill.

He carried a freezing mate to his cave, and nursed him, for all I know,
When Europe was mainly a sheet of ice, thousands of years ago.
He has stuck to many a mate since then, he is with us everywhere
    still –
He loves and gambles when he is young, and the girls stick up for
    Bill.

He has thirsted in deserts that others might drink, he has given
    lest others should lack,
He has staggered half-blinded through fire or drought with a sick
    man on his back.
He is first to the rescue in tunnel or shaft, from Bulli to Broken
    Hill,
When the water breaks in or the fire breaks out, a leader of men is
    Bill!

He wears no Humane Society's badge for the fearful deaths he
 braved;
He seems ashamed of the good he did, and ashamed of the lives he
 saved.
If you chance to know of a noble deed he has done, you had best
 keep still;
If you chance to know of a kindly act, you mustn't let on to Bill.

He is fierce at a wrong, he is firm in right, he is kind to the weak
 and mild;
He will slave all day and sit up all night by the side of a
 neighbour's child.
For a woman in trouble he'd lay down his life, nor think as another
 man will;
He's a man all through, and no other man's wife has ever been
 worse for Bill.

He is good for the noblest sacrifice, he can do what few men can:
He will break his heart that the girl he loves may marry a better
 man.
There's many a mother and wife tonight whose heart and eyes will
 fill
When she thinks of the days of the long-ago when she might have
 stuck to Bill.

Maybe he's in trouble or hard up now, and travelling far for work,
Or fighting a dead past down tonight in a lone camp west of
 Bourke.
When he's happy and flush, take your sorrow to him and borrow as
 much as you will:
But when he's in trouble or stony-broke, you never will hear from
 Bill.

And when, because of its million sins, this earth is cracked like a
 shell,
He will stand by a mate at the Judgment Seat and comfort him
 down in – Well –
I haven't much sentiment left to waste, but let cynics sneer as they
 will,
Perhaps God will fix up the world again for the sake of the likes of
 Bill.

Flinders
John Bernard O'Hara

He left his island home
For leagues of sleepless foam,
For stress of alien seas,
Where wild winds ever blow;
For England's sake he sought
Fresh fields of fame, and fought
A stormy world for these,
A hundred years ago.

And where the Austral shore
Heard southward far the roar
Of rising tides that came
From lands of ice and snow,
Beneath a gracious sky,
To fadeless memory
He left a deathless name,
A hundred years ago.

from . . . Bill the Bullock Driver
Henry Kendall

The leaders of millions – the lords of the lands
Who sway the wide world with their will,
And shake the great globe with the strength of their hands,
Flash past us – unnoticed by Bill.

The singers that sweeten all time with their song –
Pure voices that make us forget
Humanity's drama and marvellous wrong,
To Bill are as mysteries yet.

By thunders of battle and nations uphurled,
Bill's sympathies never were stirred:
The helmsmen who stand at the wheel of the world
By him are unknown and unheard.

What trouble has Bill for the ruin of lands,
Or the quarrels of temple and throne,
As long as the whip that he holds in his hands,
And the team that he drives, are his own?

For the kings of the earth — for the faces august
Of princes, the millions may shout:
To Bill as he lumbers along in the dust,
A bullock's the grandest thing out.

His four-footed friends are the friends of his choice —
No lover is Bill of your dames;
But the cattle that turn at the sound of his voice
Have the sweetest of features and names.

Of course he must dream; but be sure that his dreams,
If happy, must compass — alas!
Fat bullocks at feed by improbable streams,
Knee-deep in improbable grass.

No poet is Bill; for the visions of night
To him are as visions of day;
And the pipe that in sleep he endeavours to light
Is the pipe that he smokes on the dray.

Through beautiful, bountiful forests that screen
A marvel of blossoms from heat —
Whose lights are the mellow and golden, and green —
Bill walks with irreverent feet.

The manifold splendours of mountain and wood
By Bill like nonentities slip;
He loves the black myrtle because it's good
As a handle to lash to his whip.

And thus through the world, with a swing in his tread,
Our hero self-satisfied goes;
With a cabbage-tree hat on the back of his head,
And the string of it under his nose.

Poor bullocky Bill! In the circles select
Of the scholars he hasn't a place;
But he walks like a *man* with his forehead erect,
And he looks at God's day in the face.

Edmund Barton
Victor Daley ('Creeve Roe')

A full, rich-brained, rich-blooded man,
Who, when the doubting cliques
Exclaim 'We might,' says out 'I *can*' –
And knows more than he speaks.

Alfred Deakin
Victor Daley ('Creeve Roe')

A man of talent and of clean good sense,
Who speaks with polished air.
On silver floods of his own eloquence
He floats to God knows where.

The Brigalow Brigade
Harry Morant ('The Breaker')

There's a band of decent fellows
On a cattle-run outback –
You'll hear the timber smashing
If you follow in their track;
Their ways are rough and hearty,
And they call a spade a spade;
And a pretty rapid party
Are the Brigalow Brigade.

They are mostly short of 'sugar'
And their pockets, if turned out,
Would scarcely yield the needful
For a decent four-man 'shout'.
But they'll scramble through a tight place
Or a big fence unafraid,
And their hearts are in the right place
In the Brigalow Brigade.

They've painted Parkes vermilion
And they've coloured Orange blue,
And they've broken lots of top-rails
'Twixt the sea and Dandaloo;
They like their grog and palings
Just as stiff as they are made –
These are two little failings
Of the Brigalow Brigade.

The Brigalow Brigade are
Fastidious in their taste
In the matter of a maiden
And the inches of her waist;
She must be sweet and tender
And her eyes a decent shade –
Then her Ma may safely send her
To the Brigalow Brigade.

But women, men, and horses,
With polo in between,
Are mighty potent forces
In keeping purses lean;
But spurs are never rusty,
Though they seldom need their aid –
For 'the cuddies ain't too dusty'
In the Brigalow Brigade.

Fred

CJ Dennis

Do you know Fred? Now there's a man to know
These days when politics are in the air,
An' argument is bargin' to an' fro
Without a feller gittin' anywhere.
Fred never argues; he's too shrewd for that.
He's wise. He knows the game from A to Z.
All politics is talkin' thro' the hat;
An' everyone is wrong – exceptin' Fred.

Fred says there ain't no sense in politics;
Says he can't waste his time on all that rot.
Trust him. He's up to all their little tricks,
You'd be surprised the cunnin' schemes he's got.
Fred says compuls'ry voting is a cow.
He has to vote, or else he would be fined.
But he just spoils his paper anyhow,
An' laughs at 'em with his superior mind.

But when a law comes in that hits Fred's purse,
You ought to hear him then. Say, he does rouse;
Kicks up an awful row an' hurls his curse
On every bloomin' member in the House.
He gives 'em nothin'; says they all are crook,
All waitin' for a chance to turn their coats;
Says they are traitors; proves it by the book.
An' can you wonder that he never votes?

Aw, say, you must know Fred. You'll hear his skite
Upon street corners all about the place.
An' if you up an' say it serves him right,
He answers that it only proves his case:
Them politicians wouldn't tax him so
Unless they were all crooked, like he said,
Where is the sense in votin' when they go
An' rob a man like that. Hurray for Fred!

Brave Ben Hall

Anon

Listen all Australian sons
A hero has been slain,
Yes, he was butchered in his sleep
Upon the Lachlan Plain.

Pray do not stay your seemly grief,
But let a tear-drop fall;
For manly hearts will always mourn
The fate of Bold Ben Hall.

No brand of Cain e'er stamped his brow,
No widow's curse did fall;
When tales are read, the squatters dread
The name of Bold Ben Hall.

He never robbed a needy man –
His records best will show –
Staunch and loyal to his mates,
And manly to the foe.

They found his place of ambush,
And cautiously they crept,
And savagely they murdered him
While their victim slept.

No more he'll mount his gallant steed,
Nor range the mountains high.
The widow's friend in poverty,
Bold Ben Hall! Good-bye!

The Stockyard Liar
Will Ogilvie

If you're ever handling a rough one
There's bound to be perched on the rails
Of the stockyard some grizzled old tough one
Whose flow of advice never fails:
There are plenty, of course, who aspire
To make plain that you're only a dunce,
But the most unsupportable liar
Is the man who has ridden 'em once.

He will tell you a tale and a rum one,
With never a smile on his face,
How he broke for old Somebody Someone
At some unapproachable place:
How they bucked and they snorted and squealed,
How he spurred 'em and flogged 'em, and how
He would gallop 'em round till they reeled –
But he's 'getting too old for it now'.

How you're standing too far from her shoulder,
Or too jolly close to the same,
How he could have taught you to hold her
In the days when he 'followed the game',
He will bustle, annoy and un-nerve us
Till even our confidence fails –
O shade of old Nimrod! preserve us
From the beggar that sits on the rails!

How your reins you are holding too tightly,
Your girth might as well be unloosed;
How 'young chaps' don't handle them rightly,
And horses don't buck 'like they used';
Till at last, in a bit of a passion,
You ask him in choicest 'Barcoo'
To go and be hanged, in a fashion
That turns the whole atmosphere blue!

And the chances are strong the old buffer
Has been talking for something to say,
And never rode anything rougher
Than the shaft of old Somebody's dray;
And the horses he thinks he has broken
Are clothes-horses sawn out of pine,
And his yarns to us simply betoken
The start of a senile decline.

There are laws for our proper protection
For murder and theft and the rest,
But the criminal wanting inspection
Is riding a rail in the West;
And the Law that the country requires
At the hands of her statesmen of sense,
Is a Law to make meat of the liars
That can sit a rough buck – on the fence!

An Australian Advertisement

Henry Lawson

We want the man who will lead the van,
The man who will pioneer.
We have no use for the gentleman,
Or the cheating Cheap-Jack here;
We have no room for the men who shirk
The sweat of the brow. Condemn
The men who are frightened to look for work
And funk when it looks for them.

We'll honour the man who can't afford
To wait for a job that suits,
But sticks a swag on his shoulders broad
And his feet in blucher boots,
And tramps away o'er the ridges far
And over the burning sand
To look for work where the stations are
In the lonely Western land.

He'll brave the drought and he'll brave the rain,
And fight his sorrows down,
And help to garden the inland plain
And build the inland town;
And he'll be found in the coming years
With a heart as firm and stout,
An honoured man with the pioneers
Who lead the people out.

Victor Trumper

Victor Daley ('Creeve Roe')

Statesmen, patriots, bards, make way!
Your fame has sunk to zero;
For Victor Trumper is today
Our one Australian hero.

Is there not, haply, in the land,
Some native-born Murillo
To paint, in colours rich and grand,
This wielder of the willow?

Evo, Trumper! As for me,
It all ends with the moral
That fame grows on the willow tree,
And no more on the laurel!

The Maitland Wonder

Peter Fenton

Was there ever such a wonder
Flailing fists that crack like thunder
As the smiling boy from Maitland
In his faded dressing gown?

Was there ever such a fighter
Ever modest not a skiter
As the smiling boy from Maitland
Now the pride of Sydney town?

Will we ever see his equal
Will there ever be a sequel
To the smiling boy from Maitland
Beating men of such renown?

How his foes have come to fear him
How the crowds have come to cheer him,
Cheer the smiling boy from Maitland
As he wears his boxing crown.

As he stands for his ovation
He's the pride of all the nation,
He's the great James Leslie Darcy;
He's a god in Sydney town.

Gate Gossip

Max Fatchen

I like our gate,
Its sturdy charm
That guards the entrance
To our farm.

It's nice when shut,
Or open wide,
To sit upon
Or sit astride.

But gates are there
With things to do
Like letting sheep
And cattle through.

Our gate has bars
With several bends
From careless cars
Of farming friends.

The gateposts lean,
A little tired,
With fences stretching
Rusty-wired.

A country gate
Is surely best
To prop a farmer
For his rest.

With one foot up,
And elbows flat
Now who could pass
A man like that?

While every bit
Of iron will ring,
With all the
Rural gossiping.

The magpies fly
To sunset tree.
A voice impatient
Calls to tea.

Then, whistling,
Home the farmer goes
As gate
And conversation
Close.

A Tribute to Sir Donald

Damien Morgan ('Dib')

This is a sporting nation as we love it more than most
We play with pride and passion from the outback to the coast
Our record tells the story – it often tells we've won
If second must be taken, we'll take second place to none.

But of the magic moments and '*the greats*' that there have been
Who would be the greatest that this country's ever seen?
This question that I'm asking will require a lot of thought
Our past is overflowing with heroics found in sport.

But really it's not difficult – to sort one from the rest
That's not to name a 'one off'' – but to name – the very best
As through our sporting hist'ry, there's a record that has shone
The record is of Bradman or the man we call 'The Don'.

He wasn't just a batsman, but a lesson to be taught
His attitude to winning doesn't just apply to sport
He re-defined the barriers and dared to chase his dream
He did it for his country and his love of baggy green.

So, Sir Donald – if you hear this – thanks for all you've done
Not just for beating England or for scoring all those runs
But for all you've done for cricket and this country both the same
We'll always feel a sense of pride, at mention of your name.

Bradman at the Test

Peter Fenton

When I was only ten years old
My dad took me to town,
By train and tram we travelled
To the Sydney Cricket ground.

And it was very different then
But I can see it still
With its classic wooden grandstands
And its famous, spacious hill.

Now this would be a special day
With forty thousand more
We'd come to watch Don Bradman play
The first time since the war.

And the thunderous roar that met him
When he came onto the ground
Is something I cannot forget
I still can hear that sound.

He must have had some butterflies
Some kind of trepidation
That he would still bat well enough
To warrant this ovation.

For he was just on thirty-eight
And in his fortieth test,
And by his own admission
He was some years past his best.

But who were we to worry
If Don could get a score?
He set about the bowling
And he made two thirty-four.

Then just on twelve months later
Again he held the stage,
He made his hundredth century
This marvel of our age.

He played against the Indians
Keith Miller tempted fate
They ran the sharpest single
When the Don was ninety-eight.

And when he reached his hundred
The crowd let out a roar,
The pride they had in Bradman
I hadn't seen before.

Our Don went on the England
In nineteen forty-eight,
He brought us back unbeaten
And his batting still was great.

And he led such a mighty team
Perhaps the best we've had
With Lindwall, Miller, Morris
And Neil Harvey as a lad.

We'd sit up in the evening
To hear the A.B.C.
On quaint old-fashioned radios
With thermos flasks of tea.

Reception wasn't all that good
Sometimes you'd hear a roar
You'd think you'd lost a wicket,
But you found you'd hit a four.

You woke up in the morning
And you turned the wireless on,
You hardly even spoke
Until you'd checked up on the Don.

You can have your instant replays
And what the experts think
And those endless one-day series
That may drive us all to drink.

My memories of Bradman
And that epic sporting scene
Are worth a thousand pictures
On a television screen.

By train and tram we travelled
As we made our way to town,
We saw Don Bradman batting
On the Sydney Cricket Ground.

Cathy
Jim Haynes

Cathy Freeman we're all proud of you.
You're a real Aussie girl through and through,
'Cos you're sometimes a dag
And you know that one flag
Doesn't quite mean the same thing as two.

To a Mate
Roland Robinson

He was a man who, with his hand,
would make the language of the sand
that showed where piccaninny walked,
where emu trod or dingo stalked.

Euro's pad or writhe of snake,
or brolga's imprint he could make.
And he was one to booze and brawl
and lie beside the fire asprawl.

He was a man, when moved, who spoke
of how at Innaminka soak,
when the molten west grew dim,
the creatures from the desert's rim

came in to drink and play as he
lay watching by a hakea tree,
where stars and dingo howls, he swore
were solitude not known before.

Wherever now with swag outspread
he camps by soak or river-bed,
would that I saw his camp-fire's sparks
and hailed him through the paper-barks.

When the Army Prays for Watty

Henry Lawson

When the kindly hours of darkness, save for light of moon and
    star,
Hide the picture on the signboard over Doughty's Horse Bazaar;
When the last rose-tint is fading on the distant mulga scrub,
Then the Army prays for Watty at the entrance of his pub.

Now, I often sit at Watty's when the night is very near,
With a head that's full of jingles and the fumes of bottled beer,
For I always have a fancy that, if I am over there
When the Army prays for Watty, I'm included in the prayer.

Watty lounges in his arm-chair, in its old accustomed place,
With a fatherly expression on his round and passive face;
And his arms are clasped before him in a calm, contented way,
And he nods his head and dozes when he hears the Army pray.

And I wonder does he ponder on the distant years and dim,
Or his chances over yonder, when the Army prays for him?
Has he not a fear connected with the warm place down below,
Where, according to good Christians, all the publicans should go?

But his features give no token of a feeling in his breast,
Save of peace that is unbroken and a conscience well at rest;
And we guzzle as we guzzled long before the Army came,
And the loafers wait for 'shouters' and – they get there just the
    same.

It would take a lot of praying – lots of thumping on the drum –
To prepare our sinful, straying, erring souls for Kingdom Come;
But I love my fellow-sinners, and I hope, upon the whole,
That the Army gets a hearing when it prays for Watty's soul.

The Drifters
Jack Davis

We are the drifters, the faceless ones.
Turn your heads as we walk by.
We are the lost, forgotten sons,
Bereft in a land of plenty.

Where is the spear of the days gone by?
No more the chant of the hunting song:
The laughing face and the laughing eyes,
So sad in a land of plenty.

We have lost the peal of the Mission bell,
Drowned out by the sounds of the city streets.
We have lots to say and none to tell
Of hell in a land of plenty.

Oh, this earth! This sun! This sky I see
Is part of my heart, my heritage!
Oh God, I cry. Cry God for me.
For a place in a land of plenty.

Women Knitting
Jack Sorensen

Once in purl and once in plain,
The miracle is performed again,
And the work-dreary mother mind
Leaves all its careless care behind,
'Mrs Fitzflutin, it's half-past three
I should have made you a cup of tea.'
You know about the Wilkinsons,
You've read all that,
'What do you think of her latest hat?'
Once in purl and once in plain,
The miracle is performed again,
And when the afternoon has gone,
The human race is carried on.

The Woman at the Washtub

Victor Daley ('Creeve Roe')

The Woman at the Washtub,
She works till fall of night;
With soap, and suds and soda
Her hands are wrinkled white.
Her diamonds are the sparkles
The copper-fire supplies;
Her opals are the bubbles
That from the suds arise.

The Woman at the Washtub
Has lost the charm of youth;
Her hair is rough and homely,
Her figure is uncouth;
Her temper is like thunder,
With no one she agrees —
The children of the alley
They cling around her knees.

The Woman at the Washtub
She too had her romance;
There was a time when lightly
Her feet flew in the dance.
Her feet were silver swallows,
Her lips were flowers of fire;
Then she was Bright and Early,
The Blossom of Desire.

O Woman at the Washtub,
And do you ever dream
Of all your days gone by in
Your aureole of steam?
From birth till we are dying
You wash our sordid duds,
O Woman of the Washtub!
O Sister of the Suds!

One night I saw a vision
That filled my soul with dread,
I saw a Woman washing
The grave-clothes of the dead;
The dead were all the living,
And dry were lakes and meres,
The Woman at the Washtub
She washed them with her tears.

I saw a line with banners
Hung forth in proud array –
The banners of all battles
From Cain to Judgment Day.
And they were stiff with slaughter
And blood, from hem to hem,
And they were red with glory,
And she was washing them.

'Who comes forth to the Judgment,
And who will doubt my plan?'
'I come forth to the Judgment
And for the Race of Man.
I rocked him in his cradle,
I washed him for his tomb,
I claim his soul and body,
And I will share his doom.'

Banjo
Ted Harrington

Don't tell me that The Banjo's dead – oh yes, I've heard the tale –
But Banjo isn't dead at all, he's caught the Western Mail.
He has a lot of friends you know, among the western men,
He wants to look into their eyes and clasp their hands again;
He longs to spend some quiet nights beneath the western stars
And hear the evening wind again among the green belars.
So if they tell you Banjo's dead just say that it's a lie:
He comes from where they breed 'em tough and Banjo will not
   die.

They say that Clancy sent him word, he's at the Overflow
With many more old mates of his who knew him long ago.
The man from Snowy River's there, from Kosciuszko's side,
Who brought the wild mob in alone and taught them how to ride.
He's got his mountain pony, too, as tough and wiry yet
As when he chased the brumby mob and colt from old Regret.
Another chap, now what's his name? He comes from Ironbark,
He thought the barber cut his throat and didn't like the lark.

All these old mates of his are there, with others on the way,
And when he got a call from them, well, how could Banjo stay?
There's Gundagai and Saltbush Bill, a rough and rugged pair,
I bet that there will be some fun when Banjo meets them there.
Old Trooper Scott is coming, too, to represent the force,
And Andy Regan (or his ghost) on Father Riley's horse.
They're making for the Overflow, and when they all arrive,
You'll see that Banjo isn't dead, he's very much alive.

Then glasses clink, and healths are drunk, and many a tale is told
Of roving days and droving days that never will grow old.
The seasons come, the seasons go, and little here abides,
But good old Banjo will not die as long as Clancy rides
As long as bushmen love a horse or wild, black swans go by,
As long as there's a Southern Cross, the Banjo will not die.
So send the joyous news abroad, through hut and shearing shed,
And tell the bushmen not to grieve, for Banjo is not dead!

The Girl at the Gate

Kenneth Slessor

Out of the bush behind her,
You come in your scornful car;
There on the gate you'll find her,
Looking for Lochinvar.
But sentiment rarely rankles,
And nobody wishes to wait,
When she dances on little brown ankles
To open –
How very obliging! –
To open the Nine Mile Gate.

Open and shut, open and shut –
Lochinvar scorns to wait.
He's vanished, alas, in a cloud of gas,
Poor little Girl at the Gate!

Cars that go past in thunder,
How can they understand?
Open the gate, and wonder –
Close it, and wave your hand.
Can you pin your heart to a placard,
Or wish that he struck you dead,
When a Prince in a fairy Packard
Throws you a coin –
How generous! –
Throws you a coin instead?

Open and shut, open and shut,
Nobody wants to wait,
You're a speck on the track, and they never look back,
Poor little Girl at the Gate.

Gus

CJ Dennis

Do you know Gus? Now, he should interest you.
The girls adore him – or he thinks they do.
He owns a motor bike, not of the sort
That merely cough a little bit, or snort.
His is a fiery, detonating steed
That makes the town sit up and take some heed –
A thunderous thing, that booms and roars a treat,
With repercussions that awake the street.

That's Gus. Dead flash. One of the rorty boys,
Whose urge is to express themselves with noise,
He wakes the midnight echoes, when to sleep
We vainly strive, with detonations deep.
And Gus has visions, as he thunders by,
Of maidens who sit up in bed, and sigh,
'It's Gus! It's Gus, the he-man. What a thrill!
'Mid Jovian thunders riding up the hill!'

You can't blame Gus. He has to make a row.
He's got to get publicity somehow.
How else could he stir consciousness in us
That in this world there really is a Gus?
You can't blame Gus. But oft I long, in bed,
That some kind man would bash him on the head –
A hard, swift blow to give him pain for pain.
It would be quite safe. It couldn't hurt his brain.

Jeff Fenech
Jim Haynes

Jeff Fenech sure knew how to brawl,
As a fighter he always stood tall.
He was a jaw-rattler,
A real Aussie battler,
And of course he said, 'I love youse all!'

Ain't No Better!
Val Read

I'm the bloody best at everythin' I flamin' bloody do.
I catch the biggest bloody fish (and single-handed, too).
I've shorn a zillion bloody sheep without a twinge of pain,
I've driven thirsty cattle over miles of dry terrain.
I've ridden all the wildest bulls the rodeos have seen,
I've jogged across old Uluru. I'm big and bloody mean.
I'll down a keg in seconds flat and never blink an eye.
I'll take on any bloke who says that I'm not dinky-di.
I'm noted for my prowess when it comes courtin' gals,
There ain't no lack of evidence ter prove that we were pals.
I've done me bit ter populate, yeah, truly done my share,
Each one a replica of me, with freckles and red hair.
I reckon I could run this place and do it bloody well,
I'd tell those politicians ter go ter bloody hell.
It wouldn't take me very long ter make Orstralia grand,
Just give me 'alf a bloody chance ter organise this land.
'Cos I'm the best you'll ever find, the bloody best yer'll see,
So says the wisest man you'll meet . . . Who is he? *Bloody me!*

The Postman
CJ Dennis

I'd like to be a postman, and walk along the street,
Calling out, 'Good Morning, Sir,' to gentlemen I meet;
Ringing every door-bell all along my beat,
In my cap and uniform so very nice and neat,
Perhaps I'd have a parasol in case of rain or heat;
But I wouldn't be a postman if . . .
The walking hurt my feet.
Would you?

Post-Hole Mick
GM Smith ('Steele Grey')

A short time back, while over in Vic.,
I met with a chap called Post-Hole Mick.
A raw-boned, loose-built son of a Paddy;
And at putting down post-holes he was a daddy!

And wherever you'd meet him, near or far,
He had always his long-handled shovel and bar.
(I suppose you all know what I mean by a bar?
It's a lump of wrought iron the shape of a spar.

With one chisel end for digging the ground,
Its average weight about twenty pound.)
He worked for the cockies around Geelong,
And for some time they kept him going strong.

He would sink them a hundred holes for a bob,
And, of course, soon worked himself out of a job;
But when post-hole sinking got scarce for Mick,
He greased his brogues and cut his stick.

And one fine day he left Geelong,
And took his shovel and bar along;
He took to the track in search of work,
And struck due north, en route to Bourke.

It seems he had been some time on tramp,
When one day he struck a fencers' camp.
The contractor there was wanting a hand,
As post-hole sinkers were in demand.

He showed him the line, and put him on,
But while he looked round, sure Mick was gone –
There were the holes, but where was the man?
Then his eye along the line he ran.

Mick had already done ninety-nine,
And at hunting rate was running the line.
The Boss had some sinkers he thought were quick,
Till the day he engaged one, Post-Hole Mick.

When the job was finished, Mick started forth,
And appears to have set his course due north,
For I saw a report in the 'Croydon Star',
Where a fellow had passed with a shovel and bar.

To give an idea of how he could walk,
A day or two later he struck Cape York!
If they can't find him work there, putting down holes.
I'm afraid he'll arrive at one of the Poles!

Booberoi
Jack Moses

When old Jackie Booberoi
Bumped his dusky head,
They took him to the hospital,
Where he lay in bed.
When nurse asked Jackie Booberoi
To spell his name, he said:
'By cripes, you can't spell "Booberoi" –
Just put it down instead.'

Dost Mahomet

Graham Fredriksen

Dost Mahomet was a camel driver brought out with twenty-four camels from Peshawar and Afghanistan for the Burke and Wills expedition (1860–61). He is buried at Menindee on the Darling River.

He walks the dreary desert way
beside his dromedary team –
a player in a grander scheme
where only heroes get to play.

The brutes obey his cool command –
with: *Hooshta Rajah! Golah Sindh!*
a pilgrim in the Cooper wind . . .
a stranger in a stranger land . . .

an ancient land of gidgee stones . . .
and distance dancing in the air . . .
and mirage oceans of despair . . .
and fierce black men with pointed bones . . .

a Mecca: those who worship seek
the answers which so long deceive –
the searchers . . . who in time will leave
their bones along the hallowed creek.

And so he walks the desert ways
and guides the burdened desert ships
that Men's ambition may eclipse
the deeds of former glory days.

A pawn of greater men than he –
but deeds are weighed by higher lot;
he tends the beasts and questions not –
his greatest strength: predestiny.

He prays to Allah in the gloom;
he sees the earth and stars collide –
the darkling silence magnified
through temples where the strongest roam.

He lays his blanket on the sand,
and ghost gums whisper to the night;
and – he, a drifting satellite –
he dreams perhaps another land.

Concerning Sweepers
CJ Dennis

The other day I walked abroad,
While fierce winds howled and leapt;
And lo! I came upon a man
Who swept, and swept, and swept.

Along the street he swept the dust –
Stray refuse. But, alack!
Each time a broom-full forth he thrust,
The mad winds swept it back.

And still he swept, tho' naught he gleaned –
A patient man was he.
To me his wild endeavour seemed
But sheer futility.

'Good fellow,' I exclaimed, 'why sweep,
And sweep, and sweep again,
While teasing gales that howl and leap
Make all your sweeping vain?'

The surly fellow answered, 'Keep
Your block! What's that to you?
I sweep because I have to sweep;
The council pays me to.'

Just then a gust caught up his heap,
And sent it swirling high.
'See that! What profits it to sweep
On such a day?' said I.

'Your task is hopeless, man!' I cried.
I argued, pleaded, wept!
But he, poor fellow, turned aside
And swept,
And swept,
And swept.

The Girl in the Gods

Kenneth Slessor

All the din of Donizetti,
All the singers, high and low,
They are merely there for Betty,
Upper Circle, second row;
They are merely there to thunder
(Even Mr Rossi nods)
For a girl with eyes of wonder
In the twilight of the gods.

Like the damsel of Rossetti,
She is leaning from the sky,
And her name it may be Betty,
But there's Carmen in her eye.
Boom your mellowest, Apollo,
Till the prima donna purrs –
She may grab the flowers that follow,
But the magic isn't hers.

All the dainty allegrettos,
Airs that ripple, notes that foam,
Full of passion and stilettos,
Turning Roseville into Rome,
All the altos and contraltos,
All the beauty and the pain,
Leave her dreaming in Rialtos
When she's really in the train.

Then the night is full of daggers
And a thousand torches glow,
And the Prince of Parma swaggers
Down the path to 'Mon Repos' –
Oh, it's hard to face Artarmon,
Bricks and mortar, tiles and stones,
When a girl who should be Carmen
Has to act like Betty Jones!

The Things Old Men Collect

JW Gordon (Jim Grahame)

My shelf is crammed with broken pipes and old tobacco tins;
The lapel of my vest is bright with shining rows of pins;
I fear that I am growing old by signs that I detect,
For I am hoarding odds and ends – the things old men collect.

I seem to love a shabby coat with elbows frayed and torn;
I have a dozen styles in hats that someone else has worn;
And hanging round are shirts and pants that all show some defect;
And here and there a walking stick – the kind old men collect.

I've tins of nails and bolts and screws and little coils of twine;
A score of keys for lock and latch that fit no door of mine;
My shaving mirror lacks a frame, it's dim, and can't reflect
Those lines and wrinkles on my face that all old men collect.

I keep two old and faithful dogs and some domestic pets;
One likes to see these things about the older that one gets.
I'd have them all inside with me but someone might object;
They do not know the joy there's in the friends old men collect.

Though time is flying swiftly on, its haste does not annoy.
There's lots of good things in the world – the things old men
    enjoy.
And life is passing fair to me: I still can walk erect,
And have no hankering to rest where old men's bones collect.

Namatjira

Anon

Namatjira first showed us, first hand,
The magic and truth of our land.
His paintings could speak
Of a beauty unique,
Perhaps one day we'll all understand.

Warru

Jack Davis

Fast asleep on the wooden bench,
Arms bent under the weary head,
There in the dusk and the back-street stench
He lay with the look of the dead.

I looked at him, then back through the years,
Then knew what I had to remember –
A young man, straight as wattle spears,
And a kangaroo hunt in September.

We caught the scent of the 'roos on the rise
Where the gums grew on the Moore;
They leaped away in loud surprise,
But Warru was fast and as sure.

He threw me the fire-stick, oh what a thrill!
With a leap he sprang to a run.
He met the doe on the top of the hill,
And he looked like a king in the sun.

The wattle spear flashed in the evening light,
The kangaroo fell at his feet.
How I danced and I yelled with all my might
As I thought of the warm red meat.

We camped that night on a bed of reeds
With a million stars a-gleaming.
He told me tales of Noong-ah deeds
When the world first woke from dreaming.

He sang me a song, I clapped my hands,
He fashioned a needle of bone.
He drew designs in the river sands,
He sharpened his spear on a stone.

I will let you dream – dream on, old friend –
Of a boy and a man in September,
Of hills and stars and the river's bend –
Alas, that is all to remember.

Our Bert

Jim Haynes

Think of all the Aussie features that have been around forever,
Uluru and Kakadu – the lonely Never-Never.
Then there are the icons – the Akubra and the thong,
And the legends like the swaggie down beside the billabong,
The drovers and the shearers – lifesavers by the sea,
The cricketers and footballers who've graced the MCG.
Each one truly Aussie, each a dinkum cert,
And when it comes to Aussie legends . . . what about our Bert?
I reckon that Bert Newton is as Aussie as you get,
He's been around forever and he hasn't worn out yet.

Bert's friendly, smiling face is there each day on our TV
Eternal, like a mountain or a giant redgum tree.
You see his face each morning, you know everything's OK,
The sun and moon are shining and you'll live another day.
It doesn't matter what life brings, victory or failure,
Bert's still smiling from the screen and this is still Australia.
Let's re-design the coat of arms – we'll keep the kangaroo,
Put the Southern Cross across the top, we'll keep the emu too,
But Bert's an Aussie icon, like the Hills Hoist and the ute,
His smiling face right in the middle – wouldn't that look beaut?

Kylie

Anon

There's a cute pocket rocket called Kylie
Who's talented t'riffic and smiley.
She can dance, act and sing.
She can do anything!
And she never does anything shyly.

'Erb

CJ Dennis

Do you know 'Erb? Now, there's a dinkum sport.
If football's on your mind, why, 'Erb's the sort
To put you wise. It's his whole end an' aim.
Keen? He's as keen as mustard on the game.
Football is in his blood. He thinks an' schemes
All through the season; talks of it an' dreams
An' eats an' sleeps with football on his mind.
Yes: 'Erb's a sport – the reel whole-hearted kind.

'A healthy, manly sport.' That's wot 'Erb says.
You ought to see his form on football days:
Keyed up, reel eager, eyes alight with joy,
Full of wise schemes for his team to employ.
Knows all about it – how to kick a goal,
An' wot to do if they get in a hole.
Enthusiasm? Why, when 'Erb gets set
He is a sight you couldn't well forget.

There ain't a point about it he don't know –
All of the teams an' players, top to toe.
The rules, the tricks – it's marvellous the way
He follers – Wot? Good Lord, no, he don't play.
'Erb? Playin' football? Blimey! Have a heart!
Why, he'd drop dead before he got a start.
Aw, don't be silly. 'Erb don't have to play;
He knows more than them players any day.

He's never had a football in his hand,
'Cept once, when it was kicked up in the stand.
No, 'Erb ain't never played; he only sits
An' watches 'em, an' yells, an' hoots, and splits
His sides with givin' mugs some sound advice
An' tellin' umpires things wot ain't too nice.
Aw, look; your ejication ain't complete
Till you know 'Erb. You reely ought to meet.

The Girl in the Window

Kenneth Slessor

The girl in the window
Looks over the square
At a girl in a window
With pearls in her hair,
With diamonds to dangle
And feathers to preen,
A comb and a bangle,
As proud as a queen,
In a flat so becoming,
So smooth and so sleek,
With hot and cold plumbing
(Ten guineas a week),
Where life is no harder
For paying a price,
With fowls in the larder
And Heidsieck on ice.
No need to be thrifty
Or spend and repent,
With 'Papa' aged fifty
To fix up the rent.

The girl in the window
Looks over the square
And she sees, in a mirror,
Herself standing there!

The girl in the window
Looks over the square
At a girl in a window
With eyes of despair,
In a cheap little attic,
A cheap little dress,
All cotton and batik
(Ten shillings or less),
A trunk with no label,
A rickety bed,
A broken-down table,
A banquet of bread,
The wallpaper peeling,
A crack in the door,
Dirt on the ceiling,
And dust on the floor;
No hope for tomorrow,
The money all spent,
A fortnight of sorrow
Behind in the rent.

The girl in the window
Looks over the square
At a girl in a window –
Herself – standing there.

The Old Jimmy Woodser

Henry Lawson

The old Jimmy Woodser comes into the bar,
Unwelcomed, unnoticed, unknown,
Too old and too odd to be drunk with, by far;
And he glides to the end where the lunch baskets are
And they say that he tipples alone.

His frock-coat is green and the nap is no more,
And the style of his hat is at rest.
He wears the peaked collar his grandfather wore,
The black-ribboned tie that was legal of yore,
And the coat buttoned over his breast.

When first he came in, for a moment I thought
That my vision or wits were astray;
For a picture or page out of Dickens he brought,
'Twas an old file dropped in from the Chancery Court
To the wine vault just over the way.

But I dreamed as he tasted his bitters to-night,
And the lights in the bar-room grew dim,
That the shades of the friends of that other day's light,
And the girls that were bright in our grandfather's sight,
Lifted shadowy glasses to him.

And I opened the door as the old man passed out,
With his short, shuffling steps and bowed head;
And I sighed, for I felt as I turned me about,
An odd sense of respect – born of whisky no doubt –
For the life that was fifty years dead.

And I thought – there were times when our memory trends
Through the future, as 'twere, on its own –
That I, out of date ere my pilgrimage ends,
In a new fashioned bar to dead loves and dead friends
Might drink like the old man alone:
While they whisper, 'He boozes alone.'

SECTION FIVE

Longing and Lust
The Way of the World

In many anthologies of verse you are quite likely to find that relationships between men and women provide subject material for a sizeable percentage of the poetry included. This is not quite the case with this collection. Australian rhymed verse has tended to concentrate on rather blokey subject material. There is certainly not as big a percentage of love poetry in Australian rhymed verse as there is in poetry generally.

Having said that, the material in this section should put to rest the well-worn furphy that intimate emotional issues have been totally neglected in Australian rhymed verse; there is far too much evidence to the contrary. Apart from the more lyrical poems of such writers as Hugh McCrae and Victor Daley, the collected works of many 'bush' poets, such as Morant and Ogilvie, certainly contain their fair share of 'love' poems.

True, it is tempting to observe that much of the verse included here tends to focus more on the gender war and humour than it does on the tender bonds of love and intimacy. That is, perhaps, merely a reflection of the compiler's tastes, but I feel that there is enough genuine love poetry included here to convince most readers that this has not been a totally neglected subject in Australian rhymed verse.

Needless to say, the poems in this section also provide a social history of changing values and attitudes.

The Way of the World

Henry Lawson

When fairer faces turn from me,
And gayer friends grow cold,
And I have lost through poverty
The friendship bought with gold;
When I have served the selfish turn
Of some all-worldly few,
And Folly's lamps have ceased to burn,
Then I'll come back to you.

When my admirers find I'm not
The rising star they thought,
And praise or blame is all forgot
My early promise brought;
When brighter rivals lead a host
Where once I led a few,
And kinder times reward their boast,
Then I'll come back to you.

You loved me, not for what I had
Or what I might have been.
You saw the good, but not the bad,
Was kind, for that between.
I know that you'll forgive again –
That you will judge me true;
I'll be too tired to explain
When I come back to you.

Song

Victor Daley ('Creeve Roe')

What shall a man remember
In days when he is old,
And Life is a dying ember
And Fame a story told?

Power – that came to leave him?
Wealth to the wild winds blown?
Fame – that came to deceive him?
Ah, no! Sweet Love alone!

Honour, and Wealth, and Power
May all like dreams depart,
But Love is a fadeless flower,
Whose roots are in the heart.

Non-Event
John Bray

Let's agree to sever
Saving grief and gloom.
You want a freehold property.
I want a motel room.

Better abort the friendship
Before it's too old to kill.
You want a Joan and Darby.
I want a Fanny Hill.

We would never have been concordant,
Either in heart or head.
You want a lifelong union.
I want an hour in bed.

You can't say I deceived you.
I never promised rings.
You want Tristan and Isolde
I want a twang upon the strings.

His Masterpiece

Harry Morant ('The Breaker')

Never before was daughter of Eve endowed with a face so fair,
There be none of God's holy angels with a beauty half so rare
As thine, nor dreamer has ever dreamed the loveliness you wear.
There's a gleam in your golden tress, Lieb! a light in your melting
    eye!
There is witchery in your smile, Lieb! and a magic in your sigh
That may lure the strong ones to your shrine to worship and –
    to die.
And I – when you whispered softly, Lieb – perchance would have
    worshipped, too,
Had bowed to the spell of your beauty – an' it were not that
    I knew
The Devil had wrought his masterpiece what time he fashioned
    you.

Sammy's Verse about the Maid

Anon

Tom an' me a-fishin' went an' two live crabs we caught:
We put 'em inter Mary's bed an' waited for some sport.
Mum went out to tea that night but dad come home too late,
An' Mary, she went orf to bed jest shortly after eight.

An' then there was some life you bet, for Mary she did yell;
Her screams was louder than fog-horns or our new fire-bell.
Then dad went into Mary's room to try and stop the row,
An' jest then mum comes in an' sings out, 'What's the matter now?'

When dad come out from Mary's room I thought I should'a died
To see the way mum went for him, I laughed until I cried.
She says, 'You wretch!' He says, 'My dear, jest listen to me, pray!'
...An' then they sent me orf to bed ... an' Mary left next day.

Change of Heart
Wilbur G Howcroft

I watched her, graceful as a doe,
Amid the flowers rare
And envied those she chose to pluck
To twine into her hair.

Her fragile charm and loveliness
Went to my head like wine
And how I yearned with all my heart
That I could make her mine.

Years later, when I chanced to pass
And heard the language hot
She bellowed at her unwashed kids
I thanked the Lord I'd not!

Eh There!
Glenny Palmer

The yard is overgrown, the weeds are poking through the floor,
And all he says is, 'Yeah, I know, you told me twice before!'
Just twice he says! Well that's a joke; it's more like twenty-two,
It's funny how his hearing fails when there are jobs to do.

He says he just can't hear me when I'm standing by his side,
But one word said against him from some forty yards outside,
Well, out he comes, 'What's that you said?' (His hearing's
   working then),
I think it's called 'selective', and it sure applies to men.

When we were young I whispered my sweet-nothings in his ear,
And nothing's what they came to 'cause he didn't bloody hear!
It makes me wonder, when the preacher told him, 'Say, "I do".'
If he thought that he'd just asked him would he like a beer or two.

It doesn't matter what I do or what I have to say,
His conversation culminates repeatedly in. 'Eh?'
And like a silly bugger I repeat myself again,
And earn myself the title of a nagging harridan.

And if I want agreement all I have to do is ask,
'Cause he'll agree to anything, no matter what the task,
Provided that I time it when he's sprawled out in his chair,
And watching golf or cricket; 'cause he always answers, 'Yeah.'

Now I could ask him if he'd like me Mum to come and stay,
Or for a thousand bucks to feed the pokies every day,
And once I asked him, 'Wanna make a baby?' then and there,
I'm fifty, and still waiting, but the bugger answered, 'Yeah.'

And heaven help me if he takes a message on the phone,
I ask him who it was and he begins to grunt and groan,
He rubs his chin and frowns a lot, 'Now was it Jean or Jill?'
His mother could have saved us all by staying on the pill.

I found a clue to his complaint while cutting off his hair,
I looked inside his ear and saw a jungle growing there,
It must depend on just which way the wind decides to blow,
And if it blows from me that's when he doesn't want to know.

I've had enough; it's time I found an active listening mate,
Someone who can understand what I enunciate,
He'll need to be intelligent, committed, and a thriller,
I've found myself a ripper . . . he's a silver-backed gorilla!

Pain in the Neck

Anon

A young bloke from West Wyalong,
Complained to his doc loud and long,
'Love leaves me a wreck,
It's a pain in the neck!'
Said the doctor, 'You're doing it wrong!'

The Girl at Native Dog

GM Smith ('Steele Grey')

There was a gay young cattle-man
Who drove to Campbell's Hill,
He used to drove from Congewai
And I think he does so still.

He flirted with the maidens
Who lived along the route,
For he was a lady-killer and
Knew how to play the flute.

There was one he much admired
Who lived upon the rise,
He praised her form and figure
And raved about her eyes.

Her home was on the hilltop
Away from swamp and bog
In a high and dry locality – they
Call it Native Dog.

And every time when passing,
Or so I hear them say,
With her he'd spend an hour or two
To pass the time away.

She thought that he meant business
And so did many more,
But it seems she made a slight mistake,
As girls have done before.

Alas, for his sincerity,
This cattle-man so gay,
It seems that he was one of those
Who love and ride away.

He wooed her in the starlight,
And won her in the fog,
But he never popped the question
To the girl at Native Dog.

And now she's sad and lonely
And wears a sullen frown,
Since she heard that he is flirting
With another girl in town.

And I fancy when she meets him
She will scald him like a hog,
For the hair is somewhat ginger
On that girl at Native Dog.

Gladys
Grahame Watt

By cripes! I'm keen on Gladys. I got my eye on her.
She's the bestest woman I have seen, without a doubt, for sure!
When I pass her old man's farm, in daytime or at night,
I tips me hat and squints me eyes, in case she's there in sight.
Last Friday when I went to town to get some stores and duds,
I met her in the grocer's — between the pollard and the spuds.
I took a real good look around — there's no sign of her dad,
Then, in a sort of 'toffy' voice, said, 'How yer goin', Glad?'
Well, you could have knocked me over when she looked up kinda
    slow,
And she set me heart a'quiver when she said, 'I'm real good-oh.'
We talked about the latest things that happen here and there,
And I would'a said some more to her if the grocer didn't stare!
I got me week's provisions and headed for the door,
Then waved me hand at Gladys, 'Be seeing ya some more.'
I reckon if I catch her, next week there, just by chance,
I'll ask her to go out with me, to the pictures, or a dance.
So keep your eyes off Gladys, I saw her first, by gee!
By cripes! I'm keen on Gladys. I hope she still likes me.

Pretty Sally
CJ Dennis

The diggers came from Bendigo,
From Albury the drovers,
From where the Goulburn waters flow
Came bearded teamsters travelling slow,
And all the brown bush rovers;
And where the road goes winding still
To drop to Melbourne valley,
They sought the shanty by the hill,
And called for beer and drank their fill,
And sparked with Pretty Sally.

The teamsters halted by the door
To give their horses water,
And stood about the bar-room floor
To ogle, while they had one more,
The shanty keeper's daughter.
Diggers with gold from creek and claim
About her used to rally,
Shearers and booted stockmen came
And to the hill they gave her name,
For all loved Pretty Sally.

I see her now; a sparkling lass
Brim-full of fun and laughter.
And where the slow teams used to pass,
And swagmen paused to beg a glass,
Now motor cars speed after.
And when I seek the road anew
That dips down to the valley,
I see again that bearded crew,
And, of the lovers, wonder who
At last wed Pretty Sally.

Reedy River

Henry Lawson

Ten miles down Reedy River
A pool of water lies,
And all the year it mirrors
The changes in the skies,
And in that pool's broad bosom
Is room for all the stars;
Its bed of sand has drifted
O'er countless rocky bars.

Around the lower edges
There waves a bed of reeds,
Where water rats are hidden
And where the wild duck breeds;
And grassy slopes rise gently
To ridges long and low,
Where groves of wattle flourish
And native bluebells grow.

Beneath the granite ridges
The eye may just discern
Where Rocky Creek emerges
From deep green banks of fern;
And standing tall between them,
The grassy she-oaks cool
The hard, blue-tinted waters
Before they reach the pool.

Ten miles down Reedy River
One Sunday afternoon,
I rode with Mary Campbell
To that broad bright lagoon;
We left our horses grazing
Till shadows climbed the peak,
And strolled beneath the she-oaks
On the banks of Rocky Creek.

Then home along the river
That night we rode a race,
And the moonlight lent a glory
To Mary Campbell's face;
And I pleaded for my future
All thro' that moonlight ride,
Until our weary horses
Drew closer side by side.

Ten miles from Ryan's Crossing
And five miles below the peak,
I built a little homestead
On the banks of Rocky Creek;
I cleared the land and fenced it
And ploughed the rich red loam,
And my first crop was golden
When I brought Mary home.

Now still down Reedy River
The grassy she-oaks sigh,
And the waterholes still mirror
The pictures in the sky;
And over all for ever
Go sun and moon and stars,
While the golden sand is drifting
Across the rocky bars;

But of the hut I builded
There are no traces now.
And many rains have leveled
The furrows of the plough;
And my bright days are olden,
For the twisted branches wave
And the wattle blossoms golden
On the hill by Mary's grave.

from . . . The Castlereagh
Charles Souter ('Dr Nil')

Give me the Bush Girl, the Bush Girl for me,
That's used to soap and sunshine as anyone can see.
You wouldn't get a town girl to stop a single day
In a pine-slab cottage on the Old Castlereagh!

Do I Love Thee?
Thomas E Spencer

I ask my heart, 'Do I love thee?' But how can I e'er forget?
The feelings of joy and rapture that thrilled me when first we met?
The memory of each glad meeting is treasured within my heart,
Which has well-nigh ceased its beating, since, in sorrow, we had to
    part.

Each night, as I seek my pillow, I murmur a prayer for thee
I breathe thy name as the sunbeams flash red on the eastern sea.
Thy spirit is still the beacon that guides me 'mid care and strife,
And there 'twill remain for ever, my darling, my love, my life.

Coogee Bay
Tip Kelaher

The smell of salt on a fresh sea breeze,
Day dies and the light grows dim,
While up on the point the tall pine trees
Are sighing their evening hymn.
The lights glow out on the concrete street
Where the shop fronts face the sea,
But where a boy and his young love meet
The night is cool and free.

Your eyes are shining, my love, my love,
With the old, old haunting light –
I'd give my chance of Heaven above
To hold you again tonight,
With the scattered clouds and the moon above,
The sand, and the wind-blown spray.
Why do I think of you now, old love,
Long buried and far away?

Stirrup Song

Harry Morant ('The Breaker')

We've drunk our wine, we've kissed our girls, and funds are getting
    low,
The horses must be thinking it's a fair thing now to go.
Sling up the swags on Condamine, and strap the billies fast,
And stuff a bottle in the bag, and let's be off at last.

What matter if the creeks are up? – the cash, alas, runs down! –
A very sure and certain sign we're long enough in town;
The nigger rides the 'boko', and you'd better take the bay,
Quartpot will do to carry me the stage we'll go today.

No grass this side the border fence, and all the mulga's dead;
The horses for a day or two will have to spiel ahead;
Man never yet from Queensland brought a bullock or a hack
But lost condition on that God-abandoned border track.

But once we're through the rabbit-proof, it's certain since the rain
There's whips of grass and water, so it's 'west-by-north' again;
There's feed on Tyson's country, we can spell the mokes a week
Where Billy Stevens last year trapped his brumbies, on Bough
    Creek.

The Paroo may be quickly crossed – the Eulo Common's bare –
And anyhow it isn't wise, old man, to dally there!
Alack-a-day! far wiser men than you or I succumb
To woman's wiles and potency of Queensland wayside rum!

Then over sand and spinifex! and on o'er range and plain!
The nags are fresh; besides they know they're westward-bound
    again!
The brand upon old Darkie's thigh is that upon the hide
Of bullocks we shall muster on the Diamantina side.

We'll light our campfires while we may, and yarn beside the blaze,
The jingling hobble-chains shall make a music through the days;
And while the tucker-bags are right and we've a stock of weed
The swagman will be welcome to a pipeful and a feed.

So fill your pipe, and ere we mount we'll drain a parting nip:
Here's now that west-by-north again may prove a lucky trip;
Then back once more, let's trust you'll find your best girl's merry
    face,
Or, if she jilts you, may you get a better in her place!

Nylons

Anon

Nylons are the strangest things
I find them rather shocking.
For the bottom always seems to be
At the top of every stocking!

from . . . When Matilda Hangs the Washing

WT Goodge ('The Colonel')

There are diverse blooming damsels who reside at Number Eight,
And Matilda is the servant maid and sweet to contemplate;
She has arms of alabaster and an eye of heavenly blue,
And her hair is crisp and curly and of lovely auburn hue
And we watch her from the window of our humble domicile
And are frequently rewarded with a sunny little smile,
And we sometimes feel our sorrows we are apt to over-rate,
When Matilda hangs the washing on the line at Number Eight!

Though our general existence is a dull and weary waste
Of the clicking of the scissors and the splashing of the paste,
And of writing little paragraphs concerning Mr Brown
And the wonderful improvements he's effected in the town;
We have still a lurking hopefulness for better days in store,
With a gleam of sunshine breaking the monotony of yore,
Of a pleasure in existence, of a glimpse of earthly Heaven
With Matilda hanging washing on the line at Number Seven!

Ruptured Romance

Wilbur G Howcroft

I took my sweetheart for a stroll
Along a moonlit shore,
But soon I had to call a cab
Because her feet were sore.

I asked her up to have a drink
And started wine to pour,
But very soon she called a halt
And said her throat was sore.

I hired a tandem bicycle,
We mounted at her door
And after riding half a mile
She claimed her seat was sore.

One night I clasped her in my arms,
A kiss or two to score;
She quickly wrenched herself away
And said her lips were sore.

I'd thought to ask could we be wed,
Our full love to explore,
But dammit I can't take the risk –
'Cos I've been caught before!

My Girl Gladys

Grahame Watt

Strewth! I'm feeling chirpy! Me feet is in the air,
It's a bonzer sort of feelin' and I haven't got a care.
If you're wondrin' what has hit me, what has made me like a
   clown,
It's Gladys that I told you 'bout, the one I met in town.
Her father's got the corner place down by the three mile creek.
Glad was workin' down there when I called 'round last week.
She was muckin' out the pig sty, and gawd she looked a treat,
In a dress of red with flowers on, and gum boots on her feet.
Her hair was sort of wind-blown, and her eyes, her eyes, they
   smiled.
And when she said g'day to me it nearly drove me wild.
I put me foot up on the rail and tried to act real calm.
I said, 'Snifter sort o' weather for us blokes on the farm.'
I kept talkin' lots of rubbish 'bout wheat and crops and stuff,
Tryin' to sound important and not to be too rough!
And she looked real interested, stopped shovellin' for a while.
She said, 'It's good to see you, Dave,' and she gave a crackin' smile.
I thought, it's now or never. I said, 'How'd you like to go
To the dance down at Goomalibee? It'll be a bonzer show!'
Well, stone the crows, she nodded. She'd go! She said, 'Alright!
It sounds real good, it does, Dave, I'll see you Sat'dy night.'
I can hardly wait for Sat'dy, the days are just a blur,
I'm moonin' round and dreamin'. Me and Gladys! Me and her!
I've polished up me hobnail boots, dusted down the gig,
I even sneaked down to the barn and practised at a jig.
I'll have a bath, and oil me hair, I hope I look alright.
I can't wait for me and Gladys goin' out on Sat'dy night!

Last Night

Harry Morant ('The Breaker')

Last night when the moon rose, round and white,
Over the crest of the distant hill,
You sang your song to us there last night
When the sleeping world lay hushed and still.

Oh! why did the scented breezes shake
The oak-trees' foliage then! I vow
It was that the envious birds should wake
And hear your song 'neath the leafy bough!

They say, in this sunlit southern land
The birds thereof have been silent long;
Why did they sing no more I understand –
For you have stolen the wind birds' song.

Ah, I saw the bright stars wane – and swoon,
And heard the murmurous night-wind sigh!
You sang your song, and the placid moon
Trembled and paled in the soft grey sky.

You sang last night, and the saddened bird
Away to her leaf-hid nestlings flew,
Knowing their music would ne'er be heard
Since Heaven had given their songs to you.

The Bush Girl

Henry Lawson

So you rode from the range where your brothers select,
Through the ghostly, grey bush in the dawn.
You rode slowly at first, lest her heart should suspect
That you were so glad to be gone.
You had scarcely the courage to glance back at her,
By the homestead receding from view,
And you breathed with relief when you rounded the spur,
For the world was a wide world to you.

Grey eyes that grow sadder than sunset or rain,
Fond heart that is evermore true,
Firm faith that grows firmer for watching in vain,
She'll wait by the slip-rails for you.

Ah! the world is a new and a wide one to you,
But the world to your sweetheart is shut,
For a change never comes to the lonely bush homes
Of the stockyard, the scrub, and the hut;
And the only relief from its dullness she feels,
When the ridges grow softened and dim,
And away in the dusk to the slip-rails she steals,
To dream of past hours 'with him'.

Do you think, where, in place of bare fences, dry creeks,
Clear streams and green hedges are seen –
Where the girls have the lily and rose in their cheeks,
And the grass in mid-summer is green –
Do you think, now and then, now and then, in the whirl
Of the town life, while London is new,
Of the hut in the bush and the freckled-faced girl
Who waits by the slip-rails for you?

Grey eyes that are sadder than sunset or rain,
Bruised heart that is evermore true,
Fond faith that is firmer for trusting in vain,
She waits by the slip-rails for you.

from . . . Over the Wine
Victor Daley ('Creeve Roe')

Long ago I did discover it was fine to be a lover,
But the heartache and the worry spoil the game;
Now I think, like an old vandal,
That the game's not worth the candle,
And I know some other vandals think the same.

The Mouse
Hugh McCrae

All Christmas night upon the shelf;
Among the apples yellow-faced,
There played a pretty maiden mouse,
Divinely slim and very chaste.

Who, when I held my candle up,
Did twink her little eyes at me . . .
So mad, so bright, so mischievous;
I thought of you, dear Dorothy!

Skis and Shes

Kenneth Slessor

I sing about Women and Winter,
The rapture of 30 degrees,
The damsel who waits with a bundle of skates
And the girl who goes riding on skis;
And, oh for the flight of an eagle
To see where she happens to go –
But waving a wing is a difficult thing
When you lie with you face in the snow.

Poo-pooh to your ice, Kosciuszko,
A fig for your cucumber air,
Your peaks, I'm informed, are sufficiently warmed
By the presence of Annabel there;
But this I'm unable to warrant,
The fact is, I really don't know –
Wherever I climb I spend most of my time
With my face in a puddle of snow.

I know she has wings on her ankles,
I know she can leap like a trout,
The hoi-polloi thrill when she whistles downhill
And the guides find their eyes popping out;
For this I'll accept without question
The word of the Tourist Bureau –
My personal view is a trifle askew
Due to banging my face in the snow.

If only my skis wouldn't wobble,
If only my feet would go straight,
I'd chase her with hope down a nursery slope
And leave introductions to Fate;
But something has doomed me to grovel,
I crawl on all fours down below,
She catapults by like a bird in the sky,
And I lie with my face in the snow.

The Best Bait

Anon

'What bait do you use,' said a saint to the devil
'When you fish where the souls of men abound?'
'Well, for general use,' said the King of Evil,
'Gold and fame are best I've found.'

'But for special use?' asked the saint. 'Ah! Mate,'
Said the devil, 'I'll give you advice that's sound.
A thing I hate is to change my bait,
So I fish with woman the whole year round.'

Why Doherty Died

Thomas E Spencer

It was out on the Bogan near Billabong Creek
Where the sky shines like brass seven days in the week,
Where the buzzin' mosquitoes annoy you all night
And the blowflies come wakin' you up at daylight;
Where the people get weary and sad and forlorn
Till they wish they had died long before they were born;
There's a flat near the river, I knew the place well,
For 'twas there Dinny Doherty kept the hotel.

Dinny Doherty died. 'Twasn't aisy to say
Just the cause of the trouble that tuk him away;
If 'twas measles or whoopin' cough, croup or catarrh,
Or the things dochters pickle and put in a jar.

Not a dochter was nigh when he come to his death
So we reckoned he died just through shortage of breath –
We didn't know how these fine points to decide;
What we did know for certain was: Doherty died.

The coroner came up from Bottle-nose Flat,
And twelve of us wid him on Doherty sat.
The hate was intense; there was whisky galore –
When we'd finished we weren't as wise as before.
We were roastin'; yet there, wid a shmile on his face,
Lay poor Dinny, the only cool man in the place.
Yet divil a one in the crowd could decide
Or even imagine why Doherty died.

The old pub it seemed lonesome whin Dinny was gone,
Lavin' poor Kitty Doherty grievin' alone.
Every time that I called she cried: 'Phwat will I do?
Darlin' Dinny, come back to me, Cushla! Wirroo!
Faith it's lonely I am today, Dinny, ashore!
Don't be sayin' you're dead, that I'll see you no more.'
Whin I tried to console her, she bitterly cried,
'I have no one to love me since Doherty died.'

'I kape pinin',' says she, 'till I'm mere shkin and bone.'
(Poor Kitty! She only weighed siventeen shtone.)
'Sure, life widhout love is like bread widhout yaste.'
Poor Kitty! Her heart was as big as her waist.
And what is the pain? – 'tisn't iveryone knows
Whin a big heart like Kitty's wid love overflows.
Kitty's love was as broad as the ocean is wide,
But she'd no one to share it since Doherty died.

'Twas a hot summer's day when a visit I paid,
For the hate was hundhred and tin in the shade;
Poor Kitty looked sad as I inthered the gate,
And her cheeks were quite moist wid her tears (and the hate);
But 'twas cosy she looked as she sat in the bar,
And I whispered, 'Poor girl, is it lonely ye are?'
'Bedad! Lonely's no name for it,' Kitty replied.
'I'm just frettin' me heart out since Doherty died.'

Then, says I, 'Faith, this isn't the weather to fret!'
And I wiped her plump cheeks, that were clammy and wet;
'Sure, Kitty,' says I, 'you must hould up your head,
For the world isn't impty if one man is dead.
To be livin' and pinin' alone's a disgrace;
Can you find no good man to take Doherty's place?'
Then she shmiled through her tears, and she said as she sighed:
'Ah! the good men are scarce since poor Doherty died.'

'Och,' says I, 'to talk that way is fiddle-de-dee;
There are good men left yet, Kitty – what about me?'
Then, before you'd say 'Jack', o'er the bar she had leapt,
And she flung herself onto me bosom and wept.
'Twas in vain that I thried to get out to get cool,
She was harder to shift than a big bale of wool.
And I thought, as she lay on me bosom and cried:
'Faith! 'Tis now that I know why poor Doherty died.'

Mink
Anon

Said a bimbo from Balwyn, 'I think
This coat I've been given is mink.
I hope that it is,
If it isn't, gee whizz
There's going to be quite a stink!'

Census
Janine Haig

I was filling out the census form;
It asked me what I did –
'Occupation' boldly printed –
How it is I earn a quid.

'Housewife' doesn't cover it,
'Mother's' not enough;
To find my job description
Was a choice almighty tough.

Finally I found it!
The answer was right there;
I lifted up my pencil
And I wrote it down with care:

Jus'cm'ere and hold this ladder,
Jus'cm'ere and switch this on,
Jus'cm'ere and hold this up,
Jus'cm'ere – now where's she gone?

It is hard to find a title
For my job and make it clear;
So I'll stick to what's familiar:
Occupation: *Jus'cm'ere.*

The Free-Selector's Daughter

Henry Lawson

I met her on the Lachlan Side –
A darling girl I thought her,
And ere I left I swore I'd win
The free-selector's daughter.

I milked her father's cows a month,
I brought the wood and water,
I mended all the broken fence,
Before I won the daughter.

I listened to her father's yarns,
I did just what I 'oughter',
And what you'll have to do to win
A free-selector's daughter.

I broke my pipe and burnt my twist,
And washed my mouth with water;
I had a shave before I kissed
The free-selector's daughter.

Then, rising in the frosty morn,
I brought the cows for Mary,
And when I'd milked a bucketful
I took it to the dairy.

I poured the milk into the dish
While Mary held the strainer,
I summoned heart to speak my wish,
And, oh! her blush grew plainer.

I told her I must leave the place,
I said that I would miss her;
At first she turned away her face,
And then she let me kiss her.

I put the bucket on the ground,
And in my arms I caught her;
I'd give the world to hold again
That free-selector's daughter!

Names

Hugh McCrae

Long ago, when I was young,
I had trolled upon my tongue
Words like white or golden wine,
Names of ladies fair and fine;
That my loved one might be glad
To be called so by her lad.

All through Monday she would be
Darling Helena to me;
Tuesday found her Christabel;
Every day that we could tell
Brought another silver sound
To ring her pretty presence round.

Unaware, came surly Time,
Dried our blood, and spoiled our prime,
Drew the gallant sunlight down,
Shoved it in his ugly gown;
Stole our bread and cheese and kisses –
Christabel's now just 'The Missus'.

from . . . Down in Honolulu

EJ Brady

'Twas down in Honolulu,
Way off one night afar,
The sea-breeze comin' cooler
Across the coral bar,
When Lulu's eyes were brighter
Than any girl's I knew,
When Lulu's teeth were whiter
Than any coral, too.
Oh! Lulu, Lulu, Lulu,
My warm Pacific pearl!
My lovely, lively Lulu –
My own Kanaka girl!

For, oh! your heart was beatin'!
For, oh! your breath was sweet!
And you was good for eatin',
If gals was good to eat –
And, oh! your lips were cherry!
And, oh! your teeth *was* white –
I've tried in vain to bury
The memory of that night.
Ah! Lulu, Lulu, Lulu,
I'd give my life, I vow,
To live that starlight over –
I know I loved you, *now*!

The sea-breeze, perfume-laden,
It rustled through the palms
That night, that night I laid in
Your warm, soft twining arms.
You swore to love me ever,
I swore to love you true
Forever an' forever –
The way we used to do.
Oh! Lulu, Lulu, Lulu,
'Twas years and years ago;
I don't forget it, somehow,
Although I ought, I know.

I feel your arms still clinging –
Oh! what's the use to cry?
It's 'Homeward Bound' they're singing –
I'll come back by-and-by.
Eight bells! It's done and over;
While ships still sail the sea,
A sailor man's a rover –
Good-bye, and think of me!
Oh! Lulu, Lulu, Lulu,
I broke the sailor's vow.
I want to live it over,
I know I loved you, *now*!

'Twas down in Honolulu,
Way back in other years,
I left you, lovely Lulu,
The starlight and the tears.
But, oh! your face was fairer
Than any face I've met,
And, oh! your charms were rarer
Than any woman's yet.
And, Lulu, Lulu, Lulu,
Wherever you may be,
My brown Kanaka Lulu –
Do you remember me?

Sweethearts Wait on Every Shore

Henry Lawson

She sits beside the tinted tide,
That's reddened by the tortured sand;
And thro' the East, to ocean wide,
A vessel sails from sight of land.

But she will wait and watch in vain,
For it is said in Cupid's lore,
'That he who loved will love again,
And sweethearts wait on ev'ry shore.'

You A-Wantin' Me

Mary Gilmore

You a-wantin' me, me a-wantin' you!
What's we waitin' for? Life is wearin' through.
What's we waitin' for? Lookin' still and sad?
Life ain't watchin' round, hopin' we'll be glad.

Time's no good to us, life ain't nothin' sweet,
Me a-mopin' here, you across the street!
What should come between, partin' of us two –
You a-wantin' me, me a-wantin' you!

Kiss me on the mouth, kiss me lovin'-fair?
What's we waitin' for? No one else will care!
What's we waitin' for? Kiss me fair and true;
You a-wantin' me, me a-wantin' you!

Love Me and Never Leave Me

Ronald McCuaig

Love me, and never leave me,
Love, nor ever deceive me,
And I shall always bless you
If I may undress you:
Which I heard a lover say
To his sweetheart where they lay.

He, though he did undress her,
Did not always bless her;
She, though she would not leave him,
Often did deceive him;
Yet they loved, and when they died
They were buried side by side.

from . . . Players

Victor Daley ('Creeve Roe')

And after all – and after all
Our passionate prayers, and sighs and tears
Is Life a reckless carnival?
And are they lost, our golden years?

Ah, no; ah, no; for, long ago,
Ere time could sere, or care could fret,
There was a youth called Romeo,
There was a maid called Juliet.

The players of the past are gone;
The races rise; the races pass;
And softly over all is drawn
The quiet curtain of the grass.

But when the world went wild with Spring,
What days we had! Do you forget?
When I of all the word was king,
And you were my Queen Juliet?

There lives (though time should cease to flow,
And stars their courses should forget)
There lives a grey-haired Romeo,
Who loves a golden Juliet.

Spellbound

Robert Webb

The mysterious ways of women I'll never understand
How their modesty prevails away from ocean sand.
When skirts rise up with sudden breeze with frantic hands they
    clutch
Holding down their billowing skirts for fear they'll show too
    much.
Yet, spellbound by the ocean, they show their boobs and bum
With just a smear of sun-screen to protect them from the sun.

Sarah Dow

EJ Brady

'Er mother kep' a lodgin' place —
I got to know 'er there —
She 'ad the sunrise on 'er face,
The sunset in 'er 'air.
To other wimmen that I've met
I'd rather not refer,
But I'd 'ave sold (an' paid the debt!)
My willin' soul for 'er!

Oh, Sarah Dow! Oh, Sarah Dow!
You were too good for me, I vow;
But if I could 'ave died, I would —
To serve you, Sarah Dow!

I mustered up the pluck one day —
'Twas pretty 'ard to do;
I 'adn't 'arf the 'eart to say
One 'arf I wanted to; —
I asked 'er if she'd be my wife —
I 'ad no chance, I know,
But it was, somehow, death in life
To 'ear 'er tell me – 'No!'

I've been like sailormen ashore
To spend my 'ard-earned pence;
I'd been a reckless dog before
An' little better since;
I never saw 'er face again,
The face that 'urt me so,
I never saw 'er face since then —
She died ten year ago.

But I've a picture in my bunk
I don't let no one see,
An' when I'm done an' drowned an' sunk
That picture goes with me.
I've been an' hid it in my kit,
I wouldn't 'ear them laugh,
An' onst a while I looks at it,
An old tin photograrf.

Oh, Sarah Dow! Oh, Sarah Dow!
It's gettin' brown an' faded now;
But you are there still young an' fair,
My Sarah, Sarah Dow!

The Road to Gundagai

AB Paterson ('The Banjo')

The mountain road goes up and down,
From Gundagai to Tumut town.

And branching off there runs a track,
Across the foothills grim and black,

Across the plains and ranges grey
To Sydney city far away.

It came by chance one day that I
From Tumut rode to Gundagai.

And reached about the evening tide
The crossing where the roads divide;

And, waiting at the crossing place,
I saw a maiden fair of face,

With eyes of deepest violet blue,
And cheeks to match the rose in hue –

The fairest maids Australia knows
Are bred among the mountain snows.

Then, fearing I might go astray,
I asked if she could show the way.

Her voice might well a man bewitch –
Its tones so supple, deep, and rich.

'The tracks are clear,' she made reply,
'And this goes down to Sydney town,
And that one goes to Gundagai.'

Then slowly, looking coyly back,
She went along the Sydney track.

And I for one was well content
To go the road the lady went;

But round the turn a swain she met –
The kiss she gave him haunts me yet!

I turned and travelled with a sigh
The lonely road to Gundagai.

Streamer's End

Kenneth Slessor

Roses all over the steamer,
Paper all over the sky,
And you at the end of a streamer
Smiling goodbye, goodbye.
It isn't to me you dangle,
It isn't to me you smile,
But out of the rainbow tangle
Our lines have crossed for a while.

Somebody's benediction
Pitches a streamer – whizz! –
Under the firm conviction
You're on the end of his.
Others may claim attention,
Rolling away to sea,
But nobody's there to mention
The cove at this end is me!

Don't you consider the danger
Of setting a heart on fire
By tossing a perfect stranger
Your 10,000 volt live-wire?
I'm only a face on the skyline,
Something the wharf obscures –
But you're on the end of my line,
And I'm on the end of yours!

Off in the vast *Orsova*,
Soon you will wave in vain;
I could be Casanova,
You could be Queen of Spain –
I must go back to the city,
You must go back to the King.
Blow me a kiss for pity,
Girl at the end of the string!

Shearer's Song

Henry Lawson

The season is over;
The shearing is done;
The wages are paid; and
The 'sprees' have begun.
But never a shanty
Gets sight of my cheques;
For far down the Murray
My Annie expects
A heart that is faithful,
A head that is clear,
And sufficient provisions
To last for a year!

from . . . The Haunted Lagoon

Thomas E Spencer

There was once a man who came from Bundanoon,
And a maiden from the town of Kangaloon,
And each evening in the gloaming,
They would go together roaming
Down the winding track that led to a lagoon,
Where they'd spoon
And talk nonsense by the glimmer of the moon.

He was 'wood-and-water-joey' at the 'Star'
Where she waited and attended at the bar;
He was fair and tall and slender,
She was dark and plump and tender;
And he told her that her eyes were brighter far
Than a star,
Which remark proves just how stupid lovers are.

But, through sitting in the moonlight on a log,
Or meandering 'mid the bracken in a fog,
With the glass approaching zero,
Influenza gripped our hero,
Which resulted in his talking like a frog,
Or a hog,
Whilst his cough was like the barking of a dog.

And the falling dew descending from the trees,
With the moisture that was borne upon the breeze,
Caused a bronchial inflammation,
So our hero's conversation
Was a cross between a snuffle and a wheeze,
While his sneeze
Used to shake him from his elbows to his knees.

And he'd sit and court and spoon until he froze,
Till he couldn't tell his fingers from his toes.
Yet he'd plead with her and flatter,
Whilst his teeth would snap and chatter,
And his speech was punctuated by the blows,
Of his nose.
(In his wretched state he called his nose his 'dose'.)

But she positively spurned his fond refrain,
Though she said she never wished to give him pain,
Hot-baked hearts she'd seen a-many,
But she wasn't taking any,
Then she added that he'd water on the brain,
That was plain.
And she cocked her little nose up in disdain.

So the man from Bundanoon, in his despair,
Cried, 'Cads't thou be false add yet – *Atchoo!* – so fair?
Burst – *Atchoo!* – ye clouds asudder!
Flash ye lightdigs! Boob thou thudder!
It's edough to bake a bortal – *Tishoo!* – swear,
I declare.'
And the man from Bundanoon then tore his hair.

And they parted by the germ-infested shore
Of the lake that 'skylark never warbled o'er'.
And the wild fowl left its waters
And the possum changed its quarters,
So the pool became more silent than before,
For the roar
Of that sneeze disturbed the echoes – never more.

For they found his sodden corpse in the lagoon,
Where he floated, calmly staring at the moon,
And some folks who went there boating
Said they heard, '*Ah-Tishoo!*' floating
O'er its waters; so they ceased to go and spoon,
Very soon,
And especially the maid from Kangaloon.

Wings

Grahame Watt

Some people say when madly in love,
'Oh! For the wings, the wings of a dove.'
When I'm with Gladys my heartbeat does quicken,
And I yearn for the wings . . . of her lovely roast chicken.

from . . . The Lady with the Laugh
Charles Souter ('Dr Nil')

Sing a song of simples, of chiffons, and of sighs,
Of pearly teeth and dimples, and baby-gazing eyes!
The maiden with the ringlets may cut your heart in half,
But, Lord! she's not a patch upon the lady with the laugh!

Sing a song of sometime, and tresses growing grey,
The everlasting glum time, when age will have his way!
The charms of eyes and ankles have gone, like autumn chaff,
But, thank the gods, she's still with us . . . the lady with the laugh!

The Gay Cavalier
(from . . . Old Acquaintances)
Charles Thatcher

The Gay Cavalier's serenading
Has been suddenly brought to a close;
Instead of the room of the maiden,
Beneath her pa's window he goes;
'Twas a scene for a good artist's pencil,
For him 'twas a most unkind cut,
For the old bloke pitched out a utensil
Right slap on the cavalier's nut.

Taxi Cab!
Anon

The Taxicab Driver sits in his car,
He waits for calls from near and far;
He knows all the sorrows, he knows all the joys,
He knows all the girls who are chasing the boys;
He knows all our troubles, he knows all our strife,
He knows every man who ducks from his wife;
If a Taxicab Driver told half that he knows
He would turn all our friends into bitterest foes.

The Boss's Wife

Anon

The Boss went each night to the stockmen's hut,
For word of the day's work done,
And he'd stay for a smoke, or a yarn and a joke,
And talk of the outside run.

And the boss's wife she'd wait and watch
In loneliest contemplation
Of the lot and life of a station wife
And the ways of an outback station.

And she'd gaze at the stockmen's hut below,
And across to the servant's light,
And she'd wait and brood in the doleful mood
That comes with the silent night.

And out of the darkness a notion grew,
A dim little gleaming dart,
And the housemaid's light when it sank each night,
Struck doubt in the wifely heart.

She gave no sign, but she watched each night,
Till there wasn't much room for doubt,
And she timed when the boss came in at night,
From the time that the lights went out.

And she hid the hurt with a woman's skill,
And she studied the housemaid's lighting;
To be betrayed for an artless maid –
'Twas time to be up and fighting.

When the boss was gone to the stockmen's hut
She lost no time in going,
And using a smile and a bit of guile,
Got the maid to come help with the sewing.

And the wife, when the work was well in swing,
Slipped off to the housemaid's room,
And safe in the camp she blew the lamp,
And waited there in the gloom.

Till the footsteps soft on the beaten track
Turned in at the darkened door,
With scarce a rap, or the slightest tap,
For he'd been there often before.

In a silent style with a wifely wile,
She played the maid of the quarters,
She played with the skill and the strength of will,
And the guile of Eve's own daughters.

She played, then suddenly flashed a torch,
Just one horrified glance she took;
Then she dropped the light and she fainted quite,
Twas Chin-ti, the Chinese cook!

Her Dying Wish

Anon

Shone the moonbeams very faintly
On a face serene and saintly;
On a girl's face like a flower far too fair for long to last,
And their pallid silver fingers –
Lo! how lovingly each lingers! –
Touched her cheeks and told the story she was dying – dying fast.

At her bedside stood her lover,
Stood and bent him down above her;
Stricken sore with bitter sorrow, writhing in the clutch of grief;
Then she whispered, 'Best and nearest,
Do not mourn for me, my dearest;
I shall soon be up in Heaven, where all pain finds sure relief!

'But, before I do forsake you,
I've one last request to make you.'
'Name it, dear,' he said: 'I'll do it if it's in the power of man.'
Then once more he bent above her,
And she whispered to her lover:
'When the funeral takes place, dear, keep as sober as you can!'

from . . . To Many Ladies

Charles Souter ('Dr Nil')

When you raise your gentle eyes
All the blue fades from the skies.
When your tones so softly ring
All the birds forget to sing.
When you smile, the sea smiles too.
'Tis the same, whate'er you do:
Nature takes her cue from you.

SECTION SIX

Gambling and Grog
Betting, Boxing, Booze

Please do not assume, gentle reader, that this section appears here due to any predilection of mine for these particular subjects. I plead that the overwhelming amount of this material in the Australian rhymed verse genre makes it essential that this section be included.

I have only once pulled on a pair of boxing gloves, as a boy, and I had my opponent, my mate and next-door neighbour, very worried very quickly. A sharp rap on my nose produced blood and watering eyes and the very real thought that he'd damaged me beyond repair and was about to get a real hiding for his efforts – from his mother. Luckily I was relatively unhurt and we covered up the whole sordid incident with the usual boyish lies.

While I can think of few things I'd rather do than waste time (and money) pleasurably on Australia's beautiful thoroughbred racetracks (especially as I get older) I hold to my claim that there is no favouritism at work here.

Such a wealth of Australian rhymed verse about horse-racing and drinking exists that they are truly unavoidable as topics for a section in this collection. All the 'great' verse writers tackled the subject of booze and the granddaddy of all Aussie verse writers, Adam Lindsay Gordon, was a fine racetrack rider, as was Paterson. Ogilvie and Morant loved racing and lived with horses, CJ Dennis loved the flavour of the racetrack, and so it goes on. Boxing is included simply because I had a couple of boxing poems and they had to fit somewhere.

And anyway, in my defence, at least not all the poems here actually condone the subject material.

Betting, Boxing, Booze
Anon

There is no surer wager, you know he'll always lose,
That bloke who wastes his hard-earned cash on betting, boxing,
   booze.
Instead of wife and family, the stadium he'll choose,
After Randwick and the pub – betting, boxing, booze.
Sunday he'll just sleep all day, he'll lay in bed and snooze,
A burden to his wife and kids from betting, boxing, booze.

The Shanty by the Way
Traditional/EJ Overbury

In the first-rate business section
Where two well-known roads do meet,
Stands a very grand erection,
Welcome rest to weary feet.

If a moment you should linger,
'Tis a case for all that day,
For your cash they'll surely finger
In the shanty by the way.

Rows of bottles standing empty
Labelled with bright blue and gold –
Beer's so cold it needs no icing
From the cellars damp and cold.

Cards and billiards always ready,
Landlord presses us to stay,
How the deuce can man keep sober
In the shanty by the way?

Shoulder up your swag and wander
Thirsty, penniless you'll stray,
For your cash you'll surely squander
In the shanty by the way.

Lambed Down

Anon

The shades of night were falling fast,
As down a steep old gully passed
A man whom you could plainly see
Had just come off a drunken spree,
Lambed down.

He'd left the station with his cheque,
But two days later he's a wreck;
At Ryan's pub he felt all right,
And yet he was, before next night,
Lambed down.

'Oh, stay!' old Ryan said, 'and slip
Your blanket off, and have a nip;
I'll cash your cheque and send you on.'
He stopped, and now his money's gone –
Lambed down.

He's got the shakes and thinks he sees
Blue devils lurking in the trees;
Oh, shearers! if you've any sense
Don't be on any such pretence
Lambed down.

Life in a Glass of Beer

Thomas Curyer

I look into a glass of beer; I see the amber liquid clear;
A thousand other things I also see.
I see the dark, I see the light, I see romance, I see a fight,
And visions of what man would like to be.

I take a small sip from the glass and straightaway I'm in a class
Where friendship, love and hate are all abrew.
Arguments and friendships broken, new friends made with few
    words spoken,
Reality takes on a different view.

Near the middle of the drink it's getting hard to stop and think,
I'll tell the world at large I'm ten foot high.
Why should I dally with the rest? I'm equal to the very best!
I'll pass the time of day and pass them by.

I see the bottom of the glass; reality has come to pass.
Just one more sip, my glass of life is dry.
I live to drink, I drink to live, I've nothing in this world to give.
It's time I cashed my chips and said goodbye.

Whether it took months or years of brandy, whisky, gin or beers,
My glass of life cannot be filled anew.
Like me it is now cast aside, devoid of humour, worth or pride,
Both victims of an alcoholic brew!

Rowdy Boys
Anon

Listen here you rowdy boys,
Why don't you drink and make less noise?
It's after hours you'll bring the police,
Just stand there and drink in peace!

Bluey Brink
Anon

There once was a shearer, by name Bluey Brink,
A devil for work and a demon for drink;
He'd shear his two hundred a day without fear,
And drink without blinking four gallons of beer.

Now Jimmy the barman who served out the drink,
He hated the sight of this here Bluey Brink,
He stayed much too late, and he came much too soon,
At evening, at morning, at night and at noon.

One morning as Jimmy was cleaning the bar,
With sulphuric acid he kept in a jar,
In comes Old Bluey a'yelling with thirst:
'Whatever you've got Jim, just hand me the first!'

Now it ain't down in history, it ain't down in print,
But that shearer drank acid with never a wink,
Saying, 'That's the stuff, Jimmy! Well, strike me stone dead,
This'll make me the ringer of Stevenson's shed!'

Now all that long day as he served out the beer,
Poor Jimmy was sick with his trouble and fear;
Too worried to argue, too anxious to fight,
Seeing the shearer a corpse in his fright.

When early next morning, he opened the door,
Then along came the shearer, asking for more,
With his eyebrows all singed and his whiskers deranged,
And holes in his hide like a dog with the mange.

Says Jimmy, 'And how did you like the new stuff?'
Says Bluey, 'It's fine, but I've ain't had enough!
It gives me great courage to shear and to fight,
But why does that stuff set my whiskers alight?

'I thought I knew drink, but I must have been wrong,
For that stuff you gave me was proper and strong;
It set me to coughing, you know I'm no liar,
And every cough set my whiskers on fire!'

Something I Ate

Russell Hannah

A home brewer from Bogan Gate,
Drank his own brew and so tempted fate.
From his deathbed
He cheerfully said,
'It must have been something I ate.'

The Fellow from Sydney

Anon

There was a young fellow from Sydney
Who drank till he ruined his kidney.
It shrivelled and shrank
As he sat there and drank,
But he had a good time at it, didn't he?

The Pub that Lost its Licence

Henry Lawson

The pub that lost its licence
Was very quaint and old;
'Twas built before the railway,
Before the days of gold.
The pub that lost its licence
Was built of solid stone
And good Australian hardwood
In fashion all its own.

They build of bricks and softwood
Their narrow shells and high;
They build with iron girders
And build 'em to the sky:
The 'joiners' rush and hurry,
Time-hunted men they are –
And 'decorators' chase them
To 'fit' the shoddy bar.

The little inn with gables
Rose slowly in the past,
In days when ships and houses
And men were built to last;
In dove-tailed days, and polished,
When 'slumming' was a sin:
They fashioned it for comfort,
And called it 'Fig Tree Inn'.

Deep windowed and deep seated,
And fire-places deep,
With a stone wall round the garden,
Where the vines of ages creep;
And sunny nooks and corners,
Where one might doze and sleep.
And seats on broad verandahs,
And a bar-room cool and deep.

Our public bars are seatless
In days of greed and rush –
Where fat casks stood, and tables,
Now men must stand and 'lush'.
The pub that lost its licence
Gave time to talk and think,
But now-a-days old cronies
Must elbow up and drink.

Still round the ancient fig tree
The rustic table stands,
Surrounded by its benching
As 'twas in other lands;
Beneath it smiles the harbour,
The shippin' and all that;
And there, on summer Sundays,
Our fathers' fathers sat.

The publicans were stout men,
With manners wise and slow –
And so I sat with cronies
Not very long ago.
The stout and bustling landlady –
While slowly ran the sands
Of life, where arm-chaired 'granny'
Would doze with folded hands.

The furniture was ancient,
 And heavy as 'twas strong –
Above hung water colours
Of scenes, ah! vanished long –
Of blacks, and teams, and windmills,
Of homes beyond the seas:
And stern, unyielding pictures
Of old celebrities.

And boomerangs and waddies,
And sharks' teeth and whales' corns,
And, velveted and polished,
Some mighty bullock horns.
And spears in thongs of greenhide,
And tomahawks of stone,
And ancient guns and pistols –
And other things unknown.

The old pub lost its licence,
Not for its sins at all.
But because it was a free house
(They said it was too small)
'Twas let to other people
That grind and grub, and wowse –
They turned it into 'lodgings'
And called it 'Fig Tree House'.
(They opened it for boarders
And called it 'Fig Tree House'!)

But 'twas haunted by the spirits
Of a better braver day,
They could not let the lodgings,
The boarders would not stay.
And so it stands deserted,
While, through new paint cheap and thin,
You might discern by moonlight
 The old sign, 'Fig Tree Inn'.

The Local Pub
Wilbur G Howcroft

I must go down to the pub again,
Though you'll surely wonder why,
When all I'll get is some tepid beer
And a musty, tooth-marked pie.

Yes, I must go down to that filthy hole
But the reason's plain, you see,
Though I hate the sight of the lousy dump –
I'm the hotel licensee.

The Fallen Tree Hotel
'The Prooshan'

On the lonesome line of traffic
Where the Tumbarumba track
Forks for Bargo, and for Taradale as well,
Where the wallabies and wombats
And the kangaroos have combats,
I once beheld the Fallen Tree Hotel.

The owners of the hostel
Were two coachmen of the line,
Jack Galvin, and another known as 'Ned',
Who bravely ploughed the highways
And the lonesome tracks and by-ways
With lots of falling timber overhead.

Now the pub was never licensed,
There were boarders never one,
No billiards and no tap-room, and for bar
There was just the muddy highway,
And the lamps hung in the skyway,
The ever-changing moon or gleaming star.

Once a mighty tree had fallen,
Was it gum? I cannot tell,
But 'twas partly burnt and hollow at the end,
And into this a frisky
Little bottle of good whisky
Was hidden well from sight, you may depend.

And twice a week 'twas empty,
And twice a week 'twas full,
Both Jack and Ned maintained the measure well,
And nightly drank and boasted
To the wallabies, and toasted
Each other at the Fallen Tree Hotel.

But alas, some drovers voted
For 'reduction' and the tree –
The Fallen Tree Hotel was soon in flames;
But the language isn't printed
That could register unstinted
The record of those adjectival names

That the drivers called the drovers,
That the drovers called their luck,
That burnt a flask of whisky! But there fell
A cloud of gloom – a sadness,
And a momentary madness
Round the embers and the ashes of the Fallen Tree Hotel.

from . . . The Sick Poet
AG Stephens

Lay the bottle there beside me: put the glass upon the chair:
You had better fill it up before you go;
For my hand's a bit unsteady, and I wouldn't like to swear –
And if I spilt a drop I should, I know.
Ah! Many's the good bottle I have buried to the world
In obedience to an honest drinker's code:
Now I've come to the last bottle that shall ever wet my throttle;
And the dead marines are calling down the road.

Fate Worse than Death

Anon

He grabbed me by my slender neck, I could not beg or scream.
He took me to a dingy room where we could not be seen.
He tore away my flimsy wrap and gazed upon my form,
I felt so damp and clammy while he was bold and warm.
His hungry lips he pressed on me – I gave him every drop.
He drained me of my very soul – I could not make him stop.
He made me what I am today, that's why you find me here,
An empty bottle, thrown away, that once was filled with beer!

Mulligan's Shanty

WT Goodge ('The Colonel')

Things is just the same as ever,
On the outer Never-Never,
And you look to find the stock of liquor scanty,
But we found things worse than ord'nry,
In fact, a bit extraord'nry,
When meself and Bill the Pinker struck his shanty.
'Shanty?' says you, 'what shanty?'
'Why, Mulligan's shanty.'

I says, 'Whisky'; Bill says 'Brandy';
But there wasn't either handy,
For the boss was out of liquor in that line.
'We'll try a rum,' says Billy.
'Got no rum,' he answers chilly,
'But I'd recommend a decent drop o' tine.'
'Tine?' says Bill, 'what tine?'
'Why, turpentine!'

'Blow me blue!' says Bill the Pinker,
'Can't you give us a deep-sinker?
Ain't yer got a cask o' beer behind the screen?'
Bill was getting pretty cranky,
But there wasn't any swanky.
Says the landlord, 'why not try a drop o' sene?'
'Sene?' says Bill, 'what sene?'
'Why, kerosene!'

Well, we wouldn't spend a tanner,
But the boss's pleasant manner
All our cursing couldn't easily demolish.
Says he, 'Strike me perpendic'lar
But you beggars are partic'lar.
Why, the squatter's in the parlour drinking polish.'
'Polish?' says Bill, 'what polish?'
'Why, furniture polish!'

The Publican Stood at the Pearly Gate

Anon

A publican stood at the Pearly Gate,
His head was bent, and low;
He meekly asked the Man in White
'Which way, mate, do I go?'

'What have you done,' Saint Peter said,
'That you should come up here?'
'I kept a public house below
For many and many a year.'

Saint Peter opened wide the gate
And gently pressed the bell.
'Come right inside and choose a harp –
You've had your share of hell!'

Casey's Beer

Ted Harrington

It happened many years ago in Dan Magee's hotel.
A crowd was gathered round the bar – I knew the fellows well.
Magee had something up his sleeve (he had the sergeant's ear –
The sergeant liked a pot himself and swore by Danny's beer).

Tim Casey dropped along one night – a thirsty soul was Tim –
And Dan Magee took down a pot and filled it to the brim,
A pot of lovely bitter ale, foam-capped and amber-clear –
Tim placed it gently on the bar, for Casey loved his beer.

His cherrywood was in his hand – its bowl was like a jug.
He had a look around the bar and borrowed someone's plug.
It was a habit Casey had, the weed was far too dear,
He couldn't waste his cash on that – he wanted it for beer.

What happened next I can't explain, I really hate to tell:
The like was never seen before in Dan Magee's hotel.
It might have been an accident; a stranger standing near –
A chimpanzee in human form – knocked over Casey's beer.

The pot plonked down upon the floor, it sounded like a knell,
And on the crowd around the bar an awful silence fell.
A swagman in the corner swooned; the stranger shook with fear,
But never stayed to pay the price for spilling Casey's beer.

The ale went trickling down the bar, and Casey stood like stone,
Till somewhere from his chest there came a dreadful, muffled moan.
The sound that came from Casey's throat I never hope to hear –
It shook the bottles on the shelf: ''E spilt me pint o' beer!'

The look of pain on Casey's face it pierced us to the core,
As with a last despairing moan he sank upon the floor.
We stopped to hear his last faint words – we knew the end was
    near.
He closed one eye and gave a sigh: ''E spilt me pot o' beer!'

The graveyard lies across the road, a stone throw from the pub,
And poor Tim Casey lies asleep beneath a big, green shrub;
And on the stone above his head you'll read in letters clear:
'Here lies Tim Casey; R.I.P. *A stranger spilt his beer.*'

I Allus Has Wan at Eleven

Anon

I allus has wan at eleven,
It's a duty that has to be done.
If I *don't* have wan at eleven
I *must* have eleven at wan.

The City of Dreadful Thirst

AB Paterson ('The Banjo')

The stranger came from Narromine and made his little joke –
'They say we folks in Narromine are narrow-minded folk.
But all the smartest men down here are puzzled to define
A kind of new phenomenon that came to Narromine.

'Last summer up in Narromine 'twas gettin' rather warm –
Two hundred in the water bag, and lookin' like a storm –
We all were in the private bar, the coolest place in town,
When out across the stretch of plain a cloud came rollin' down.

'We don't respect the clouds up there, they fill us with disgust,
They mostly bring a Bogan shower – three raindrops and some dust;
But each man, simultaneous-like, to each man said, "I think
That cloud suggests it's up to us to have another drink!"

'There's clouds of rain and clouds of dust – we'd heard of them
    before,
And sometimes in the daily press we read of 'clouds of war':
But – if this ain't the Gospel truth I hope that I may burst –
That cloud that came to Narromine was just a cloud of thirst.

'It wasn't like a common cloud, 'twas more a sort of haze;
It settled down about the streets, and stopped for days and days,
And not a drop of dew could fall and not a sunbeam shine
To pierce that dismal sort of mist that hung on Narromine.

'Oh, Lord! we had a dreadful time beneath that cloud of thirst!
We all chucked-up our daily work and went upon the burst.
The very blacks about the town that used to cadge for grub,
They made an organised attack and tried to loot the pub.

'We couldn't leave the private bar no matter how we tried;
Shearers and squatters, union men and blacklegs side by side
Were drinkin' there and dursn't move, for each was sure, he said,
Before he'd get a half a mile the thirst would strike him dead!

'We drank until the drink gave out, we searched from room to
    room,
And round the pub, like drunken ghosts, went howling through the
    gloom.
The shearers found some kerosene and settled down again,
But all the squatter chaps and I, we staggered to the train.

'And, once outside the cloud of thirst, we felt as right as pie,
But while we stopped about the town we had to drink or die.
But now I hear it's safe enough, I'm going back to work
Because they say the cloud of thirst has shifted on to Bourke.

'But when you see those clouds about – like this one over here –
All white and frothy at the top, just like a pint of beer,
It's time to go and have a drink, for if that cloud should burst
You'd find the drink would all be gone, for that's a cloud of thirst!'

We stood the man from Narromine a pint of half-and-half;
He drank it off without a gasp in one tremendous quaff;
'I joined some friends last night,' he said, 'in what *they* called a
    spree;
But after Narromine 'twas just a holiday to me.'

And now beyond the western range, where sunset skies are red,
And clouds of dust, and clouds of thirst, go drifting overhead,
The railway train is taking back, along the western line,
That narrow-minded person on his road to Narromine.

A Good Head

Anon

Unto the barmaid fair, 'My dear,'
The artless Johnnie said,
'There is no head upon this beer,
Nor any sign of head.'

The barmaid, Oh, her voice was kind,
And, oh . . . her words were true,
Said, 'Drink it, sonny, and you'll find
'Twill put a head on you.'

Tim Dooley

Thomas E Spencer

Tim Dooley lives down near the end of the town,
With his wife, and a horse, and a dray;
He'll fetch you a cartload of wood for a crown,
Or he'll go out to work by the day;
As a rule, Tim is one of the mildest of men,
And he drinks nothing stronger than tea,
But now and again something happens, and then,
Tim Dooley breaks out on the spree;
Then you hear the folks say:
'Quick! Get out of the way,
For Tim Dooley is out on the spree.'

Then we hear a loud yell, that we all know full well,
'Tis a sound like a wild dingo's bray;
And the deafest old man in the township can tell
It is Dooley in search of his prey;
All business stops, for the folks close their shops,
Women snatch up their children and flee,
And the Methodist parson with fear almost drops,
When Tim Dooley gets out on the spree.
Our policeman turns pale,
And stops inside the gaol,
When he knows Dooley's out on the spree.

Now, the dread of a fray would not cause this dismay,
Or give rise to such panic and fear,
But who can his courage or valour display,
When he feels his last moment is near?
When Dooley gets tight he is mighty polite,
Wants to kiss everyone he may see,
And a whiff from his breath causes sure, sudden death,
When Tim Dooley is out on the spree;
So we hide, or we fly
When the rumour goes by,
That Dooley is out on the spree.

Rum
Anon

'Rum,' he said, 'Is good for some,
But you know it makes me frown.
How can we keep our spirits up,
If we keep those spirits down?'

The Guile of Dad McGinnis
WT Goodge ('The Colonel')

When McGinnis struck the mining camp at Jamberoora Creek
His behaviour was appreciated highly;
For, although he was a quiet man, in manner mild and meek,
Not like ordinary swagmen with a monumental cheek,
He became the admiration of the camp along the creek
'Cause he showed a point to Kangaroobie Riley!

Both the pubs at Jamberoora had some grog that stood the test
(Not to speak of what was manufactured slyly!)
And the hostel of O'Gorman, which was called The Diggers' Rest,
Was, O'Gorman said, the finest house of any in the west;
But it was a burning question if it really was the best,
Or the Miners' – kept by Kangaroobie Riley.

Dad McGinnis called at Riley's. Said he 'felt a trifle queer',
And with something like a wan and weary smile, he
Said he 'thought he'd try a whisky'. Pushed it back and said, 'I fear
I had better take a brandy.' Passed that back and said: 'Look here,
Take the brandy; after all, I think I'll have a pint of beer!'
And he drank the health of Kangaroobie Riley!

'Where's the money?' asked the publican; 'you'll have to pay,
    begad!'
'Gave the brandy for the beer!' said Dad the wily,
'And I handed you the whisky when I took the brandy, lad!'
'But you paid not for the whisky!' answered Riley. 'No,' said Dad,
'And you don't expect a man to pay for what he never had!'
– 'Twas the logic flattened Kangaroobie Riley!

'See,' said Kangaroobie Riley, 'you have had me, that is clear!
But I never mind a joke,' he added dryly.
'Just you work it on O'Gorman, and I'll shout another beer.'
'I'd be happy to oblige yer,' said McGinnis with a leer,
'But the fact about the matter is – O'Gorman sent me here! –
So, good morning, Mr Kangaroobie Riley!'

Drunks

'Syd Swagman'

Wild drunks, mild drunks, weary drunks and sad,
Drunks that 'knowed your dad, me son, when he was a lad,'
Tall drunks, small drunks, tubby drunks and thin.
Drunks that seem to cheek the cops until they get run in;

Square drunks, lair drunks, moody drunks and loud,
Drunks that will not drink with drunks because they are too
    proud.
Tough drunks, rough drunks, dirty drunks and fat,
Drunks that shicker with the flies and shicker on their pat;

Poor drunks, sore drunks – heads as big as tanks,
Drunks that keep the town alive with their funny pranks;
Glad drunks, mad drunks, yellow drunks and white –
Somehow I meet a lot of drunks whenever I get tight.

Lovely Beer – A Toast

Anon

Here's to lovely beer, golden, cold and clear,
Not as sweet as a woman's lips – but a damn sight more sincere!

One Wish

Frank Daniel

We had fished with little luck out on Lake Burrinjuck
And Jack me mate said, 'Hell, we're out of grog.'
We hadn't had much fun, just sittin' in the sun,
And now we had to row ashore, a tidy slog.

We each reeled in our line, there was a jug attached to mine,
While my cobber only had a wormless hook.
As the sun continued glaring, we both just sat there staring
At the only catch we'd made we couldn't cook.

When I gave the thing a rub, so help me, from the jug
A spook appeared before us in a cloud.
And both us fishin' blokes yelled, 'Holy flamin' smokes,
We'll have three wishes now if we're allowed.'

But the genie said, 'Oh no, you only get one go
I'm just a learner, I can't grant you three.
But with one I'll do my best, it'll be a little test,
And with one wish you'll surely have a spree.'

But me mate, perhaps remissful, was a little over-wishful
And he said, 'I wish this lake was full of beer.'
In a flash, to our surprise, the lake turned amber 'fore our eyes,
And we watched that novice genie disappear.

I was cranky with old Jack; I wished the Genie would come back,
Though my mate, now in his element, did gloat.
But I reckon Jack disgraced us – 'cos the problem now that faced us,
Was that we'd both have to pee *inside* the boat!

My Wife
David Nicholson

I met my wife in the pub last night,
I couldn't believe she was there.
She's supposed to be home looking after the kids,
Not knockin' back pots for a dare!
I told her she shouldn't be drinking.
She replied, 'Well, I don't give a damn,
And actually I'm not as far gone
As most thinkle peep that I am!'

It was funny the way that her mood changed,
Going home 'neath a star-laden sky,
She went all soppy and sheepish
And looked longingly into me eye.
I placed her head on my shoulder
And I told her she looked really sweet.
And we made our way home in the moonlight,
(Someone else helped to carry her feet!)

from . . . Over the Wine
Victor Daley ('Creeve Roe')

Very often when I'm drinking,
Of the old days I am thinking,
Of the good old days when living was a joy,
And each morning brought new pleasure,
And each night brought dreams of treasure,
And I thank the lord that I was once a boy.

For not all the trains in motion,
All the ships that sail the ocean
With their cargoes; all the money in the mart,
Could purchase for an hour
Such a treasure as the flower,
As the flower of Hope that blossomed in my heart.

Now I sit and smile and listen
To my friends whose eyes still glisten
Though their beards are showing threads of silver-grey,
As they talk of fame and glory,
The old, old pathetic story,
While they drink 'Good luck' to luck that keeps away.

And I hate the cant of striving,
Slaving, planning and contriving,
Struggling onward for a paltry little prize.
Oh, it fills my heart with sorrow
This mad grasping for Tomorrow,
While Today from gold to purple dusks and dies.

Very often when I'm drinking,
Of the old days I am thinking,
Of the good old days when living was a joy,
When I see folk marching dreary
To the tune of *Miserere*
Then I thank the Lord that I am still a boy.

You Can't Take It with You
Anon

There are many good reasons for drinking –
And one has just entered my head:
If a man doesn't drink when he's living,
How the hell can he drink when he's dead!

When Is a Man Drunk?
Anon

He is not drunk who from the floor
Can rise and drink and ask for more;
But drunk is he who speechless lies
Without the strength to drink or rise.

King Whiskey

WT Goodge ('The Colonel')

King Whiskey's father down in Hell, he rubbed his hands with
  glee,
'My son on earth is doing well, extremely well,' said he.
'Pile up the logs upon the blaze and let the furnace roar.
Another batch of Whiskey's slaves is hammering at the door.'

The flames shot up a brilliant red, the grid was white with heat,
A basting pot of boiling lead was placed on every seat.
'Ha, ha,' said Satan, 'this is neat; we have no cause to fear
That they'll complain they did not meet a warm reception here.'

King Whiskey sat upon his throne, his courtiers standing round,
All meek, subservient in tone, they bowed them to the ground.
In tribute then they handed up their stores of golden wealth,
And from the reeking poison cup they drank King Whiskey's
  health.

And out beyond the palace gates the wives and mothers stand,
And, breadless, loudly curse the fates that Whiskey rules the land.
The courtiers dimly hear the cry but Whiskey dulls their ears,
'Fill up, let revelry run high, we'll drown these childish fears!'

And men there are in Whiskey's land complaining things are bad
And money getting scarcer and but little to be had;
And yet however bad is trade and things however flat,
King Whiskey's tribute must be paid, they can't go short of that!

King Whiskey's courtiers soon grow old and tribute's falling short,
The strength is gone, the blood is cold, the once-clear mind
  distraught!
And demons, imps, and grinning apes, and glaring reptiles yell
And loathsome forms and fearsome shapes all point the road to
  Hell!

But Whiskey's court is bright and gay, nor do the ranks grow thin,
For as the old are borne away the younger ones come in.
King Whiskey's father down in Hell, he rubs his hands with glee
'My son on earth is doing well, extremely well,' says he.

Bottle Queen

Traditional/Jim Haynes

We bred her in the suburbs and we trained her after dark,
Sometimes down the Botany Road and sometimes in the park,
And the way we used to feed her, it often led to rows,
We pinched the chaff from stables and the green stuff from the
  Chows.

Now her sire was imported but we never knew from where
And her mother Black Moria, was a bottle dealer's mare.
We bought a set of colours, they were second hand and green,
And we had to call her something, so we called her Bottle Queen.

In the evenings when we galloped her I usually took the mount,
We didn't have a stop-watch, so me mate, he used to count.
She showed us four in forty-nine, one-forty for the mile,
But she coulda done much better, she was pulling all the while.

Now that's something like a gallop, on the sand with ten stone up,
It'd win the English Derby! Or the Wagga Wagga Cup!
And when we thought we had her just as fit as she could be,
Me mate, he bit his sheila for the nomination fee.

We bunged her in a maiden and they dobbed her seven stone,
Talk about a 'jacky', she was in it on her own!
So we worked her on the bottles when the cart was good and light,
It was bottles every morning and training every night.

We walked her down to Kenso on the morning of the race,
The books had never heard of her, we backed her win and place,
Then we rubbed her down and saddled her and led her to the
  track,
And told that hoop his fee was good . . . if he brought a winner
  back!

Well, they jumped away together but The Queen was soon in
  front,
As for all the others, they were never in the hunt!
She was romping past the leger, she was fighting for her head,
When some bastard waved a bottle . . . and our certainty stopped
  dead!

Now when folks who know hear, 'Bottle-Oh', they say, 'There's
   poor old Jim,
He mighta made a fortune, but the bottle did him in.'
Yes we shoulda made a motza, my bloody oath we should,
Except I guess you might say that The Queen was trained too
   good!

So, don't talk to me of racing, you can see I've had enough.
It's a game for men with money and for blokes who know their
   stuff.
And if someone tries to tell you that the racing game is clean . . .
Just remember what I told you, my tale of Bottle Queen.

Not on It
AB Paterson ('The Banjo')

The new chum's polo pony was the smartest pony yet –
The owner backed it for the Cup for all that he could get.
The books were laying fives to one, in tenners; and you bet
He was on it.

The bell was rung, the nags came out their quality to try,
The band played, 'What Ho! Robbo!' as our hero cantered by,
The people in the Leger Stand cried out, 'Hi, mister, hi!
Are you on it?'

They watched him as the flag went down; his fate is quickly told –
The pony gave a sudden spring, and off the rider rolled.
The pony finished first all right, but then our hero bold
Was not on it.

from . . . How We Beat the Favourite
Adam Lindsay Gordon

'Aye, squire, said Stevens, 'they back him at evens;
The race is all over, bar shouting, they say;
The Clown ought to beat her; Dick Neville is sweeter
Than ever – he swears he can win all the way.

'But none can outlast her, and few travel faster,
She strides in her work clean away from The Drag;
You hold her and sit her, she couldn't be fitter,
Whenever you hit her she'll spring like a stag.

'And p'rhaps the green jacket, at odds though they back it,
May fall, or there's no telling what may turn up.
The mare is quite ready, sit still and ride steady,
Keep cool; and I think you may just win the cup.'

Dark brown and tan muzzle, just stripped for the tussle,
Stood Iseult, arching her neck to the curb,
A lean head and fiery, strong quarters and wiry,
A loin rather light, but a shoulder superb.

We started, and Kerr made a strong run on Mermaid,
Through furrows that led to the first stake-and-bound,
The crack, half extended, looked bloodlike and splendid,
Held wide on the right where the headland was sound.

I pulled hard to baffle her rush with the snaffle,
Before her two-thirds of the field got away;
All through the wet pasture where floods of the last year
Still loitered, they clotted my crimson with clay.

The fourth fence, a wattle, floored Monk and Bluebottle;
The Drag came to grief at the blackthorn and ditch,
The rails toppled over Redoubt and Red Rover,
The lane stopped Lycurgus and Leicestershire Witch.

She passed like an arrow Kildare and Cock Sparrow
And Mantrap and Mermaid refused the stone wall;
And Giles on The Greyling came down at the paling,
And I was left sailing in front of them all.

She rose when I hit her, I saw the stream glitter,
A wide scarlet nostril flashed close to my knee,
Between sky and water The Clown came and caught her,
The space that he cleared was a caution to see.

And forcing the running, discarding all cunning,
A length to the front went the rider in green;
A long strip of stubble, and then the quick double,
Two stiff flights of rails with a quickset between.

She came to his quarter, and on still I brought her,
And up to his girth, to his breastplate she drew,
A short prayer from Neville just reached me, 'The Devil!'
He muttered – locked level the hurdles we flew.

A hum of hoarse cheering, a dense crowd careering,
All sights seen obscurely, all shouts vaguely heard;
'The green wins!' 'The crimson!' The multitude swims on,
And figures are blended and features are blurred.

On still past the gateway she strains in the straightway,
Still struggles, 'The Clown by a short neck at most!'
He swerves, the green scourges, the stand rocks and surges,
And flashes, and verges, and flits the white post.

Aye! So ends the tussle, I knew the tan muzzle
Was first, though the ring men were yelling, 'Dead heat!'
A nose I could swear by, but Clarke said, 'The mare by
A short head.' And that's how the favourite was beat.

How We Backed the Favourite

CJ Dennis

'Sure thing,' said the grocer, 'as far as I know, sir,
This horse, Peter Pan, is the safest of certs.'
'I see by the paper,' commended the draper,
'He's tipped and he carries my whole weight of shirts.'
The butcher said, 'Well, now, it's easy to tell now
There's nothing else in it except Peter Pan.'
And so too the baker, the barman, bookmaker,
The old lady char and the saveloy man.

'You stick to my tip, man,' admonished the grip-man,
'Play up Peter Pan; he's a stayer with speed.'
And the newspaper vendor, the ancient road mender,
And even the cop at the corner agreed.
The barber said, 'Win it? There's nothing else in it.
I backed Peter Pan with the last that I had.'
'Too right,' said the lift man. 'The horse is a gift, man.'
The old jobbing gardener said, 'Peter Pan, lad!'

I know nought of racing. The task I was facing,
It filled me with pain and unreasoning dread.
They all seemed so certain, and yet a dark curtain
Of doubt dulled my mind . . . But I must keep my head!
I went to the races, and I watched all their faces.
I saw Peter Pan's; there was little he lacked.
And as he seemed willing, I plancked on my shilling
And triumphed! And that's how the favourite was backed.

Carbine's Melbourne Cup, 1890

Anon

The race is run, the Cup is won, the great event is o'er.
The grandest horse that strode a course has led them home once
  more.
I watched with pride your sweeping stride before you ranged in
  line,
For far and near a ringing cheer was echoed for Carbine.

The start was made, no time delayed before they got away,
Those horses great, some thirty-eight, all eager for the fray.
No better start could human heart to sportsmen ever show
As Watson did, each jockey bid get ready for to go.

With lightning speed, each gallant steed along the green track tore;
Each jockey knew what he must do to finish in the fore.
But Ramage knew his mount was true, though he had 10-5 up,
For Musket's son great deeds had done before that Melbourne
  Cup.

No whip, nor spur, he needs to stir a horse to greater speed;
He knew as well as man can tell when he could take the lead.
So on he glides with even strides, though he is led by nine;
But Ramage knows before they close he'll try them with Carbine.

The bend is passed; the straight at last: he takes him to the fore.
The surging crowd with voices loud the stud's name loudly roar.
The jockey too, he full well knew the race was nearly o'er,
As on his mane he slacked the rein: no need to urge him more.

Brave horse and man who led the van on that November day!
Your records will be history still when ye have passed away.
For such a race, for weight and pace, has never been put up
As that deed done by Musket's son in the 1890 Cup.

In Memory of Phar Lap
Anon

He was a mighty horse indeed, alas, he's passed away,
But sportsmen will remember him until the latest day.
He was the marvel of the age, the swiftest beast on earth,
New Zealand loved his lightning name, the land that gave him
   birth.
Australia too was proud of him, this land of sun and shine,
For his owner and his partner he was a rich gold mine.
Five hundred years may come and go before another's bred,
To equal noble Phar Lap, now numbered with the dead.

The Day Our Trotter Kicked Aunt Kate
Wilbur G Howcroft

The day our trotter kicked Aunt Kate was one we won't forget,
Our family was dazed with grief and things ain't normal yet.
Oh, what a tragedy it was! For days we hardly slept!
Poor Uncle took it very hard – in fact he up and wept.

The neighbours, though, were very kind and visited for weeks.
Mum gave them tea and buttered scones while tears rolled down
   her cheeks.
The womenfolk, their voices hushed, brought sandwiches and
   cakes,
While long-time enemies of ours called in for old-time sakes.

Our Dad was in a dreadful state, we feared he'd lose his mind,
Till parson spoke of courage and the faith of humankind.
So now Dad's quietened down a bit, says no one was to blame –
'Twas just the cruel hand of Fate that made our trotter lame . . .

Out of Sight

AB Paterson ('The Banjo')

They held a polo meeting at a little country town,
And all the local sportsmen came to win themselves renown.
There came two strangers with a horse, and I am much afraid
They both belonged to what is called 'the take-you-down brigade'.

They said their horse could jump like fun, and asked an amateur
To ride him in the steeplechase, and told him they were sure,
The last time round, he'd sail away with such a swallow's flight
The rest would never see him go – he'd finish out of sight.

So out he went; and, when folk saw the amateur was up,
Some local genius called the race 'the dude-in-danger cup'.
The horse was known as Who's Afraid, by Panic from The Fright,
But still his owners told the jock he'd finish out of sight.

And so he did; for Who's Afraid, without the least pretence,
Disposed of him by rushing through the very second fence;
And when they ran the last time round the prophecy was right –
For he was in the ambulance, and safely out of sight.

Bert

CJ Dennis

Did you ever meet Bert? 'E's all over the town,
In offices, shops an' in various places,
Cocky an' all; an' you can't keep 'im down.
I never seen no one so lucky at races.
Backs all the winners or very near all;
Tells you nex' day when the races are over.
'E makes quite a pot, for 'is wagers ain't small;
An' by rights 'e 'ad ought to be livin' in clover.

But, some'ow or other — aw, well, I dunno.
You got to admit that some fellers is funny.
'E don't dress too well an' 'is spendin' is low.
I can't understand wot 'e does with 'is money.
'E ought to be sockin' a pretty fair share;
An' tho' 'e will own 'e's a big money-maker,
'E don't seem to save an' 'e don't seem to care
If 'e owes a big wad to 'is butcher an' baker.

'E don't tell you much if you meet on the course;
But after it's over 'e comes to you grinnin',
Shows you 'is card where 'e's marked the first 'orse,
An' spins you a wonderful tale of 'is winnin'.
Can't make 'im out, 'e's so lucky an' that.
Knows ev'ry owner an' trainer an' jockey;
But all of 'is wagerin's done on 'is pat.
Won't spill a thing, even tho' 'e's so cocky.

Oyster, that's Bert. 'E's as close as a book.
But sometimes I've come on 'im sudden an' saw 'im
Lip 'angin' down an' a reel 'aggard look,
Like all the woes in the world come to gnaw 'im.
But, soon as 'e sees you, 'e brightens right up.
'Picked it again, lad!' 'e sez to you, grinnin'.
'A fiver at sevens I 'ad in the Cup!
That's very near sixty odd quid that I'm winnin'.'

Mystery man — that's 'is style for a cert,
Picks the 'ole card, yet 'e's shabby and seedy;
'E must 'ave some sorrer in secrit, old Bert —
Some drain on 'is purse wot is keepin' 'im needy.
A terrible pity. Some woman, no doubt.
No wonder 'e worries in secrit an' souses.
If I 'ad 'is winnin's, year in an' year out,
Why I'd own a Rolls Royce an' a terris of 'ouses.

O for Octagonal

Jim Haynes

You hear blokes talk of champions, you see 'em come and go,
A real champion may come along each ten years or so.
I've read of Carbine and Phar Lap, those legends from the past,
And I saw Tulloch and Gunsynd and they were tough and fast,
Kingston Town was brilliant, so strong the mare Sunline,
But for toughness and sheer courage there's just one champ for
    mine!
No champion that ever strode the turf could make me feel
The way I felt about that gallant brown son of Zabeel.

O for Octagonal to be racing once again,
O for Octagonal, on him you could depend,
He never gave up trying, he'd stick right to the end,
O for Octagonal, he was the punter's friend.

Derby Day in '96 you should have heard the cheers,
From the biggest crowd that Randwick had seen for thirty years.
With Saintly, Nothing Leica Dane, Filante down the straight,
I won't see a race like that again however long I wait.
It was his class and courage that wore the others down,
His will to win that drove him on to win the triple crown.
His stamina unparalleled, his action was sublime,
Oh what I'd give to see old Ocky race just one more time!

O for Octagonal to be racing once again,
O for Octagonal, on him you could depend,
He never gave up trying, he'd stick right to the end,
O for Octagonal, he was the punter's friend.

Bart

Jim Haynes

There's a trainer of horses named Bart
And there's two things that set him apart,
His hair's silver grey
And he trains 'em to stay,
He's won ten Melbourne Cups for a start.

Royal Randwick

Tip Kelaher

Are the two-year-olds still racing down the Randwick mile,
Do thudding hoofs still shake the Randwick turf,
Do flower-beds and gardens still produce their springtime smile,
Does the ring-roar match the booming of the surf?

Are there still some lovely ladies to beautify the scene,
Is the band still playing marches 'neath the stand,
Is the sunshine just as brilliant and the couch grass just as green
As when we sailed to fight on foreign strand?

Is the stale cigar smell drifting, and do gripping hands denote
Glad meetings and a move towards the bar,
Is there movement, life and laughter from the 'birdcage' to the tote
As the old friends congregate from near and far?

Have you any colts like Gold Rod or Avenger or High Caste,
Or a miler like proud Ajax at his best,
Could the new lot hope to foot it with the champions of the past,
With Eurythmic, Gloaming, Poitrel and the rest?

Oh, the bay, the black, the chestnut – rippling muscles in the sun!
Close finishes! The crowd's loud, vibrant roar!
A day of keen, hard racing, stirring contests every one,
Brings a tingle to a horseman's blood once more.

Now Randwick stands a symbol of the life we left behind,
And 'twill compensate for loss and parting pain,
When the war is safely over if I have the luck to find
I can spend a day at Randwick again.

Old Pardon, the Son of Reprieve

AB Paterson ('The Banjo')

You never heard tell of the story? Well now, I can hardly believe!
Never heard of the honour and glory of Pardon, the son of
    Reprieve?
But maybe you're only a Johnnie and don't know a horse from hoe?
Well, well, don't get angry, my sonny, but, really, a young 'un
    should know.

They bred him outback on the 'Never', his mother was Mameluke
    breed,
To the front and then stay there was ever the root of the
    Mameluke creed.
He seemed to inherit their wiry strong frames – and their pluck to
    receive –
As hard as a flint and as fiery was Pardon, the son of Reprieve.

We ran him at many a meeting, at crossing and gully and town,
And nothing could give him a beating – at least when our money
    was down.
For weight wouldn't stop him, nor distance, nor odds, though the
    others were fast;
He'd race with a dogged persistence and wear them all down at the
    last.

At Turon the Yattendon filly led by lengths at the mile-and-a-half,
And we all began to look silly, while her crowd were starting to
    laugh;
But the old horse came faster and faster, his pluck told its tale, and
    his strength,
He gained on her, caught her, and passed her, and won it, hands
    down, by a length.

And then we swooped down on Menindee to run for the
    President's Cup.
Oh! that's a sweet township – a shindy to them is board, lodging
    and sup.
Eye-openers they are, and their system is never to suffer defeat;
It's 'win, tie or wrangle' – to best 'em, you must lose 'em, or else
    it's 'dead-heat'.

We strolled down the township and found 'em at drinking and
    gaming and play;
If troubles they had, why they drowned 'em, and betting was soon
    under way.
Their horses were good uns and fit uns, there was plenty of cash in
    the town;
They backed their own horses like Britons, and, Lord! how we
    rattled it down!

With gladness we thought of the morrow, we counted our wages
    with glee,
A simile homely to borrow – 'there was plenty of milk in our tea'.
You see we were green and we never had even a thought of foul
    play,
Though we well might have known that the clever division would
    'put us away'.

Experience *docet*, they tell us, at least so I've frequently heard;
At 'dosing' or 'stuffing', those fellows were up to each move on the
    board.
They got to his stall – it is sinful to think what such villains will
    do –
They gave him a regular skinful of barley – green barley – to chew.

He munched it all night and we found him next morning as full as
    a hog –
The girths wouldn't nearly meet round him; he looked like an
    overfed frog.
We saw we were done like a dinner – the odds were a thousand to
    one
Against Pardon turning up winner, 'twas cruel to ask him to run.

We got to the course with our troubles, a crestfallen couple were we;
And we heard the 'books' calling the doubles – a roar like the surf
    of the sea;
And over the tumult and louder rang, 'Any price Pardon, I lay!'
Says Jimmy, 'The children of Judah are out on the warpath today.'

Three miles in three heats. Ah, my sonny, the horses in those days
    were stout,
They had to run well to win money; I don't see such horses about.
Your six-furlong vermin that scamper half-a-mile with a
    feather-weight up,
They wouldn't earn much of their damper in a race like the
    President's Cup.

The first heat was soon set a-going; The Dancer went off to the
    front;
The Don on his quarters was showing, with Pardon right out of
    the hunt.
He rolled and he weltered and wallowed – you'd kick your hat
    faster I'll bet.
They finished all bunched, and he followed all lathered and
    dripping with sweat.

But troubles came thicker upon us, for while we were rubbing him
    dry,
The stewards came over to warn us, 'We hear you are running a
    bye!
If Pardon don't spiel like tarnation and win the next heat, if he
    can,
He'll earn a disqualification; just think over *that* now, my man!'

Our money all gone and our credit, our horse couldn't gallop a
    yard;
And then people think that *we* did it. It really was terribly hard.
We were objects of mirth and derision to folks in the lawn and the
    stand,
And the yells of the clever division of, 'Any price Pardon!' were
    grand.

We still had a chance for the money, two heats still remained to be
    run:
If both fell to us, why, my sonny, the clever division were done.
And Pardon was better, we reckoned, his sickness was passing away,
So we went to the post for the second and principal heat of the
    day.

They're off and away with a rattle, like dogs from the leashes let
  slip,
And right at the back of the battle he followed them under the
  whip.
They gained ten good lengths on him quickly, he dropped right
  away from the pack.
I tell you it made me feel sickly to see the blue jacket fall back.

Our very last hope had departed – we thought our old fellow was
  done,
When all of a sudden he started to go like a shot from a gun.
His chances seemed slight to embolden our hearts; but, with teeth
  firmly set,
We thought, 'Now or never! The old 'un may reckon with some of
  them yet.'

Then loud rose the war-cry for Pardon; he swept like the wind
  down the dip,
And over the rise by the garden the jockey was done with the
  whip.
The field was at sixes and sevens – the pace at the first had been
  fast –
And hope seemed to drop from the heavens, for Pardon was
  coming at last.

And how he did come! It was splendid; he gained on them yards
  every bound,
Stretching out like a greyhound extended, his girth laid right down
  on the ground.
A shimmer of silks in the cedars as into the running they wheeled,
And out flashed the whips of the leaders, for Pardon had collared
  the field.

Then right through the ruck he was sailing – I knew that the
  battle was won –
The son of Haphazard was failing, the Yattendon filly was done
He cut down The Don and The Dancer, he raced clean away from
  the mare –
He's in front! Catch him now if you can, sir! And up went my hat
  in the air!

Then loud from the lawn and the garden rose offers of 'Ten to one
  on!'
'Who'll bet on the field? I back Pardon!' No use; all the money
  was gone.
He came for the third heat light-hearted, a-jumping and dancing
  about;
The others were done ere they started, crestfallen and tired, worn
  out.

He won it, and ran it much faster than even the first, I believe;
Oh, he was the daddy, the master, was Pardon the son of Reprieve.
He showed 'em the method of travel – the boy sat as still as a
  stone –
They never could see him for gravel; he came in hard-held, and
  alone.

But he's old and his eyes have grown hollow like me, with my
  thatch of the snow;
When he dies, then I hope I may follow, and go where the
  racehorses go.
I don't want no harping or singing, such things with my style don't
  agree;
Where the hoofs of the horses are ringing there's music sufficient
  for me.

And surely the thoroughbred horses will rise up again and begin
Fresh races on faraway courses and p'rhaps they might let me slip in.
It would look rather well on the race-card, 'mongst cherubs and
  seraphs and things,
'Angel Harrison's black gelding, Pardon, blue halo, white body and
  wings'.

And if they have racing hereafter, (and who is to say they will not?)
When the cheers and the shouting and laughter proclaim that the
  battle grows hot;
As they come down the racecourse a-steering, he'll rush to the
  front, I believe;
And you'll hear the great multitude cheering for Pardon, the son
  of Reprieve.

Foley and the Green

Anon

This fight took place in 1871 and lasted two hours forty minutes or 140 rounds, depending which account you choose to believe. One thing that's certain is that it ended in a draw, so the writer cheated here, although Foley did win the rematch at Port Hacking some weeks later. The fights were bare-knuckle and illegal, thus the secluded locations. The Catholic/Protestant division in our society was very real back then. Larry Foley, the 'father of Australian boxing', died in 1917.

Now Paddy dear and did you hear the news that's going 'round,
That Sandy Ross has lost the fight at George's River ground?
No more his crowing will be heard, no more his colour seen,
I think he's had enough this time of Foley and the green.

The green the colour of the brave we raise high in the air,
And to our enemies we show the colour that we wear.
The orange flag has been pulled down, the battle fought out keen,
And Sandy Ross has lost the fight at George's River green.

The orange ties they mustered strong upon that Tuesday morn,
As Sandy he came up to scratch with head and beard all shorn.
His orange scarf around his waist was plainly to be seen,
As Foley stepped into the ring wearing Ireland's green.

'Sinn Fein, Sinn Fein!' he cried aloud to all his friends close by,
'I've come to fight for Ireland's cause and for that cause I'll die.
And to deny her colours, I ne'er would be so mean,
So in this ring I'll die or win for dear old Ireland's green.

'Here's to Him lads, here's to Him boys,' then Sandy Ross did say,
'I've come to fight for Old King Bill upon this glorious day.
The orange scarf around me waist will soon come into bud,
'Twill be dyed red upon this ground by this poor Fenian's blood!'

They both shook hands, you'd really think no feeling lay between
The colours bright that made this fight, the orange and the green.
For three long hours that fight did last till seconds came between,
And threw the sponge high in the air in favour of the green.

Every Saturday Night

Anon

Never seen his like before,
Upon the old stadium floor,
They called him a skiter,
But, Lord, what a fighter!
Every Saturday night.

Maitland's fighting boy,
The battlers' pride and joy,
How he'd beat 'em,
He'd simply eat 'em,
Every Saturday night.

And all I wish tonight,
Is to see Les Darcy fight,
Middleweights feared him,
Lord! How we cheered him,
Every Saturday night.

Simpson and Lithgow

Jim Haynes

The only drawn match in history where both boxers were knocked out!

They're not there in the hall of fame, their names you may not
    know,
But they made boxing history, Simpson and Lithgow.
They fought at St George League's Club, and in the second round,
They clinched and tumbled from the ring and both heads hit the
    ground.
'Twas on September twenty-first in nineteen-sixty-five
Each man landed heavily, was lucky to survive.
But they made boxing history, of that there is no doubt,
The only drawn match ever . . . where both men were knocked
    out!
They're not there in the hall of fame, their names you may not
    know,
But they made boxing history, Simpson and Lithgow.

SECTION SEVEN

Toilers and Travellers
The Men Who Made Australia

Here are verses about the people who worked and travelled the land. These are the kinds of poems that most people expect to find in any collection of what is loosely known as 'bush verse'. Critics of our folk verse tradition, those who say that these are the only topics ever covered by the genre, will find plenty to support their view here.

It is true that many of these verses contain outmoded ideas and attitudes that are quite politically incorrect these days. Many are museum pieces that show how pioneers lived and worked in the bush, others display attitudes and lifestyles still prevalent in the towns and suburbs of twenty-first-century Australia. While some of these poems take a light-hearted or comic look at rural life, many are quite tragic and lugubrious. This is a good section to dip into if you are feeling gloomy and melancholy.

Here are Aussie icons like the shearer, drover, gold-digger, bullocky and stockman. The themes of these poems range from the pro-colonial attitudes of Gordon and Dyson to the typical *Bulletin* approach – anti-British, pro-worker, fiercely Australian/Republican (and often very much racist and pro 'white-Australia') – found in Lawson, Daley and Boake.

But, if you leave aside the politics and attitudes of the time, you will find a collection of verses that capture something of the professions, lifestyles, hopes and aspirations of the people of rural Australia.

from . . . The Men Who Made Australia

Henry Lawson

Written on the occasion of the Royal visit to Australia 1901

There'll be royal times in Sydney for the Cuff and Collar Push,
There'll be lots of dreary drivel and clap-trap
From the men who own Australia, but who never knew the Bush,
And who could not point their runs out on the map.
Oh, the daily Press will grovel as it never did before,
There'll be many flags of welcome in the air,
And the Civil Service poet, he shall write odes by the score –
But the men who made the land will not be there.

You shall meet the awful Lady of the latest Birthday Knight –
(She is trying to be English, don't-cher-know!)
You shall hear the empty mouthing of the champion blather-skite,
You shall hear the boss of local drapers blow.
There'll be 'majahs' from the counter, tailors' dummies from the
    fleet,
And to represent Australia here today,
There's the toady with his card-case and his cab in Downing Street;
But the men who made Australia – where are they?

Call across the blazing sand wastes of the Never-Never Land!
There are some who will not answer yet awhile,
Some whose bones rot in the mulga or lie bleaching on the sand,
Died of thirst to win the land another mile.
Thrown from horse, ripped by cattle, lost on deserts: and the weak,
Mad through loneliness or drink (no matter which),
Drowned in floods or dead of fever by the sluggish slimy creek –
These are men who died to make the Wool-Kings rich.

There are carriages in waiting for the swells from over-sea,
There are banquets in the latest London style,
While the men who made Australia live on damper, junk and tea –
But the quiet voices whisper, 'Wait a while!'
For the sons of all Australia, they were born to conquer fate –
And, where charity and friendship are sincere,
Where a sinner is a brother and a stranger is a mate,
There the future of a nation's written clear.

Aye, the cities claim the triumphs of a land they do not know,
But all empty is the day they celebrate!
For the men who made Australia federated long ago,
And the men to rule Australia – they can wait.
Though the bed may be the rough bunk or the gum leaves or the
    sand,
And the roof for half the year may be the sky –
There are men among the Bushmen who were born to save the
    land!
And they'll take their places sternly by-and-by.

A Toast to Pioneer Women

Fred Rutter

And here's to the ladies, God bless 'em,
They never got statues or fame.
Their menfolk went off into new worlds
And, God bless the women, they came.

They were doctors and cooks for their menfolk
As they made a new home in the wild.
They aged from the harsh style of living
And often died birthing a child.

They cared for their menfolk and families,
As the gentlemen bragged of their deeds.
They faced all the dangers their men did,
Put aside all their personal needs.

And what did they get for their troubles,
In the wilderness they helped to tame?
A greening bronze statue of husband,
In a city that bears a man's name.

So here's to the pioneer women –
The men couldn't do it alone,
'God bless the pioneer women',
It ought to be carved into stone.

from . . . Men of Australia

Edward Dyson

Men of all the lands Australian from the Gulf to Derwent River,
From the Heads of Sydney Harbour to the waters of the West,
There's a spirit loudly calling where the saplings dip and quiver,
Where the city crowds are thronging, and the range uplifts its crest!
Do ye feel the holy fervour of a new-born exultation?
For the task the Lord has set us is a trust of noblest pride
We are named to march unblooded to the winning of a nation,
And to crown her with a glory that may evermore abide.

Bushmen, roaming on the ridges tracking 'colours' to their sources,
Swinging axes by the rivers where the millsaws rend and shriek,
Smoking thoughtful pipes, or dreaming on your slow, untroubled
    horses,
While the lazy cattle feed along the track or ford the creek,
Ye have known our country's moods in all her wild and desert
    places,
Ye have felt the sweet, strange promptings that her solitudes
    inspire;
To have breathed the spirit of her is to love her – turn your faces,
Ride like lovers when the day dawns, ride to serve her, son and
    sire!

Miners in the dripping workings, farmers, pioneers who settle
On the bush lands, city workers of the benches and the marts,
Swart mechanics at the forges, beating out the glowing metal,
Thinkers, planners, if ye feel the love of country stir your hearts,
Help to write the bravest chapter of a fair young nation's story
Great she'll be as Europe's greatest, more magnificent in truth.
That our children's children standing in the rose light of her glory
May all honour us who loved her and who crowned her in her
    youth!

The New Country

Mary Hannay Foott

Condé had come with us all the way
Eight hundred miles, but the fortnight's rest
Made him fresh as a youngster, the sturdy bay!
And Lurline was looking her very best.

Weary and footsore, the cattle strayed
'Mid the silvery saltbush well content;
Where the creeks lay cool 'neath the gidya's shade
The stock-horses clustered, travel-spent.

In the bright spring morning we left them all
Camp, and cattle, and white, and black
And rode for the Range's westward fall,
Where the dingo's trail was the only track.

Slow through the clay-pans, wet to the knee,
With the cane-grass rustling overhead;
Swift o'er the plains with never a tree;
Up the cliffs by a torrent's bed.

Bridle on arm for a mile or more
We toiled, ere we reached Bindanna's verge
And saw — as one sees a far-off shore —
The blue hills bounding the forest surge.

An ocean of trees, by the west wind stirred,
Rolled, ever rolled, to the great cliff's base;
And its sound like the noise of waves was heard
'Mid the rocks and the caves of that lonely place.

We recked not of wealth in stream or soil
As we heard on the heights the breezes sing;
We felt no longer our travel-toil;
We feared no more what the years might bring.

Westward Ho!

Harry Morant ('The Breaker')

There's a damper in the ashes, tea and sugar in the bags,
There's whips of feed and shelter on the sand-ridge for the nags,
There's gidya wood about us and water close at hand,
And just one bottle left of the good Glenlivet brand.

There are chops upon the embers, which same are close-up done,
From as fine a four-tooth wether as there is on Crossbred's run;
'Twas a proverb on the Darling, the truth of which I hold:
'That mutton's ay the sweetest which was never bought nor sold.'

Out of fifty thousand wethers surely Crossbred shouldn't miss
A sheep or so to travellers – faith, 'tis dainty mutton, this –
Let's drink a nip to Crossbred; ah, you drain it with a grin,
Then shove along the billy, mate, and, squatted, let's wade in.

The night's a trifle chilly, and the stars are very bright,
A heavy dew is falling, but the fly is rigged aright;
You may rest your bones till morning, then if you chance to wake,
Give me a call about the time that daylight starts to break.

We may not camp tomorrow, for we've many a mile to go,
Ere we turn our horses' heads round to make tracks for down below.
There's many a water-course to cross, and many a black-soil plain,
And many a mile of mulga-ridge ere we get back again.

That time five moons shall wax and wane we'll finish the work,
Have the bullocks o'er the border and truck 'em down from
  Bourke,
And when they're sold at Homebush, and the agents settle up,
Sing hey! a spell in Sydney town and Melbourne for the 'Cup'.

The Ballad of the Drover

Henry Lawson

Across the stony ridges,
Across the rolling plain,
Young Harry Dale, the drover,
Comes riding home again.
And well his stock-horse bears him,
And light of heart is he,
And stoutly his old pack-horse
Is trotting by his knee.

Up Queensland way with cattle
He travelled regions vast;
And many months have vanished
Since home-folk saw him last.
He hums a song of someone
He hopes to marry soon;
And hobble-chains and camp-ware
Keep jingling to the tune.

Beyond the hazy dado
Against the lower skies
And yon blue line of ranges
The homestead station lies.
And thitherward the rover
Jogs through the lazy noon,
With hobble-chains and camp-ware
All jingling to a tune.

An hour has filled the heavens
With storm-clouds inky black;
At times the lightning trickles
Around the drover's track;
And Harry pushes onward,
His horses' strength he tries,
In hope to reach the river
Before the flood shall rise.

The thunder from above him
Goes rolling o'er the plain;
And down on thirsty pastures
In torrents falls the rain,
And every creek and gully
Sends forth its little flood,
Till the river runs a banker,
All stained with yellow mud.

Now Harry speaks to Rover,
The best dog on the plains,
And to his hardy horses,
And strokes their shaggy manes;
'We've breasted bigger rivers
When floods were at their height,
Nor shall this gutter stop us
From getting home to-night!'

The thunder growls a warning,
The ghastly lightnings gleam,
As the drover turns his horses
To swim the fatal stream.
But, oh! the flood runs stronger
Than e'er it ran before;
The saddle-horse is failing,
And only half-way o'er!

When flashes next the lightning,
The flood's grey breast is blank,
And a cattle dog and pack-horse,
Are struggling up the bank.
But in the lonely homestead
The girl will wait in vain
He'll never pass the stations
In charge of stock again.

The faithful dog a moment
Sits panting on the bank,
And then swims through the current
To where his master sank.
And round and round in circles
He fights with failing strength,
Till, borne down by the waters,
The old dog sinks at length.

Across the flooded lowlands
And slopes of sodden loam
The pack-horse struggles onward,
To take dumb tidings home.
And mud-stained, wet, and weary,
Through ranges dark goes he;
While hobble-chains and tinware
Are sounding eerily.

The floods are in the ocean,
The stream is clear again,
And now a verdant carpet
Is stretched across the plain.
But someone's eyes are saddened,
And someone's heart still bleeds
In sorrow for the drover
Who sleeps among the reeds.

Middle Cut o' Brisket
Keith Garvey

Beef today for dinner
Onion sauce and spuds
'Strewth she looks a winner
'Light and dust your duds
Hungry riders waitin'
To enjoy the feast
Middle cut o' brisket
Best cut on the beast.
Bellies small and shrunken
Soon will fill once more
Get the bottle, Duncan,
London Bob can pour.

Middle cut o' brisket
Salted boiled and strained
Middle cut o' brisket
Illegally obtained.

Sick of eatin' tomcats
Snake and kangaroo
Brumbies, goats and wombats
Break yer heart to chew.
Hard we rode by starlight
To a neighbourin' run
Back before the far light
Heralded the sun.
Packbags full and leakin'
Salt and bloodied brine
See the old cook seekin'
Slices fat and fine.

Middle cut o' brisket
Steamin' in the pot
Middle cut o' brisket
Eat it cold or hot.

Chew the tasty tallow
Piled up on the plate
Ringers shrewd or callow
All declare it great
Have another helpin'
Never fear the traps
Hear the heelers yelpin'
Hungry for the scraps.
Johnny cake and damper
Soakin' up the grease
See how every camper
Eats in joy and peace.

Middle cut o' brisket
Temptin' every thief
Middle cut o' brisket
Finest cut o' beef.

from . . . The Sick Stockrider
Adam Lindsay Gordon

Hold hard, Ned! Lift me down once more, and lay me in the shade.
Old man, you've had your work cut out to guide
Both horses, and to hold me in the saddle when I sway'd
All through the hot, slow, sleepy, silent ride.
The dawn at 'Moorabinda' was a mist rack dull and dense,
The sunrise was a sullen, sluggish lamp;
I was dozing in the gateway at Arbuthnot's bound'ry fence,
I was dreaming on the Limestone cattle camp.

We crossed the creek at Carricksford, and sharply through the haze,
And suddenly the sun shot flaming forth;
To southward lay 'Katawa' with the sand peaks all ablaze
And the flush'd fields of Glen Lomond lay to north.
Now westward winds the brindle path that leads to Lindisfarm,
And yonder looms the double-headed Bluff;
From the far side of the first hill, when the skies are clear and calm,
You can see Sylvester's woolshed fair enough.

Five miles we used to call it from our homestead to the place
Where the big tree spans the roadway like an arch;
'Twas here we ran the dingo down that gave us such a chase
Eight years ago – or was it nine? – last March.
'Twas merry in the glowing morn, among the gleaming grass
To wander as we've wander'd many a mile,
And blow the cool tobacco cloud, and watch the white wreaths
    pass,
Sitting loosely in the saddle all the while.

. . .

I've had my share of pastime, and I've done my share of toil,
And life is short – the longest life a span;
I care not now to tarry for the corn or for the oil,
Or for the wine that maketh glad the heart of man.
For good undone and gifts misspent and resolutions vain,
'Tis somewhat late to trouble. This I know –
I should live the same life over, if I had to live again;
And the chances are I go where most men go.

The deep blue skies wax dusky and the tall green trees grow dim,
The sward beneath me seems to heave and fall;
And sickly, smoky shadows through the sleepy sunlight swim,
And on the very sun's face weave their pall.
Let me slumber in the hollow where the wattle blossoms wave,
With never stone or rail to fence my bed;
Should the sturdy station children pull the bush flowers on my grave,
I may chance to hear them romping overhead.

Out from Noonkanbah

John Wilson ('Wilo')

The coolibahs quiver,
The snakewood moans,
And bower-birds play
With Lin Bower's bones
While the thunder rolls
In ominous tones
Out from Noonkanbah.

When piccaninnies shriek
At a spectral sight
And dingoes howl
In the ghastly light
You'll know that Lin Bower
Walks at night
Out from Noonkanbah.

Away out there
Where horizons melt
There's a pair of boots,
Some mildewed felt,
A few old buttons
And a sun-cracked belt
Out from Noonkanbah.

In articulo mortis,
Ah, forsook!
With a shovel of sand
And a leather-bound book
They buried him there
With the Chinese cook . . .
Out from Noonkanbah.

The Lights of Cobb and Co

Henry Lawson

Fire lighted; on the table a meal for sleepy men;
A lantern in the stable; a jingle now and then;
The mail-coach looming darkly by light of moon and star;
The growl of sleepy voices; a candle in the bar;
A stumble in the passage of folk with wits abroad;
A swear-word from a bedroom, the shout of 'All aboard!'
'Tchk-tchk! Git up!' 'Hold fast, there!' and down the range we go;
Five hundred miles of scattered camps will watch for Cobb and Co.

Old coaching towns already decaying for their sins;
Uncounted 'Half-Way Houses', and scores of 'Ten-Mile Inns';
The riders from the stations by lonely granite peaks;
The black-boy for the shepherds on sheep and cattle creeks;
The roaring camps of Gulgong, and many a 'Digger's Rest';
The diggers on the Lachlan; the huts of Farthest West;
Some twenty thousand exiles who sailed for weal or woe
The bravest hearts of twenty lands will wait for Cobb and Co.

The morning star has vanished, the frost and fog are gone,
In one of those grand mornings which but on mountains dawn;
A flask of friendly whisky – each other's hopes we share –
And throw our top-coats open to drink the mountain air.
The roads are rare to travel, and life seems all complete;
The grind of wheels on gravel, the trot of horses' feet,
The trot, trot, trot and canter, as down the spur we go
The green sweeps to horizons blue that call for Cobb and Co.

We take a bright girl actress through western dusts and damps,
To bear the home-world message, and sing for sinful camps,
To stir our hearts and break them, wild hearts that hope and ache
(Ah! when she thinks of *those* days her own must nearly break!)
Five miles this side the goldfield, a loud, triumphant shout:
Five hundred cheering diggers have snatched the horses out:
With 'Auld Lang Syne' in chorus, through roaring camps they go
That cheer for her, and cheer for Home, and cheer for Cobb and Co.

Three lamps above the ridges and gorges dark and deep,
A flash on sandstone cuttings where sheer the sidings sweep,
A flash on shrouded wagons, on water ghastly white;
Weird bush and scattered remnants of 'rushes in the night';
Across the swollen river a flash beyond the ford:
Ride hard to warn the driver! He's drunk or mad, good Lord!
But on the bank to westward a broad and cheerful glow
New camps extend across the plains, new routes for Cobb and Co.

Swift scramble up the siding where teams climb inch by inch;
Pause, bird-like, on the summit — then breakneck down the pinch;
By clear ridge-country rivers, and gaps where tracks run high,
Where waits the lonely horseman, cut clear against the sky;
Past haunted half-way houses — where convicts made the bricks —
Scrub-yards and new bark shanties, we dash with five and six;
Through stringybark and blue-gum, and box and pine we go —
A hundred miles shall see tonight the lights of Cobb and Co!

Horse-Bells
'BDG'

I love to lie and listen to the horse-bells' merry sound,
When the cattle are in camp and we are out-stretched on the
   ground;
There is music in the horse-bells, and I love to hear their song
As they join in happy chorus —
Tinkle! Tonkle! Tankle! Tong!

They tonkle through the brigalow, they tankle near the swamp;
They tinkle on the ridges and they wrangle round the camp;
There's little Fairy's thimble-bell and Billy's bull-frog strong,
And big and little blend in
Tinkle! Tonkle! Tankle! Tong!

As the great moon glares above the cattle rest in camp, content;
It's a pleasure just to be alive as, with the wattle scent
The soft breeze brings the music of the horse-bells' merry song,
Soothing ever and repeating
Tinkle! Tonkle! Tankle! Tong!

from . . . The Bells and Hobbles
EJ Brady

When our feet are in the stirrups, and our hands are on the reins,
When the cities lie behind us and before us spread the plains,
There's a song of night and morning that in minor music swells,
'Tis the jangle of the hobbles and the jingle of the bells.

Oh, the sun shall rouse us early, as he swings into the blue;
And we'll boil the old black billy while our world is wet with dew,
While the working world a-hurry seeks its stuffy office cells,
We'll be slipping off the hobbles and be strapping up the bells.

And the breezy tracks we travel from the sunrise to his set,
They will aid us to remember, they will help us to forget;
For the song of Night and Morning will be with us as it knells
In the message of the hobbles and the answer of the bells.

The Dying Stockman

Anon

A strapping young stockman lay dying,
His saddle supporting his head.
His comrades around him were crying,
As he leaned on one elbow and said,

'Wrap me up in my stockwhip and blanket
And bury me deep down below,
Where the dingoes and crows won't molest me,
In the shade where the coolibahs grow.

Cut down a couple of saplings,
Place one at my head and my toe.
Carve on them a stockwhip and saddle,
To show there's a stockman below.

There's some tea in the old battered billy,
Place the pannikins all in a row,
And drink to the health of a stockman,
Farewell dear old pals, I must go.'

from . . . The Golden Yesterday

Roderic Quinn

Hither they quested the young and eager,
The social misfit, the aged, the banned;
Friends were lacking and fortune meagre,
And here was promise, the Promised Land.

They had their triumphs, their gains, their losses,
Their noons of laughter, their nights of care;
Back on the hills are some rough crosses
A name . . . a date . . . and, perchance, a prayer.

They dug the clay, and they broke the boulders,
They turned the creek, and they washed the mould,
But vain as makers and vain as moulders,
They lived and wrought in the Age of Gold.

They worked and worried, their labour blotching
The land's green surface with scar and pit;
Yet, all around them the hills were watching
Flower-crowned, tree-crested and glory-lit.

A breeze comes down from the highlands smoothing
The green young wheat, and a bird makes mirth,
And Spring is here with soft hands soothing
The ruined rocks and the wounded earth.

The diggers passed: and the last red embers
Of their night-fires, they are ashen grey;
But, while hearts beat and the mind remembers,
They shall not fade as a dream away.

Cleaning Up
Edward Dyson

When the horse has been unharnessed and we've flushed the old
    machine,
And the water o'er the sluice is running evenly and clean;
When there's thirty load before us, and the sun is high and bright,
And we've worked from early morning and shall have to work till
    night,
Not a man of us is weary, though the graft is pretty rough,
If we see the proper colour showing freely through the stuff.

With a dandy head of water and a youngster at the rear
To hand along the billy, boys, and keep the tail race clear,
We lift the wash and flash the fork and make the gravel fly.
The shovelling is heavy and we're soaked from heel to thigh;
But it makes a fellow tireless and his thews and sinews tough
If the colour's showing freely as he gaily shifts the stuff.

When Geordie Best is pumping to a rollicking refrain,
And Sandy wipes his streaming brow and shakes the fork again,
The pebbles dance and rattle and the water seems to laugh
Good luck is half the battle and good will's the other half;
And no day's too long and trying and no toil is hard enough,
When we see the colour showing in each shovelful of stuff.

Can the mining speculator with a pile of golden scrip,
Or the plunger who has laid his all upon a winning tip,
Or the city man who's hit upon a profitable deal,
Know the wonderful elation that the lucky diggers feel
When Fortune's smiled but grimly and the storeman's looking
    gruff,
And at last they see the colour showing freely in the stuff?

Never, mates! It is a feeling that no other winner knows
Not the soldier marching homeward from the conquest of his foes,
Nor the scholar who's successful in his searching of the skies,
Nor the squalid miser grovelling where his secret treasure lies.
'Tis a keener, wilder rapture in the digger bold and bluff
Who feels the sluice and sees the colour shining in the stuff.

Then lift the wash, and flash the fork, and make the gravel fly!
We can laugh at all the pleasures on which other men rely,
When the water o'er the sluice is running evenly and clean,
And the loaded ripples glitter with a lively golden sheen.
No day's too long and trying, and no toil is hard enough
When we wash her down and see the colour freely through the
    stuff.

The Swagman's Rest

AB Paterson ('The Banjo')

We buried old Bob where the bloodwoods wave
At the foot of the Eaglehawk;
We fashioned a cross on the old man's grave,
For fear that his ghost might walk;
We carved his name on a bloodwood tree,
With the date of his sad decease,
And in place of 'died from effects of spree',
We wrote, 'May he rest in peace'.

For Bob was known on the Overland,
A regular old bush wag,
Tramping along in the dust and sand,
Humping his well worn swag.
He would camp for days in the river bed,
And loiter and 'fish for whales'.
'I'm into the swagman's yard', he said,
'And I never shall find the rails.'

But he found the rails on that summer night
For a better place, or worse,
As we watched by turns in the flickering light
With an old black gin for nurse.
The breeze came in with the scent of pine,
The river sounded clear,
When a change came on, and we saw the sign
That told us the end was near.

But he spoke in a cultured voice and low
'I fancy they've "sent the route";
I once was an army man, you know,
Though now I'm a drunken brute;
But bury me out where the bloodwoods wave,
And if ever you're fairly stuck,
Just take and shovel me out of the grave,
And, maybe, I'll bring you luck.

'For I've always heard . . .' here his voice fell weak,
His strength was well-nigh sped,
He gasped and struggled and tried to speak,
Then fell in a moment dead.
Thus ended a wasted life and hard,
Of energies misapplied
Old Bob was out of the 'swagman's yard'
And over the Great Divide.

The drought came down on the field and flock,
And never a raindrop fell,
Though the tortured moans of the starving stock
Might soften a fiend from hell.
And we thought of the hint that the swagman gave
When he went to the Great Unseen
We shovelled the skeleton out of the grave
To see what his hint might mean.

We dug where the cross and the grave-posts were,
We shovelled away the mould,
When sudden a vein of quartz lay bare
All gleaming with yellow gold.
'Twas a reef with never a fault nor baulk
That ran from the range's crest,
And the richest mine on the Eaglehawk
Is known as 'The Swagman's Rest'.

A Ballad of Eureka

Victor Daley ('Creeve Roe')

Stand up, my young Australian,
In the brave light of the sun,
And hear how Freedom's battle
Was in old days lost – and won.
The blood burns in my veins, boy,
As it did in years of yore,
Remembering Eureka,
And the men of 'Fifty-four.

The tyrants of the goldfields
Would not let us live in peace;
They harried us and chased us
With their horse and foot police.
Each man must show his licence
When they chose, by fits and starts:
They tried to break our spirits,
And they almost broke our hearts.

There comes a time to all men
When submission is a sin;
We made a bonfire brave, and
Flung our licences therein.
Our hearts with scorn and anger
Burned more fiercely than the flame,
Full well we knew our peril,
But we dared it all the same.

On Bakery Hill the Banner
Of the Southern Cross flew free;
Then up rose Peter Lalor,
And with lifted hand spake he:
'We swear by God above us,
While we live, to work and fight
For Freedom and for Justice,
For our Manhood and our Right.'

Then, on the bare earth kneeling,
As on a chapel-floor,
Beneath the sacred Banner,
One and all, that oath we swore:
And some of those who swore it
Were like straws upon a flood,
But there were men who swore it
And who sealed it with their blood.

I said, my young Australian,
That the fight was lost – and won –
But, oh, our hearts were heavy
At the setting of the sun.
Yet, ere the year was over,
Freedom rolled in like a flood:
They gave us all we asked for –
When we asked for it in blood.

The bitter fight was ended,
And, with cruel coward-lust,
They dragged our sacred banner
Through the Stockade's bloody dust.
But, patient as the gods are,
Justice counts the years and waits –
That banner now waves proudly
Over six Australian States.

God rest you, Peter Lalor!
For you were a white man whole;
A swordblade in the sunlight
Was your bright and gallant soul.
And God reward you kindly,
Father Smith, alive or dead:
'Twas you that gave him shelter
When a price was on his head.

Within the Golden City
In the place of peace profound
The Heroes sleep. Tread softly:
'Tis Australia's Holy Ground.
And ever more Australia
Will keep green in her heart's core
The memory of Lalor
And the Men of 'Fifty-four.

Bullocky Bill

Edward Dyson

From the river sidin' the railway town,
To the dull new port there three days down;
Forward and back on the uphill track
With a creak of the jinker and a ringin' crack;
Slow as a funeral, but sure as steam,
Bullocky Bill and his old red team.

Ploughin' around by the ti-tree scrub
Four wheels down to the bloomin' hub
Hither and fro with their heads all low,
Bally and Splodger and Banker go,
Men in the ranges much esteem,
Bullocky Bill and his old red team.

Wormin' about where the tall trees spring,
Surgin' ahead when the clay bogs cling,
A rattle of lash and a language rash,
On the narrow edge of immortal smash.
He'd thread a bead or walk a beam,
Bullocky Bill and his old red team.

Engines and stamps for the mines about,
Tools for the men who are leadin' out;
Tucker and booze and the latest news,
Back where bunyip stirs the ooze;
Pioneers with the best we deem,
Bullocky Bill and his old red team.

Climbin' a hill where the red stars ride,
Rattlin' down on the other side;
With a whistle an' grind an' a scramble blind,
And a thunderin' gumtree slung behind.
But they always get there, hill or stream,
Bullocky Bill and his old red team.

The Melodious Bullocky

WT Goodge ('The Colonel')

'Tis of the Wild Colonial Boy,
Come out of that saplin', Rat!
Brought up by honest parents, . . .
Now, Strawberry, what are you at?
He robbed them lordly squatters, . . .
Whoa Diamond! Darn your hump!
And a terror to Horstralia, . . .
Now then, Nugget, mind that stump!
'Twas at the age of seventeen, . . .
Gee back there, Dimple! Gee!
He never, . . .
Way there Baldy! Sich a cow I never did see!
He was his father's only son, . . .
Gee back there now, Rob Roy!
And fondly did his parents love the Wild Colonial Boy!

The Teams

Henry Lawson

A cloud of dust on the long white road,
And the teams go creeping on
Inch by inch with the weary load;
And by the power of the greenhide goad
The distant goal is won.

With eyes half-shut to the blinding dust,
And necks to the yokes bent low,
The beasts are pulling as bullocks must;
And the shining tires might almost rust
While the spokes are turning slow.

With face half-hid 'neath a broad-brimmed hat
That shades from the heat's white waves,
And shouldered whip with its greenhide plait,
The driver plods with a gait like that
Of his weary, patient slaves.

He wipes his brow, for the day is hot,
And spits to the left with spite;
He shouts at 'Bally', and flicks at 'Scot',
And raises dust from the back of 'Spot',
And spits to the dusty right.

He'll sometimes pause as a thing of form
In front of a settler's door,
And ask for a drink, and remark, 'It's warm,'
Or say, 'There's signs of a thunderstorm;'
But he seldom utters more.

But the rains are heavy on roads like these;
And, fronting his lonely home,
For weeks together the settler sees
The teams bogged down to the axletrees,
Or ploughing the sodden loam.

And then when the roads are at their worst,
The bushman's children hear
The cruel blows of the whips reversed
While bullocks pull as their hearts would burst,
And bellow with pain and fear.

And thus with little of joy or rest
Are the long, long journeys done;
And thus – 'tis a cruel war at the best –
Is distance fought in the mighty West,
And the lonely battles won.

The Glenburgh Wool Goes Down

Jack Sorensen

The ramp outside the woolshed door,
Holds yet another load:
So yoke the camel team once more
And take the waggon road.
The shafters prop, the leaders pull,
The wheels creak dismally,
And sixty bales of Glenburgh wool,
Roll westward to the sea.

On down the winding dusty track,
From dawn till close of day:
The punchers shout, the big whips crack,
While straining camels sway.
By stony plain, by sandhills brown,
By wattles o'er the lea,
The hard-won wool goes rolling down,
From Glenburgh to the sea.

A creek to cross, a hill to climb,
A stretch of sandy track:
They'll haul it through if given time,
Though a straw would break each back.
So a morning breaks, a bright sun wanes,
Till a day, then a week, is gone.
Yet with creaking wheels and clinking chains,
The Glenburgh wool rolls on.

Cool nights of rest while the camels swell,
As they munch the mulga near:
While the hobble chain and the doleful bell
Will lull the puncher's ear.
Two more long days from Rocky Pool,
And then Carnarvon town,
And sixty bales of Glenburgh wool,
 From inland heights go down.

Black Harry's Team

AB Paterson ('The Banjo')

No soft-skinned Durham steers are they,
No Devons plump and red,
But brindled, black, and iron-grey
That mark the mountain-bred;
For mountain-bred and mountain-broke,
With sullen eyes agleam,
No stranger's hand could put a yoke
On old Black Harry's team.

Pull out, pull out, at break of morn
The creeks are running white,
And Tiger, Spot, and Snailey-horn
Must bend their bows by night;
And axles, wheels and flooring boards
Are swept with flying spray
As, shoulder-deep, through mountain fords
The leaders feel their way.

He needs no sign of cross or kirn
To guide him as he goes,
For every twist and every turn
That old black leader knows.
Up mountains steep they heave and strain
Where never wheel has rolled,
And what the toiling leaders gain
The body bullocks hold.

Where eaglehawks their eyries make,
On sidelings steep and blind,
He rigs the good old-fashioned brake –
A tree tied on behind.
Up mountains, straining to the full,
Each poler plays his part
The sullen, stubborn, bullock pull
That breaks a horse's heart.

Beyond the furthest bridle track
His wheels have blazed the way;
The forest giants, burnt and black,
Are earmarked by his dray.
Through belts of scrub where messmates grow
His juggernaut has rolled,
For stumps and saplings have to go
When Harry's team takes hold.

On easy grade and rubber tyre
The tourist car goes through;
They halt a moment to admire
The far-flung mountain view.
The tourist folk would be amazed
If they could get to know
They take the track Black Harry blazed
A hundred years ago.

One of the Has-Beens

Anon

I'm one of the 'has-beens', a shearer I mean,
I once was a ringer and I used to shear clean,
Make the wool peel off easy, like soil from a plough,
But you may not believe me, 'cos I can't do it now.
I shore with Pat Hogan, Bill Bright and Jack Gunn,
Charlie Fergus, Tommy Layton and the great Roaring Dunn
Yes they brought to the Lachlan the best they could find,
But not one among them could leave me behind.

Now I'm old and I'm slow and I'm used to the frown
The boss often displays saying, 'Keep them blades down!'
But I once could stay with the great Jackie Howe,
Though you may not believe me, 'cos I can't do it now.
It's no use complaining, and I'll shear till I die,
Though the days of fast shearing have long passed me by,
Now I try to shear easy, shear clean and shear slow,
I merely have told you what I was long ago.

Widgegoara Joe

W Tully

I'm only a backblocks shearer as can easily be seen,
I've shorn in almost every shed on the plains of Riverine.
I've shorn in all the famous sheds and seen big tallies done,
But somehow or other, I don't know why, I never became a gun.

I've opened up the windpipe straight, I've opened behind the ear,
I've shorn in every possible style in which a man can shear.
I've studied all the cuts and drives of the famous men I've met,
But I've never succeeded in tallying up those three little figures yet!

As the boss walked down this morning I saw him stare at me,
For I'd mastered Moran's 'shoulder cut' as he could plainly see.
But I've another surprise for him that'll give him quite a shock,
Tomorrow he'll find that I have mastered Pierce's 'rang tang block'.

If I succeed as I hope to do then I intend to shear
At the Wagga demonstration which is held there every year.
And there I'll lower the colours, the colours of Mitchell and Co,
Instead of Deeming you will hear of 'Widgegoara Joe'.

Hurrah me boys me shears are set and I feel both fit and well,
Tomorrow will find me at the gate when the gaffer rings the bell,
With Haydon's patent thumb guards fixed and both o' me blades
    pulled back;
Tomorrow I go with the siding blow for a century or the sack!

The Song of the Songless Shearer
CJ Dennis

*'Back in the early days,' said the old, grey shearer, 'when we used the
blades, and were all country men, and shearing was really shearing, we
used to sing at the board the whole day through. But never a song is heard
now. The shearers are mainly city men, who talk politics; and they are all
keen on getting back to the city lights and the union meetings. We had
better times in the days when we used to sing.'*

Now, my dad 'e was a shearer an' 'e sez to me, 'Look 'ere.
There's sheep upon the run, me son; there's sheep we 'ave to shear.'
My dad 'e was a shearer, an' a country man as well,
'E sez to me, 'If they ain't shore the country goes to 'ell.'

My dad 'e was a country man (I think I told you that).
A man who knoo Australia where the sky-line's pretty flat.
'E never looked for spires an' things for cuttin' out the sky,
'E 'ad no vain desires an' things, the same as you an' I.

My dad 'e took the broader view, an' shore with dinkum shears,
An', oh, good Lord! down at the board – if any man 'ad ears –
'E'd 'ear 'em singin', singin' there while they ripped off the fleece.
An' me? Well I'm a shearer, but we've lorst them days o' peace.
For I live down in the city; an' I knows the city's streets;
I 'ave to be on tap, yeh know, wot time the Union meets.

My father was a shearer, an' 'e knoo sheep thro' an' thro'.
'E never yearned for city lights, the same as me an' you.
My father was a country man; an' I am thinkin' now
My father picked the best of it – 'e sang things, any'ow.

An' when a man can't sing at work – sing shearin' at the board.
'E's losing somethin' all the time that workmen can't afford.
Oh, me dad 'e was a shearer, an' 'e was a country man.
An' 'ere's me now, a shearer too; but sing I never can.

Fer why? I live in cities, an' the city's in me blood,
An' the Union boss 'as got me, an' it's easy understud.
I goes to Union meetin's, an' they 'ands me all the dope.
But do I know Australia? No. I 'aven't got a 'ope.

I knows the cities an' the streets; an' when the shearin's due,
If you goes up or you stays down is wot the boss tells you.
Ah, me dad 'e was a shearer; an' 'e knoo sheep thro' an' thro'.
But I don't want to know 'em less they pay a man. Do you?

Yes; I'm a city shearer, an' when I get 'ome at night –
Back 'ome from these 'ere pitcher shows, an' p'raps a little tight.
I sorter gits to wonderin' if reely, after all,
My dad weren't on the dinkum track; an' ain't I took a fall –

Fer when me father shore a sheep 'e sung there at the board,
But shearers they ain't singin' now; for songs they can't afford.
They're thinkin' of the dough they'll get, an' 'ow they'll do it in.
But me dad 'e sung to ringin' blades, an' never cared a pin.
An' this is all the change I get when all is done an' said:
If fellers cannot sing at work they might as well be dead.

The Shearer From Mudgereebah
Anon

Said a shearer from Mudgereebah,
'I never once cried out for tar!
For as long as I shore 'em
I never once tore 'em
Well, leastways not here in the bar.'

A Shearer's Dream
Henry Lawson

Oh, I dreamt I shore in a shearin' shed, and it was a dream of joy,
For every one of the rouseabouts was a girl dressed up as a boy
Dressed up as a page in pantomime, and the prettiest ever seen
They had flaxen hair, they had coal-black hair, and every shade
    between.
The shed was cooled by electric fans that was over every chute;
The pens was polished mahogany, and everything else to suit.

The huts had springs to the mattresses and the tucker was simply
    grand,
And every night by the billerbong we danced to a German band.
Our pay was the wool on the jumbuks' backs, so we shore till all
    was blue
The sheep was washed afore they was shore and the rams was
    scented too;
And all of us wept when the shed cut out, in spite of the long, hot
    days,
For every hour them girls waltzed in, with whisky and beer on
    traaays!

There was short, plump girls, there was tall slim girls, the
    handsomest ever seen,
They was four-foot-five, they was six-foot high, and every height
    between.
There was three of them girls to every chap, and as jealous as they
    could be
There was three of them girls to every chap, and six of 'em picked
    on me;
We was draftin' 'em out for the homeward track and sharing 'em
    round like steam,
When I woke with my head in the blazin' sun to find 'twas a
    shearer's dream.

The Shearer's Nightmare

Anon

Old Bill the shearer had been phoned to catch the train next day,
He had a job at Mungindi, an early start for May.
So he packed his port and rolled his swag and hurried off to bed,
But sleep? He couldn't steal a wink to soothe his aching head.

He heard the missus snoring hard, he heard the ticking clock,
He heard the midnight train blow in, he heard the crowing cock.
At last Bill in a stupor lay, a-dreaming now was he,
Of sheep and pens and belly-wool he shore in number three.

He grabbed the missus in her sleep and shore her like a ewe.
The fine performance started as up the neck he flew,
Then he turned her for the long-blow, down the whipping side he
    tore,
With his knee upon her back and a firm grip round her jaw.

Then he rolled her over, like a demon now he shore,
(She dared not kick or struggle, she had seen him shear before).
He was leading 'Jack the Ringer', he was matching 'Mick the
    Brute',
When he called for tar and dumped her, like a hogget, down the
    chute!

Then he reached to stop the shear machine and put it out of gear,
And turned the electric light on so all was bright and clear.
He was gazing out the window, now awakened from his sleep,
And down there on the footpath lay his missus in a heap!

He said, 'Blimey, I've had nightmares after boozin' up a treat,
And I've walked without me trousers to the pub across the street,
But this sure takes some beatin', and it's one I'll have to keep.
I dare not tell me mates I shore the missus in me sleep!'

Jacky Howe

Anon

When it comes to shearing, a lotta tales are spun,
Some boasting is in earnest and some of it's in fun.
But the record that's unbeaten, three hundred twenty-one,
It never will be beaten, it simply can't be done.
It was made on Alice Downs, a Central Queensland run,
By Jackie Howe from Warwick, the best under the sun.
October tenth in '92, that's when the deed was done,
And Jacky used the blades that day, that's why he's number one!

Down the River

Barcroft Boake ('Surcingle')

Hark, the sound of it drawing nearer,
Clink of hobble and brazen bell;
Mark the passage of stalwart shearer,
Bidding Monaro soil farewell.
Where is he making for? Down the river,
Down the river with eager tread;
Where is he making for? Down the river,
Down the river to seek a 'shed'.

Where is his dwelling on old Monaro?
Buckley's Crossing, or Jindaboine?
Dry Plain is it, or sweet Bolaira?
P'raps 'tis near where the rivers join.
Where is he making for? Down the river,
When, oh when, will he turn him back?
Soft sighs follow him down the river,
Moist eyes gaze at his fading track.

See, behind him his pack-horse, ambling,
Bears the weight of his master's kit,
Oft and oft from the pathway rambling,
Crops unhampered by cruel bit.
Where is he making for? Equine rover,
Sturdy nag from the Eucumbene,
Tempted down by the thought of clover,
Springing luscious in Riverine.

Dreams of life and its future chances,
Snatch of song to beguile the way;
Through green crannies the sunlight glances,
Silver-gilding the bright 'Jack Shay'.
'So long, mate, I can stay no longer,
So long, mate, I've no time to stop;
Pens are waiting me at Mahonga,
Bluegong, Grubben and Pullitop.

'What! You say that the river's risen?
What! That the melted snow has come?
What! That it locks and bars our prison?
Many's the mountain stream I've swum.
I must onward and cross the river,
So long, mate, for I cannot stay;
I must onward and cross the river,
Over the river there lies the way.'

One man short when the roll they're calling,
One man short at old Bobby Rand's;
Heads are drooping and tears are falling
Up on Monaro's mountain lands.
Where is he making for? Down the river,
Down the river of slimy bed;
Where is he making for? Down the river,
Down the river that bears him, dead.

A Sundowner's Song

Louis Esson

I've eaten bitter bread,
In sweat wrung from my brow;
And earth-bent, hunger-gripped
Scarred hands on axe and plough.
Now, when the sun is shining,
With swag slung on my back,
I laugh at soured selectors
When I pass down the track.

Whalin' up the Lachlan
By the waters grey,
Whalin' up the Lachlan
All a summer's day,
We'll drop a line to tickle
The black fish and the cod,
Whalin' up the Lachlan
Beside a lazy rod.

Some choose to crack the greenhide,
And some to sow and reap;
And some to pink with B-bows
A-shearin' greasy sheep.
But some there are, sundowners,
Who take the easy way,
Nor think of lean tomorrow
If they fare fit today.

Whalin' up the Lachlan
Done with axe and plough,
Whalin' up the Lachlan
The billy's boiling now.
We'll fill our pipes, an' yarn there,
And watch the world roll by,
Whalin' up the Lachlan
Under a starry sky.

I'll Tell You What, You Wanderers
Henry Lawson

I'll tell you what, you wanderers, who drift from town to town;
Don't look into a good girl's eye, until you've settled down.
It's hard to go away alone and leave old chums behind
It's hard to travel steerage when your tastes are more refined
To reach a place when times are bad, and to be stranded there,
No money in your pocket nor a decent rag to wear.
But to be forced from that fond clasp, from that last clinging kiss
By poverty! There is on earth no harder thing than this.

from . . . The Song of the Sundowner
Thomas E Spencer

I'm the monarch of valley, and hill, and plain,
And the king of this golden land.
A continent broad is my vast domain,
And its people at my command.

In the drought-stricken plains of the lone Paroo,
When the rainless earth is bare,
I take toll from the shepherd and jackeroo,
And I sample their humble fare.

Not a fig I care though the stock may die,
And the sun-cracked plains be brown;
I can make for the east, where the grass is high,
I'm at home when the sun goes down.

When river and creek their banks o'er leap,
And the flood rolls raging by;
When the settlers are mourning their crops and sheep,
I can watch 'em without a sigh.

I care not what others may do or think,
I'm a monarch without a crown;
I can always be sure of my food and drink,
And a home when the sun goes down.

Wanderers

James Hebblethwaite

As I rose in the early dawn,
While stars were fading white,
I saw upon a grassy slope
A camp-fire burning bright;
With tent behind and blaze before,
Three loggers in a row
Sang all together joyously
Pull up the stakes and go!

As I rode on by Eagle Hawk,
The wide blue deep of air,
The wind among the glittering leaves,
The flowers so sweet and fair,
The thunder of the rude salt waves,
The creek's soft overflow,
All joined in chorus to the words
Pull up the stakes and go!

Now by the tent on forest skirt,
By odour of the earth,
By sight and scent of morning smoke,
By evening camp-fire's mirth,
By deep-sea call and foaming green,
By new stars' gleam and glow,
By summer trails in antique lands
Pull up the stakes and go!

The world is wide and we are young,
And sounding marches beat,
And passion pipes her sweetest call
In lane and field and street;
So rouse the chorus, brothers all,
We'll something have to show
When Death comes round and strikes our tent
Pull up the stakes and go!

Out Back

Henry Lawson

The old year went, and the new returned, in the withering weeks
of drought,
The cheque was spent that the shearer earned, and the sheds were
all cut out;
The publican's words were short and few, and the publican's looks
were black
And the time had come, as the shearer knew, to carry his swag Out
Back.

For time means tucker, and tramp you must, where the scrubs and
plains are wide,
With seldom a track that a man can trust, or a mountain peak to
guide;
All day long in the dust and heat when summer is on the track
With stinted stomachs and blistered feet, they carry their swags
Out Back.

He tramped away from the shanty there, where the days were long
and hot,
With never a soul to know or care if he died on the track or not.
The poor of the city have friends in woe, no matter how much
they lack,
But only God and the swagmen know how a poor man fares Out
Back.

He begged his way on the parched Paroo and the Warrego tracks
    once more,
And lived like a dog, as the swagmen do, till the Western stations
    shore;
But men were many, and sheds were full, for work in the town was
    slack
The traveller never got hands in wool, though he tramped for a
    year Out Back.

In stifling noons when his back was wrung by its load, and the air
    seemed dead,
And the water warmed in the bag that hung to his aching arm like
    lead,
Or in times of flood, when plains were seas, and the scrubs were
    cold and black,
He ploughed in mud to his trembling knees, and paid for his sins
    Out Back.

He blamed himself in the year 'Too Late' – in the heaviest hours of
    life –
'Twas little he dreamed that a shearing-mate had care of his home
    and wife;
There are times when wrongs from your kindred come, and
    treacherous tongues attack
When a man is better away from home, and dead to the world,
    Out Back.

And dirty and careless and old he wore, as his lamp of hope grew
    dim;
He tramped for years till the swag he bore seemed part of himself
    to him.
As a bullock drags in the sandy ruts, he followed the dreary track,
With never a thought but to reach the huts when the sun went
    down Out Back.

It chanced one day, when the north wind blew in his face like a
    furnace-breath,
He left the track for a tank he knew – 'twas a short-cut to his
    death;
For the bed of the tank was hard and dry, and crossed with many a
    crack,
And, oh! it's a terrible thing to die of thirst in the scrub Out Back.

A drover came, but the fringe of law was eastward many a mile;
He never reported the thing he saw, for it was not worth his while.
The tanks are full and grass is high in the mulga off the track,
Where the bleaching bones of a white man lie by his mouldering
    swag Out Back.

For time means tucker, and tramp they must, where the plains and
    scrubs are wide,
With seldom a track that a man can trust, or a mountain peak to
    guide;
All day long in the flies and heat the men of the outside track
With stinted stomachs and blistered feet must carry their swags
    Out Back.

from . . . The People on the Land
JW Gordon (Jim Grahame)

We're the backbone of the country and the mainstay of the land,
And the destinies of people we have balanced in our hand.
They have preached it in the churches, they have taught it in the
    schools;
It's the slogan of the sages and the byword of the fools.
But the teachers and the preachers never know or understand
All the hard and bitter struggles of the people on the land.

We have seen the sweet rain falling on the fields that we have sown,
And in fancy reaped a harvest ere the first green ears have shown;
And we've heard the humming header and we've seen the bulging
    bags,
We have visited the tailor, cast aside our outworn rags;
And we've heard the crisp notes rustle, almost felt them in our hand,
As the phantom wheat went racing like a stream of golden sand!

We have peeped into the future; and we've hastily looked back
To the hard old times behind us when our fathers blazed the track,
When we all slept on the waggon and our sleep was sweet and
    sound,
And our mothers cook their dinners at a campfire on the ground.
When their washing up was finished they would come and lend a
    hand
At the drilling or the tilling as we grappled with the land.

Oh! We've dreamed and schemed and fretted as we trudged behind
  the plough;
And we've built some airy castles as the sweat dripped from our
  brow.
Life seems furrow after furrow without halt or break or bend,
Making ready for the harvest of the Reaper in the end;
And the teachers and the preachers do not know or understand
Of the Hopes, like sunken treasure, that are buried in the land!

The Shame of Going Back

Henry Lawson

When you've come to make a fortune and you haven't made your
  salt,
And the reason of your failure isn't anybody's fault
When you haven't got a billet, and the times are very slack,
There is nothing that can spur you like the shame of going back;
Crawling home with empty pockets,
Going back hard-up;
Oh! it's then you learn the meaning of humiliation's cup.

When the place and you are strangers and you struggle all alone,
And you have a mighty longing for the town where you are known;
When your clothes are very shabby and the future's very black,
There is nothing that can hurt you like the shame of going back.

When we've fought the battle bravely and are beaten to the wall,
'Tis the sneers of men, not conscience, that make cowards of us all;
And the while you are returning, oh! your brain is on the rack,
And your heart is in the shadow of the shame of going back.

When a beaten man's discovered with a bullet in his brain,
They post-mortem him, and try him, and they say he was insane;
But it very often happens that he'd lately got the sack,
And his onward move was owing to the shame of going back.

Ah! my friend, you call it nonsense, and your upper lip is curled,
I can see that you have never worked your passage through the
    world;
But when fortune rounds upon you and the rain is on the track,
You will learn the bitter meaning of the shame of going back;
Going home with empty pockets,
Going home hard–up;
Oh, you'll taste the bitter poison in humiliation's cup.

Occupations

Bruce Simpson ('Lancewood')

At many tasks we humans toil
In boom times and depression
To keep the billy on the boil
And ward off repossession.
These jobs may range across the board
From cops to sausage stuffers,
While others gain unjust reward
As pimps and cattle duffers.

Some men grow rich by growing wool
On sheep they call merinos;
While others fleece you when you're full
In places called casinos.
The shearers shear the squatters' sheep
With widened combs and cutters,
The shearing board the rousies sweep,
While some sweep city gutters.

Some blokes maintain the Harbour Bridge,
The 'Salvos' feed the needy,
Some fellows gouge at Lightning Ridge
And some at Coober Pedy –
The barmen work behind the bar
And help to make life jolly,
While some, be–wigged, before the bar
Get rich on crime and folly.

The portrait painter paints in oils,
While call girls use cosmetics,
Some doctors specialise in boils
And some in anaesthetics.
While bakers toil at kneading dough
To get the dough they're needing,
Consultants thrive who say they know
Just why you're not succeeding.

Some battlers work and cop it sweet
In places Godforsaken,
While some resort to selling meat
In bringing home the 'bacon'.
The bookies live by laying odds
While fielding at the races,
While some survive who tempt the gods
By holding hidden aces.

The builders raise our buildings high,
The wreckers knock 'em over;
The politicians rave and cry
And live like pigs on clover.
Comedians grow fat on mirth,
While others fatten cattle,
The farmers joined with Mother Earth
In unrelenting battle.

By dark the crafty burglars creep,
When honest men are sleeping,
By wicked ways they earn their keep,
But not by wicket keeping.
Some yakka calls for craft and skill
While some needs only muscle;
The taxi drivers fill the till
In metered city bustle.

Some jobs I know would numb the mind,
A worker's patience straining,
But most accept the daily grind
And toil without complaining.
Here's my advice to those who whine,
'Just tell the boss to stow it
And try this flamin job of mine –
Become a starving poet.'

The Navvy on the Line
Anon

I'm a ringer I'm a dinger I'm a navvy on the line.
I get four-and-twenty-bob a week besides me overtime.
All the ladies love the navvies and the navvies love the fun,
There'll be lots of little navvies when the railway's done!

The Flying Gang
AB Paterson ('The Banjo')

I served my time, in the days gone by,
In the railway's clash and clang,
And I worked my way to the end, and I
Was the head of the 'Flying Gang'.
'Twas a chosen band that was kept at hand
In case of an urgent need,
Was it south or north we were started forth
And away at our utmost speed.
If word reached town that a bridge was down,
The imperious summons rang
'Come out with the pilot engine sharp,
And away with the flying gang.'

Then a piercing scream and a rush of steam
As the engine moved ahead,
With a measured beat by the slum and street
Of the busy town we fled,
By the uplands bright and the homesteads white,
With the rush of the western gale,
And the pilot swayed with the pace we made
As she rocked on the ringing rail.
And the country children clapped their hands
As the engine's echoes rang,
But their elders said, 'There is work ahead
When they send for the flying gang.'

Then across the miles of the saltbush plain
That gleamed with the morning dew,
Where the grasses waved like the ripening grain
The pilot engine flew,
A fiery rush in the open bush
Where the grade marks seemed to fly,
And the order sped on the wires ahead,
The pilot *must* go by.
The Governor's special must stand aside,
And the fast express go hang,
Let your orders be that the line is free
For the boys of the flying gang.

The Tram-Man

CJ Dennis

I'd like to be a Tram-man, and ride about all day,
Calling out, 'Fares, please!' in quite a 'ficious way,
With pockets full of pennies which I'd make the people pay.
But in the hottest days I'd take my tram down to the Bay;
And when I saw the nice cool sea I'd shout 'Hip, hip, hooray!'
But I wouldn't be a tram-man if . . .
I couldn't stop and play.
Would you?

The Line

JW Gordon (Jim Grahame)

Across a strip of pasture land, when washing day is fine
I sometimes watch my neighbour's wife hang garments on the line.
They billow out like sails of ships, old ships we used to know
Great counterpanes and pillow-slips and sheets as white as snow.

My neighbour's wife is plump and fair and she's a fruitful vine,
For one-year-old to twelve-year-old have something on the line.
There, father's shirt and baby's bib are waving fresh and clean;
And romper up to dungaree, with sizes in between.

The copper boils at eight o'clock, the tubs are full at nine;
And 'ere the whistle goes at twelve the clothes are on the line.
I see the hose of every shape flung out like nimble legs
Of dancers at a festival, all straining at the pegs.

The little trousers seem to try to run out into space,
And flay the air with hasty strides which easily outpace
The cotton tweeds, threadbare and patched, the kind that workmen
   don
While red-striped towels flick and crack to urge the sprinters on!

The Old Ute

Ross Noble

There's a cocky's old ute standing out in the street
With a sleepy dog chained to the tray
And a tangle of wire and an old diesel drum
And a great chunk of mouldy old hay.

With tyres half flat and bumpers all bent,
The sides have been gored by a bull.
There's rust in the tailgate, the bonnet and doors
And mudguards with mud are packed full.

In the cabin there'll be an old bottle of drench,
Some jumper leads, tow rope and chain,
A hammer and pliers, some old hayband too
And a dirty old coat for the rain.

Stuck under the seat you'll find a grease gun
(It hasn't seen daylight for years),
A knife and an axe and deep in the dirt
A machine for tagging cow's ears.

The owner will be in the Dalgety's store
Or standing around in the street
Talking of weather and lamb drops and such
And the prices of cattle and wheat.

Although the old ute standing out in the street
Certainly looks a bit rough
It's hardly surprising he won't trade it in,
The new utes aren't nearly as tough.

So he'll keep it no doubt until it's worn out,
And drive it until it is wrecked,
Then buy a new ute, all shiny and beaut,
And treat *it* with total neglect.

The Tool Shed
Graham Fredriksen

Ratchets and wrenches and vices on benches.
Shockies and shifters and levers and lifters.
Sanders and sockets and sprayguns and sprockets.
Chisels and chippers and grinders and grippers.
Staplers and stampers and cutters and clampers.
Hacksaws and hammers and routers and rammers.
There's no 'ifs' and 'buts' – this bloody old shed
Is driving me nuts so I'm bolting to bed – goodnight.

A Tribute to Firefighters
Max Fatchen

The roar of the gale and the fury; the dust that is rolling its cloud,
The smoke of the raging inferno will wrap all the day in its shroud,
With terrible conflict of gullies wherever the firefighter goes,
Unsung in his overalled armour, the battler with helmet and hose.

The throat that is dry as a sandpit; the eyes that are red as raw meat,
He goes with a wail of a siren and into the holocaust heat.
The Bush is a time bomb of terror, the tree is a fountain of fuel,
The wind is a torrid tormentor with temper that's fickle and cruel.

The radios harsh with their chatter (remember the training and
   drills),
The holding, withdrawing, regrouping to cover the tinder-dry hills,
And sadly there's wreckage and ruin, for dreams in the ashes will lie.
You can't save it all from disaster but, man, how you go in and try!

So when, on the blackened tomorrow, the engines are back in their
   yard,
For a spell from the heat and the heartbreak, the homes and the
   people they guard,
Though the waterbag's lukewarm and gritty, a toast we would like
   to propose
To the bloke in his overalled armour: the battler with helmet and
   hose.

Where the Dead Men Lie

Barcroft Boake ('Surcingle')

Out on the wastes of the Never-Never –
That's where the dead men lie!
There where the heat-waves dance for ever –
That's where the dead men lie!
That's where the Earth's loved sons are keeping
Endless tryst: not the west wind sweeping
Feverish pinions can wake their sleeping –
Out where the dead men lie!

Where brown Summer and Death have mated –
That's where the dead men lie!
Loving with fiery lust unsated –
That's were the dead men lie!
Out where the grinning skulls bleach whitely
Under the saltbush sparkling brightly;
Out where the wild dogs chorus nightly –
That's where the dead men lie!

Deep in the yellow, flowing river –
That's where the dead men lie!
Under the banks where the shadows quiver –
That's where the dead men lie!
Where the platypus twists and doubles,
Leaving a train of tiny bubbles;
Rid at last of their earthly troubles –
That's where the dead men lie!

East and backward pale faces turning –
That how the dead men lie!
Gaunt arms stretched with a voiceless yearning –
That how the dead men lie!
Oft in the fragrant hush of nooning
Hearing again their mother's crooning,
Wrapt for aye in a dreamful swooning –
That's how the dead men lie!

Only the hand of Night can free them –
That's when the dead men fly!
Only the frightened cattle see them –
See the dead men go by!
Cloven hoofs beating out one measure,
Bidding the stockmen know no leisure –
That's when the dead men take their pleasure!
That's when the dead men fly!

Ask, too, the never-sleeping drover:
He sees the dead pass by;
Hearing them call to their friends – the plover,
Hearing the dead men cry;
Seeing their faces stealing, stealing,
Hearing their laughter, pealing, pealing,
Watching their grey forms wheeling, wheeling
Round where the cattle lie!

Strangled by thirst and fierce privation –
That's how the dead men die!
Out on Moneygrub's farthest station –
That's how the dead men die!
Hard-faced greybeards, youngsters callow;
Some mounds cared for, some left fallow;
Some deep down, yet others shallow;
Some having but the sky.

Moneygrub, as he sips his claret,
Looks with complacent eye
Down at his watch-chain, eighteen carat –
There, in his club, hard by:
Recks not that every link is stamped with
Names of men whose limbs are cramped with
Too long lying in grave-mould, camped with
Death where the dead men lie.

The Ships That Won't Go Down

Henry Lawson

We hear a great commotion
'Bout the ship that comes to grief,
That founders in mid-ocean,
Or is driven on a reef;
Because it's cheap and brittle
A score of sinners drown.
But we hear but mighty little
Of the ships that won't go down.

Here's honour to the builders –
The builders of the past;
Here's honour to the builders
That builded ships to last;
Here's honour to the captain,
And honour to the crew;
Here's double-column headlines
To the ships that battle through.

They make a great sensation
About famous men that fail,
That sink a world of chances
In the city morgue or gaol,
Who drink, or blow their brains out,
Because of 'Fortune's frown'.
But we hear far too little
Of the men who won't go down.

The world is full of trouble,
And the world is full of wrong,
But the heart of man is noble,
And the heart of man is strong!
They say the sea sings dirges,
But I would say to you
That the wild wave's song's a paean
For the men that battle through.

Creatures and Creations
Ode to a Bandicoot

Australians don't have much of a track record when it comes to protecting and preserving this continent's unique wildlife. Conservation of our rare fauna has not been a great success story, and unfortunately the same is true of our poetic attempts to capture something of the spirit of our native beasts and birds. Good serious verse about our wildlife is quite rare, which does seem rather odd when our writers of traditional rhymed verse have written thousands of poems about Australia's landscape and flora.

We are better at being silly and fanciful about our animals. Using creatures as a starting point for nonsense verse and cautionary verse has been a very popular pursuit since the Victorian era, and you will notice the influence of British writers like Hilaire Belloc and Edward Lear in many of the verses that follow.

Domestic animals have been a more popular topic. The horse and dog have a special place in the hearts of most bush folk and it is no surprise that they feature quite regularly in our verse heritage. Cattle and sheep are mostly in the background as an essential part of rural life.

So, here is a rather odd collection of poems about creatures. Some are observations and reflections on nature, some take a sentimental or humorous look at our relationships with our domestic animals and four-legged workmates. The majority, however, are silly verses that use various creatures, real and imaginary, to amuse children or for some wry adult fun.

Ode to a Bandicoot
Wilbur G Howcroft

The bandicoot is mighty cute, he lives on nuts and stew,
On cricket bats and old straw hats and doughnuts dipped in glue.
He has no cares but sits and stares and does not fret at all
At woes of State, the stings of fate, or if his stocks should fall.

He often sings and flaps his wings and hums a merry tune,
Of scores repaid or conquests made beneath the midday moon.
He loves to prance some stately dance with flowers in his hair,
A plastic pail tied to his tail and both his elbows bare.

He builds a home of bark and chrome atop a burnt-out ridge;
He has a maid, who's never paid, and strong drink in the fridge.
So think of him when life grows grim, contrive to ape his ways,
And you will find great peace of mind with happy, carefree days.

Your Friend – The Insect
Grahame Watt

I'm just a little insect, be watchful and take care,
I have six legs and silky wings, I'm really rather rare.
You may not even see me as you dash around so quick,
I hide in shady places and I look just like a stick.
I feed on bits and pieces, I keep the bush so clean,
I pollinate the plants as I fly around – unseen.
So please! Oh please! Take care of me, don't swat or wildly spray.
For I am there, though out of sight, I'm working every day.
Remember that the insects were also made by God,
I'm very, very proud to be a tiny arthropod.

Look! A Koala!
Cole Turnley/Merron Cullum

There's much agitation, excitement and talk,
And manifestations of glee.
We've found a koala ensconced in the fork
Of a branch near the top of a tree!

Meanwhile, the koala ignores all the fuss.
He sits there, and sits there some more.
We gape up at him, and he glances at us.
Is it him, us, or each, who's a bore?

The Triantiwontigongolope

CJ Dennis

There's a very funny insect that you do not often spy,
And it isn't quite a spider, and it isn't quite a fly;
It is something like a beetle, and a little like a bee,
But nothing like a woolly grub that climbs upon a tree.
Its name is quite a hard one, but you'll learn it soon, I hope.
So, try:

Tri–
Tri–anti–wonti–
Triantiwontigongolope.

It lives on weeds and wattle-gum, and has a funny face;
Its appetite is hearty, and its manners a disgrace.
When first you come upon it, it will give you quite a scare,
But when you look for it again you find it isn't there.
And unless you call it softly it will stay away and mope.
So, try:

Tri–
Tri–anti–wonti–
Triantiwontigongolope.

It trembles if you tickle it or tread upon its toes;
It is not an early riser, but it has a snubbish nose
If you sneer at it, or scold it, it will scuttle off in shame,
But it purrs and purrs quite proudly if you call it by its name,
And offer it some sandwiches of sealing-wax and soap.
So, try:

Tri–
Tri–anti–wonti–
Triantiwontigongolope.

But of course you haven't seen it; and I truthfully confess
That I haven't seen it either, and I don't know its address.
For there isn't such an insect, though there really might have been
If the trees and grass were purple, and the sky was bottle-green.
It's just a little joke of mine, which you'll forgive, I hope.
Oh, try!

Tri!
Tri-anti-wonti-
Triantiwontigongolope.

The Crafty Crocodile

Wilbur G Howcroft

The crocodile is full of guile, he loves to perch in trees
And hypnotise the bugs and flies then eat them at his ease.
He leaps with glee from tree to tree and carols merrily –
His only care his falling hair, or else his 'housemaid's knee'.

He takes great pains each time it rains to keep from getting damp;
'Cos moisture shrinks his armour links and brings on painful
    cramp.
At close of day he slinks away (he's frightened of the dark),
He creeps inside some secret hide and blocks his ears with bark.

Come morning light he might invite some lady croc to dine
On bindi-eyes and crayfish pies washed down with gum-tree wine.
The crocodile will always smile and hug himself with glee
At folk who run from having fun – like maybe you and me?

The Echidna
Leon Gellert

The male echidna with its mate
Survives the most precarious state;
He rolls her, hair and spines and all
Into an eenzy-weenzy ball –
And buries her; and in this way
Provides against a rainy day.
But, like as not, this same echidna
Forgets just if, or where, he's hidna!

The Drover's Dream
Anon

One night, while travelling sheep, my companions were asleep,
And there was no star to 'luminate the sky,
I was dreaming I suppose, for my eyes were partly closed,
When a very strange procession passed me by.
First there came a kangaroo with a swag of blankets blue,
A dingo ran beside him as a mate,
They were travelling mighty fast and they shouted as they passed,
'We'll have to run along, it's getting late!'

Some frogs from out the swamp, where the atmosphere is damp,
Came bounding in and sat upon some stones,
They each unrolled their swags and produced, from little bags,
The violin, the banjo and the bones.
The goanna and the snake, with an adder, wide awake,
And an alligator, danced the 'Soldier's Joy'.
In a spreading silky-oak the jackass cracked a joke,
And a magpie sang 'The Wild Colonial Boy'.

A pelican and a crane came in from off the plain
To amuse the company with a highland fling,
And the dear old bandicoot played a tune upon his flute
While the koalas all sat round him in a ring.

The possum and the crow sang some songs of long ago
While the frill–neck lizard listened with a smile,
And an emu, standing near, with his claw up to his ear,
Said, 'The funniest thing I've heard in quite a while!'

Some brolgas darted out from the ti–tree all about
And performed a set of Lancers very well,
Then the parrot, green and blue, gave the orchestra the cue
To strike up 'The Old Log Cabin in the Dell'.
I was dreaming, I suppose, of these entertaining shows,
And it never crossed my mind I was asleep
Till the boss, beneath the cart, woke me up with quite a start,
Yelling, 'Dreamy! Where the hell are all the sheep?'

A Platypus's Predicament

Julie Murphy

Platypus Pauly is one tricky guy
He's a muddle of animals, and this is why
Look at his beak and you'd think him a duck
Ask if he's reptile, you'd be out of luck
Think him a mammal, he'd say, 'Of a kind.'
But he's not quite the sort that you'd have on your mind
His missus lays eggs just like a snake
But they're not like a bird's which are hard and can break
They're soft and leathery like grandma's skin
And each has a little round baby within.

He has webbed feet like a duck, only four,
And the best beaver's tail that you ever saw.
Swims like a fish, with great charm and flair,
But he's not a fish – he has to breathe air.
So, when you think of Pauly, you think of a mix
Not of one animal but something like six
Reptile and duck, and beaver and fish,
And probably others to add if you wish
Because Pauly is special – he's a monotreme
And I bet he's the strangest mammal you've seen.
He is a platypus, all said and done
He's just one animal – yes, only one.

from . . . Frogs in Chorus
AB Paterson ('The Banjo')

The chorus frogs in the big lagoon
Would sing their songs to the silvery moon.
Tenor singers were out of place,
For every frog was a double bass.
But never a human chorus yet
Could beat the accurate time they set.
The solo singer began the joke;
He sang, 'As long as I live I'll croak,
Croak, I'll croak,'
And the chorus followed him, 'Croak, croak, croak!'

The Rifle Bird
Leon Gellert

'Secretive' is perhaps the word
Best fitted to the rifle bird.
Its armaments to casual eyes
Seem lighter than its name implies.
Savants to whom we have appealed;
Assure us they are well concealed;
But records do not indicate a
Very happy wealth of data;
And scientists who've lain in wait
To watch it in its native state
Have not so much as caught an eyeful
Of the furtive creature's rifle.

The Yeti
Wilbur G Howcroft

The Yeti dwells for longish spells upon some high plateau;
He lives on moss and fairyfloss and lots and lots of snow.
A troglodyte, he's impolite and wears no clothes at all,
Except a hat when dancing at the Neanderthal Spring Ball.

His hair is lank, his gaze is blank – a most unlovely brute;
He is indeed an abject breed with manners dissolute.
Although he's crude and downright rude, I really must confess
He'd pass for my Aunt Bertha if he shaved and wore a dress.

Roger the Lodger
Bob Miller

Old Roger the Lodger lives down in my shed,
You have to be careful and watch where you tread.
You have to be wary and look upwards too,
He'll swing from the rafters and smile down at you.
He'll catch all the mice that run in the hay
Old Roger the Lodger sure earns his pay.
He climbs on the benches and slides on the shelves.
Can you guess why Roger is not like ourselves?

He's lived in my shed since long, long ago
And now he's grown up . . . three metres or so.
He has two big eyes and a check-coloured coat
Some white pointy teeth and a very long throat.
He swallows his lunch when he's out on a spree,
But he's nice to his friends . . . that means you and me.
He comes out each year in a shiny new skin
Can you guess why Roger wears such a big grin?

Old Roger the lodger has no legs or arms,
His uncles and aunts live on neighboring farms.
His Mum and his Dad moved away with no fuss,
They knew he'd be happy to live here with us.
He's calm and contented, he sleeps quite a lot,
And sometimes you'll wonder if he's there or not.
Did you guess he's a python who's not underfed?
And he's happy as Larry down there in my shed.

I Worry 'Bout the Penguin
Jim Haynes

The little fairy penguin who zooms about the ocean,
On terra firma travels with an awkward waddling motion.
From burrow to the open sea each day he must commute,
Hunting for his dinner in his little dinner suit.

When dinner's caught his only thought's to get home to his
    burrow,
Have a little sleep and do it all again tomorrow.
I worry 'bout the penguin and often wonder why,
He's a bird that swims just like a fish although he cannot fly.

The reason, I was told at school, is evolutionary.
(The emu can't fly either, nor can the cassowary).
But I worry 'bout the penguin, though I know he's brave and
    bold,
'Cos his burrow is quite draughty and the ocean's very cold.

It's a wonder little fairy penguins don't all get the flu,
Swimming in the cold and eating raw fish like they do.
So next time you have fish and chips or hamburgers for tea,
Think about the fairy penguin fishing out at sea.

The Mutton Bird
Leon Gellert

Only a greenhorn (or a glutton)
Would seek the mutton-bird for mutton.
For, be it known, he might as well
Pursue the bellbird for a bell;
Or (passing on from brute to brute)
Approach the fruitbat for some fruit;
Or (getting quite beyond control)
Track down the polecat for a pole;
Which goes to prove our nomenclature
Is not in strict accord with nature.

Brumby's Run

AB Paterson ('The Banjo')

It lies beyond the western pines
Towards the sinking sun,
And not a survey mark defines
The bounds of 'Brumby's Run'.

On odds and ends of mountain land
On tracks of range and rock,
Where no one else can make a stand,
Old Brumby rears his stock —

A wild, unhandled lot they are
Of every shape and breed,
They venture out 'neath moon and star
Along the flats to feed.

But when the dawn makes pink the sky
And steals along the plain,
The Brumby horses turn and fly
Towards the hills again.

The traveller by the mountain track
May hear their hoofbeats pass,
And catch a glimpse of brown and black,
Dim shadows on the grass.

The eager stock-horse pricks his ears
And lifts his head on high
In wild excitement when he hears
The Brumby mob go by.

Old Brumby asks no price or fee
O'er all his wide domains:
The man who yards his stock is free
To keep them for his pains.

So, off to scour the mountainside
With eager eyes aglow,
To strongholds where the wild mobs hide
The gully-rakers go.

A rush of horses through the trees,
A red shirt making play;
A sound of stockwhips on the breeze,
They vanish far away!

Ah, me! before our day is done
We long with bitter pain
To ride once more on Brumby's Run
And yard his mob again.

Envoi

Harry Morant ('The Breaker')
The Breaker's farewell to his favourite horse on his enlisting for the South African War

When the last rousing gallop is ended,
And the last post-and-rail has been jumped,
And a cracked neck that cannot be mended
Shall have under the yew-tree been dumped,
Just you leave him alone in God's acre,
And drink in wine, whisky or beer:
'May the saints up above send The Breaker
A horse like good old Cavalier.'

Leave Him in the Long Yard

Kelly Dixon

Well he's looking kind of jaded and his sight is not the best,
The hair around his muzzle's turning grey,
He has seen a hundred musters and I think it's only fair
That we leave him in the long yard here today.

He was broken in the sixties, maybe sixty-three or four,
Never faltered, always seemed to be on hand.
Never have I seen him beaten by a bullock in the bush,
And at night watch he was pick of all the land.

So leave him out there in the long yard, do not rush him,
Leave him out there with his mate the baldy bay.
Leave him there till after smoko, then we'll catch him,
We'll pull his tail and turn him out today.

He's entitled to some kindness in return for all he's been,
Now he's failing and his step is getting slow.
Let him squander his last summers by the river with his mate,
In the paddock where the sweetest grasses grow.

Stop and see him when you ride the river paddock,
Watch the old chap now his youth has slipped away,
And don't tell me when you have to use the rifle,
Let's have smoko, boys, then turn him out today.

Leave him out there in the long yard. Whoa! Don't rush him,
Leave him out there with his mate the baldy bay.
His old mate that he can laze and he can graze with,
We'll trim his feet and turn him out today.

The Story of Mongrel Grey

AB Paterson ('The Banjo')

This is the story the stockman told,
On the cattle camp, when the stars were bright;
The moon rose up like a globe of gold
And flooded the plain with her mellow light.
We watched the cattle till dawn of day
And he told me the story of Mongrel Grey.

'He was a knock-about station hack,
Spurred and walloped, and banged and beat;
Ridden all day with a sore on his back,
Left all night with nothing to eat.
That was a matter of everyday –
Common occurrence to Mongrel Grey.

'Pr'aps we'd have sold him, but someone heard
He was bred outback on a flooded run,
Where he learnt to swim like a water bird,
Midnight or midday were all as one.
In the flooded ground he could find his way,
Nothing could puzzle old Mongrel Grey.

''Tis a special gift that some horses learn,
When the floods are out they will splash along
In girth-deep water, and twist and turn
From hidden channel and billabong,
Never mistaking the road to go;
For a man may guess – but the horses *know*.

'I was camping out with my youngest son,
Bit of a nipper just learnt to speak,
In an empty hut on the lower run,
Shooting and fishing in Conroy's Creek.
The youngster toddled about all day,
And with our horses was Mongrel Grey.

'All of a sudden the flood came down
Fresh from the hills with the mountain rain,
Roaring and eddying, rank and brown,
Over the flats and across the plain.
Rising and falling – fall of night –
Nothing but water apppeared in sight!

''Tis a nasty place when the floods are out,
Even in daylight, for all around
Channels and billabongs twist about,
Stretching for miles in the flooded ground.
And to move was a hopeless thing to try
In the dark, with water just racing by.

'I had to try it. I heard a roar,
And the wind swept down with the blinding rain;
And the water rose till it reached the floor
Of our highest room, and 'twas very plain
The way the water was sweeping down
We must shift for the highlands at once, or drown.

'Off to the yard I splashed, and found
The horses shaking with cold and fright;
I led them down to the lower ground,
But never a yard would they swim that night!
They reared and snorted and turned away,
And none would face it but Mongrel Grey.

'I bound the child on the horse's back,
And we started off with a prayer to Heaven,
Through the rain and the wind and the pitchy black,
For I knew that the instinct God has given
To guide his creatures by night and day
Would lead the footsteps of Mongrel Grey.

'He struck deep water at once and swam,
I swam beside him and held his mane,
Till we touched the bank of the broken dam
In shallow water – then off again,
Swimming in darkness across the flood,
Rank with the smell of the drifting mud.

'He turned and twisted across and back,
Choosing the places to wade or swim,
Picking the safest and shortest track,
The pitchy darkness was clear to him.
Did he strike the crossing by sight or smell?
The Lord that led him alone could tell.

'He dodged the timber whene'er he could,
But the timber brought us to grief at last;
I was partly stunned by a log of wood,
That struck my head as it drifted past;
And I lost my grip of the brave old grey,
And in half a second he swept away.

'I reached a tree where I had to stay,
And did a 'perish' for two days hard;
And lived on water – but Mongrel Grey,
He walked right into the homestead yard
At dawn next morning, and grazed around,
With the child on top of him safe and sound.

'We keep him now for the wife to ride,
Nothing too good for him now, of course;
Never a whip on his fat old hide,
For she owes the child to that old grey horse.
And not old Tyson himself could pay
The purchase money of Mongrel Grey.

Acrobat Birds
Joseph Tishler ('Bellerive')

Acrobat birds of beauty and grace
Are tumbler pigeons, the wonder of space.
Attractive to view is their skyward flight
And aerial feats in the evening light.
In clusters they circle and cloudward ascend,
Tumble and prance and downward descend.
Acrobat birds of beauty and grace,
They tumble and float through boundless space.

The Lyre Bird
Charles Souter ('Dr Nil')

I live in the shades where the honey-bells grow.
I sing in the sunlight; I sleep in the snow,
My song is the wild wind that blows through the rain;
The note of the magpie; the croak of the crane:
The cry of the curlew, the hum of the quail,
And all the sweet sounds of the thicket and dale!

I walk in the shadows; I dance in the sun.
I play in the gloaming, when daylight is done.
I laugh like the kookoo and trill like the wren,
And mimic the music of maidens and men.

But if we should meet in the forest, alone,
Then hush! . . . and I'll sing you a song of my own!

Spider

Col Wilson ('Blue the Shearer')

Mr Tarantula Spider,
I'm watching you crawl up the wall.
Are you living high-rise?
Are you just after flies?
I'm terrified that you'll fall.
And Mr Tarantula Spider,
If you fall off the ceiling at night,
And land on the bed,
On the top of my head,
I know that I'll die, from sheer fright.

Mrs Tarantula Spider,
Says you look quite debonair.
But you're ugly as sin,
With your fly-eating grin,
And your body all covered with hair.
They say that you're perfectly harmless,
And that you do nothing but good.
But Tarantula, please,
I'd be far more at ease,
If you'd stay in the shed, where you should.

Mr Tarantula Spider,
I know spiders often get slain,
By ignorant men.
And they'll do it again,
So spider, please let me explain.
Now Mr Tarantula Spider.
I don't want to kill you stone dead,
But you're far more appealing,
Up there on the ceiling,
Than when you're down here, on my head.

The Spider from the Gwydir

Anon

By the sluggish River Gwydir lived a vicious redback spider,
He was just about as vicious as could be,
And the place that he was camped in was a rusty Jones's Jam tin,
In a paddock by the showground at Moree.

Near him lay a shearer snoozing, he'd been on the grog and
　　boozing
All the night and half the previous day,
And the 'kooking' of the kookas and the spruiking of the spruikers
Failed to wake him from the trance in which he lay.

Then a crafty looking spieler with a dainty little sheila
Came along collecting wood to make a fire.
Said the spieler, 'Here's a boozer, and he's gonna be a loser,
If he isn't you can christen me a liar!

'Stay here and keep nit honey, while I fan the mug for money,
And we'll have some little luxuries for tea.'
Said the sheila, 'Don't be silly! You go home and boil the billy,
You can safely leave this mug to little me.'

So she circled ever nearer till she reached the dopey shearer
With his pockets bulging, still asleep and snug,
But she never saw the spider that was creepin' up beside her,
'Cos her mind was on the money and the mug.

Now the spider needed dinner, he was daily growin' thinner
He'd been fasting and was empty as an urn,
As she eyed the bulging pocket, he darted like a rocket,
And he bit the spieler's sheila on the stern.

Well the sheila raced off squealin' and her dress began unpeelin'.
As she sprinted she was feelin' quite forlorn.
On the bite one hand was pressing while the other was undressing
And she reached the camp the same as she was born.

Now the shearer pale and haggard woke and back to town he
   staggered,
Where he caught the train and gave the booze a rest,
And he never knew that spider that was camped there by the
   Gwydir,
Had saved him sixty smackers of the best!

The Brolga's Laugh

Anon

Brolgas laugh and brolgas shout
The brolga's there when there's rain about;
If it's going to rain they're sure to know,
And then they'll laugh, 'Oh, oh! oh! oh!'
They laugh all night and they laugh all day,
If it's going to rain they'll laugh and play;
If they laugh in the night it's sure to rain,
And then they'll laugh and dance again.

They'll hatch their young in the pouring rain,
And then they'll laugh and laugh again.
If a drought comes on (which it's sure to do,
The swamps all dry and the herbage too)
They'll flap their wings and away they'll soar,
And the brolga's laugh we'll hear no more
Till the rain returns will its pattering glee,
And the brolga's laugh brings joy to me!

North-East by North
(Black Swans)
Charles Souter ('Dr Nil')

North-east by north, in an inky sky,
Five hundred feet o'erhead,
With steady stroke of wing they fly
To the land where they were bred.
The scent of the far-off billabong
And the gleam of the lignum brake
Come to them as they swing along,
Led by the old grey drake.

With flash of pearly underwing
And swish of rushing wind,
The reeling miles astern they fling
And leave the sea behind.
For well they know the summer's past
And there is a sense of pain,
The winter has returned at last!
The swamps are full again!

So two by two, in echelon,
With the old grey drake ahead,
All through the night they swing along
Until the east is red;
North-east by north, on tireless wing,
All through the glaring day –
And as they go, a chorus sing,
To cheer them on their way.

And as I lie awake at night
Upon my restless bed,
And hear the black swans in their flight
Five hundred feet o'erhead,
And listen to the old grey drake
Calling his cohort forth,
I would be flying in his wake,
North-east by north, half north!

from . . . Black Swans

AB Paterson ('The Banjo')

As I lie at rest in a patch of clover
In the western park when the day is done,
I watch as the wild black swans fly over
With their phalanx turned to the sinking sun;
And I hear the clang of their leader crying
To a lagging mate in the rearward flying,
And they fade away in the darkness dying,
Where the stars are mustering one by one.

Oh! Ye wild black swans, 'twere a world of wonder
For a while to join in your westward flight,
With the stars above and the dim earth under,
Through the cooling air of the glorious night.
As we swept along on our pinions winging,
We should catch the chime of a church-bell ringing,
Or the distant note of a torrent singing,
Or the far-off flash of a station light.

From the northern lakes with the reeds and rushes,
Where the hills are clothed with a purple haze,
Where the bell-birds chime and the songs of thrushes
Make music sweet in the jungle maze,
They will hold their course to the westward ever,
Till they reach the banks of the old grey river
Where the waters wash and the reed beds quiver
In the burning heat of the summer days.

In the silent park is a scent of clover,
And the distant roar of the town is dead,
And I hear once more as the swans fly over
Their far-off clamour from overhead.
They are flying west by their instinct guided,
And for man likewise is his fate decided,
And griefs apportioned and joys divided
By a mighty power with a purpose dread.

from . . . The Magpies' Song

Frank S Williamson

Oh, I love to be by Bindi, where the fragrant pastures are,
And the Tambo to his bosom takes the trembling Evening Star,
Just to hear the magpies warble in the blue gums on the hill,
When the frail green flower of twilight in the sky is lingering still,
Calling, calling, calling to the abdicating day;
Oh, they fill my heart with music as I loiter on my way.

Over the Moon

Les Ward

If a kangaroo lived on the moon,
Where gravity is weak,
He could, I guess, jump over a dune,
Or even a mountain peak!

If a cattle dog lived on the moon,
Where cattle never do,
He would, I guess, run over the dune,
And chase the kangaroo!

Fred's Job

Peg Vickers

Fred is doing vital work and has to stay for free
At all the finest tourist spots that others pay to see.
His job is checking cockatoos and other talking birds
Making sure they do not say obnoxious-sounding words.
He treats his work with earnestness and utter dedication
Sometimes staying several weeks at some unique location.
He has the patience of a saint, forever sitting there,
Waiting hours just in case a cocky starts to swear.
He censors birds throughout the land and puts his mind right to it
Though difficult may be the task – someone has to do it.

My Kelpie

Wilbur G Howcroft

Who barks and wags his tail with glee
And greets the new day joyously
Each morning as he welcomes me?
My kelpie

Who, with his head upon his paws,
Waits patiently while I'm indoors
And plainly shows who he adores?
My kelpie

Who sticks with me the whole day through
No matter what I say or do
And does most things I ask him to?
My kelpie

Who digs great holes in garden beds
And tears his sleeping mat to shreds
And never worries where he treads?
My kelpie

Who often whimpers in the night,
Perhaps through some canine foresight
Or nightmares of a long-past fight?
My kelpie

Who looks at me with faithful eyes
And never cheats and never lies
Nor puts me off with alibis?
My kelpie

Who is my mate — not just a pet —
A mere brown dog, perhaps, and yet
I know I never shall forget?
My kelpie.

The Mongrel

Grahame Watt

'Who owns the mong in the corner?'
The bloke at the bar loudly said,
'He's breathing his last breath I reckon,
That poor blessed dog looks near dead!

'And dogs aren't allowed, where I come from,
To frequent hotels in the town.
Who owns this excuse for a canine?
He'd be much better off if put down!'

A silence hung there for a minute,
Then a whiskery old drover spoke up.
'That's my dog young feller, he's my dog,
I've had him since he was a pup.

'You're right, he's old and decrepit,
Like me he has not long to go.
But that mong as you call him's my best friend,
And no better mate could you know.

'For me and that dog have enjoyed life.
We both talked a language the same.
We shared the hot days and water-bag thirst
As we worked at the mustering game.

'And that dog saved my life in the outback
When thrown from my horse, far away,
That dog ran for help and led the men back,
I owe him my life you could say.

'I reared him on scraps from my feed bag,
I taught him to fetch and to heel.
I'd say you're a stranger to these parts
Or you'd now just the way that I feel.

'Yes, he's old, and it's cruel now to see him,
No dog should have earned such a fate.
Last Friday I picked up my rifle,
But how could I shoot my best mate?

'I even asked that young vet bloke
"How much to give my dog rest?"
"Fifty dollars", he said, "Is the fee for the job."
But with money I've never been blessed.'

The stranger grew quiet at the story,
He glanced at the bar drinking crew
He said, 'Sorry old timer, I spoke out of turn,
I can see what that dog means to you.

'Here's fifty dollars to have him put down,
And you'll have to excuse me I fear,
I know it's hard to lose a good friend,
One so close, and so near.'

The stranger shook hands with the drover
And quickly departed the room.
A silence hung over the drinkers,
A sort of a sadness and gloom.

But then the old drover said, 'Spark up!'
Things aren't that bad, for you see,
That city bloke left fifty dollars
So now all the drinks are on me!

'Drink up you blokes, name your poison,
And drink to that mong – he's a swell!
If his owner were here, well, I'd kiss him,
And shout *him* a few drinks as well!'

The Koala
Leon Gellert

The native bear is small in stature
And specially endowed by nature
With means exclusively equipped
To live on leaves of eucalypt.
Its viscera, though doubtless clean,
Must needs be very, very green.
And therefore we reveal this fact
(told *sotto voce* and with tact)
It's uphill work to get koala
Stains off carpets in your parlour.

Cane Toad
Jim Haynes

Scientists will all attest
The cane toad is a noxious pest.
With eighteen poisons on his skin,
Ugly warts and wicked grin.
He gobbles up our native creatures
And, with his ugly toxic features,
Poisons those that try to eat him,
Let's hope that science can defeat him.

(Meanwhile, when on a Queensland road,
Please don't swerve to avoid a toad.)

The Gyrating Goose
Wilbur G Howcroft

I knew a goose, his name was Joe,
Who suffered bouts of vertigo
That threw his balance out of plumb
And wrecked his equilibrium.

At certain times the bird would reel,
Then rotate like a catherine wheel,
Or, rapidly and minus fault,
Proceed to double somersault.

Whenever he'd attempt to fly
And soar, light-hearted, in the sky,
He'd flap his wings, then get up pace
And, like as not, fall on his face.

At courting time 'twas sad to see
Joe's efforts with a chickadee,
For, though he'd turn on all his charm,
His antics merely caused alarm.

So, while he acted like a clown,
The female goose would turn him down
And leave poor Joe alone and blue
To seek another mate to woo.

Some hunting dogs one day, alack
(A ravening, bloodthirsty pack),
Attacked the geese and, shades of woe!
Slew every single one but Joe.

Our hero turned an ashen white
And started to gyrate in fright.
The pack drew back in fear and dread
Then downed their tails and promptly fled.

This story proves beyond all doubt,
It doesn't pay to moon about
Or stand flat-footed in the way
Of hunting dogs in search of prey.

Weary Will

AB Paterson ('The Banjo')

The strongest creature for his size
But least equipped for combat
That dwells beneath Australian skies
Is Weary Will the Wombat.

He digs his homestead underground,
He's neither shrewd nor clever;
For kangaroos can leap and bound
But wombats dig forever.

The boundary rider's netting fence
Excites his irritation;
It is to his untutored sense
His pet abomination.

And when to pass it he desires
Upon his task he'll centre
And dig a hole beneath the wires
Through which the dingoes enter.

And when to block the hole they strain
With logs and stones and rubble,
Bill Wombat digs it out again
Without the slightest trouble.

The boundary rider bows to fate,
Admits he's made a blunder,
And rigs a little swinging gate
To let Bill Wombat under.

So most contentedly he goes
Between his haunt and burrow;
He does the only thing he knows,
And does it very thorough.

The Dove
Leon Gellert

Outside my bedroom window pane
The doves are mating once again.
They bow, they bill, they flap, they flutter
From roof to rail, from gate to gutter.
They peck and preen and scratch and scatter,
Making the most infernal clatter –
A course of conduct opportune,
No doubt, for such a month as June.
And yet, I must confess I find
Such bedlam (to the temperate mind),
When emphasised without abatement,
Merely becomes an over-statement.

The Prince
Bobby Miller

I've moved into a brand new home, a rural bush retreat.
My lonely days are over now, my life is just complete.
See, this newly married couple have come to live with me,
I think he's dull and boring, but she's a doll, you see!
I watch her daily round the house, I watch her taking showers,
Last week her husband caught me and laughed for several hours.
He always tells me where to go and it's an uphill slog,
But there's no chance of moving me . . . 'cause I'm a green
    house-frog.

He throws me daily out the door and daily I am cursed,
But I always sneak back in again, 'cause I was in here first.
Why should I live out in the scrub and climb up in the trees?
Why should I boil on summer days or shiver in the breeze?
I always use me nicest grin when people come around,
And when they're watching movies, well, I never make a sound.
He says, 'We haven't got a goldfish, or a budgie or a dog,
So, get it through your big green head, we do not need a frog.'

She really gets so raging mad when I'm swimmin' in their loo.
I ask you what's so wrong with that? Its deep and cool and blue.
The other day she chucked a fit and screamed at him to come
When all I did was shyly place . . . me cold hand on her bum.
He threw me in the dam for that, just one more of his crimes!
I've seen him do the same darn thing a hundred other times!
I sometimes wish he'd move away and join some synagogue,
And then I'd have her to myself, the princess and the frog.

She must know I'm besotted by the way I smile and pout
But every time I jump on her, she nearly passes out.
So, I keep this lonely vigil by her bedside every night,
If only I could speak to her, I know she'd see the light,
'Cause I really am a royal frog, a prince in shiny green.
I sit for hours and dream of all the things that might have been.
I could change her life forever and our future would be bliss,
If only she would give to me . . . just one wet sloppy kiss.

What a Bore!
Anon

The old sow counted her litter,
They numbered near a score.
I swear I heard her murmur,
'Good Heavens! What a bore!'

The Day Aunt Aggie Bit Our Dog
Wilbur G Howcroft

The day Aunt Aggie bit our dog
Was one of woe and strife.
You see, it was a racing dog –
The great pride of our life.

Aunt Aggie had been acting queer,
We'd noticed little things . . .
Like perching in the henhouse in
The hope that she'd grow wings.

Then voices started telling her
She was the rightful queen,
And at our Royal Show that year
She bunged on quite a scene!

The household took it well enough,
Until she went too far
And bit our famous racing dog –
It left an awful scar!

'This has to end!' Grandfather growled,
And called on Cousin Keith.
'I'll stop the silly cow', he cried,
And up and pawned her teeth.

So now Aunt's quietened down a bit
(She thinks she is a log),
But all the same we watch her close –
And so, too, does our dog!

The Rabbit
Leon Gellert

The differential calculus
May be a simple thing to us,
But rabbits on the other hand
Have found it hard to understand.
Yet they can add and multiply
More rapidly than you and I,
An aptitude which, in the rabbit,
Comes less from sex-appeal than habit.

Mad Jack's Cockatoo
Anon

There's a man that went out in the floodtime and drought,
By the banks of the outer Barcoo,
And they called him Mad Jack 'cause the swag on his back
Was the perch for an old cockatoo.

By the towns near and far, in shed, shanty and bar
Came the yarns of Mad Jack and his bird,
And this tale I relate (it was told by a mate)
Is just one of the many I've heard.

Now Jack was a bloke who could drink, holy smoke,
He could swig twenty mugs to my ten,
And that old cockatoo, it could sink quite a few,
And it drank with the rest of the men.

One day when the heat was a thing hard to beat,
Mad Jack and his old cockatoo
Came in from the West – at the old Swagman's Rest
Jack ordered the schooners for two.

When these had gone down he forked out half a crown,
And they drank till the money was spent:
Then Jack pulled out a note from his old tattered coat
And between them they drank every cent.

Then the old cockatoo, it swore red, black and blue,
And it knocked all the mugs off the bar;
Then it flew through the air, and it pulled at the hair
Of a bloke who was drinking Three Star.

And it jerked out the pegs from the barrels and kegs,
Knocked the bottles all down from the shelf,
With a sound like a cheer it dived into the beer,
And it finished up drowning itself.

When at last Mad Jack woke from his sleep he ne'er spoke,
But he cried like a lost husband's wife,
And each quick falling tear made a flood with the beer,
And the men had to swim for their life.

Then Mad Jack he did drown; when the waters went down
He was lying there stiffened and blue,
And it's told far and wide that stretched out by his side
Was his track-mate – the old cockatoo.

At Sunrise
Max Fatchen

Across the silent paddock
There comes a cautious hare,
His ears, two pointed fingers,
To probe the frosty air.
And where the wheat is growing
He pauses in his run
Along the aisles of morning,
To breakfast with the sun.

My Dog
Jack Davis

You foolish creature charging in
To flop in my chair with your lop-sided grin,
You chew my shoes and eat my socks:
I'm sure your head is made of rocks.
I plant, you dig my flowers and lawn,
You bark when the roosters crow at dawn.
You chase the baker, you bit the rector,
But you seem to adore the bill-collector.
Chaos comes with you through the door –
You are a clown and not much more.

But when I sit by the fire at night
And the world is mostly sleeping,
My thoughts caught up in fancied flight,
Then gently you come creeping.
You sit and stare at me above you,
Your tongue-tip soft as a feather,
And I stretch my hand to prove I love you –
A man and his dog together.

SECTION NINE

Deployments and Dispatches

The Anzac on the Wall

It is well documented that war has played a large role in defining the Australian character and spirit. The Boer War gave us our first inkling that we were a people quite different from our British forebears; it also took from us, in highly controversial circumstances, one of our 'great' verse writers, Harry Morant.

World War I and the Anzac campaign were defining moments in our search for national identity. World War II provided another arena for Australians to explore national priorities, character and spirit.

Some of the poetry included here, ranging from soldiers' ditties and homesick songs to beautiful reflective and poignant verse, was written by actual combatants. Two of these whose verse I find particularly moving are Leon Gellert and Tip Kelaher.

Gellert was a Gallipoli survivor, and I feel we are lucky to have had a poet of his ability on the front line at Gallipoli, for nowhere is the absolute heartbreak of that campaign better expressed than in his verse.

The Tip Kelaher story is even more poignant. The impending doom that overshadows the yearning for the mundanity of home in his verse actually overtook him during the battle for Egypt. On 14 July 1942, he refused to leave his machine gun in the face of over-whelming enemy fire and was killed in action. Kelaher's verses thus have that extra dimension of pathos and heartbreaking irony reserved for poetry that comes to us direct from the field of conflict after the death of the poet.

As poetry is very often the literary form chosen to express our heightened emotional responses to life, and given that war is naturally a time when we are dealing with elemental questions, intense emotions and self-analysis, it isn't surprising that so much poetry is written in times of war. For the combatants themselves the sense of their own mortality and their separation from homeland and loved ones provide material for verse, as does the camaraderie of armed service and the inevitable need to ponder such issues as justice and the universality of human aspirations. For those left at home the uncertainty of life in times of war, both at a private and national level, also produces emotional outpourings and questionings in the form of poetry.

The Anzac on the Wall

Jim Brown

Loitering in a country town 'cos I had time to spare;
I went into an antique shop to see what was in there.
Bikes and pumps and kero lamps, the old shop had it all,
Then I was taken prisoner by the Anzac on the wall.

Such an honest open face, a young man in his prime,
When I looked at that photograph your eyes locked onto mine.
A face so proud and confident inside a wooden frame,
I felt myself drawn to you in a way I can't explain.

'That Anzac have a name?' I asked. The old man didn't know.
He said, 'Those who could have told me passed on long ago.'
The old man kept on talking and, according to his tale,
The photo was unwanted junk bought at a clearance sale.

'I asked around,' the old man said, 'but no one knew his face,
He's been up on that wall for years, deserves a better place.
Someone must have loved him, it seems a shame somehow.'
I nodded and said quietly, 'Oh well, I'll take him now.'

So you came home with me mate – too long you'd been alone
I don't even know your name mate, but you're welcome in my
    home.
Did you fight at Flanders, or perhaps Gallipoli?
I'll never know the answer, but I know you fought for me.

I wonder where they sent you mate, when you answered the call,
Were you killed in action? Did you come home at all?
You must have had a family – will you be claimed one day?
To be honest, I hope not mate – 'cos I'm proud to have you stay.

Sometimes visitors look at you and then they question me,
And I tell a little white lie and I claim you're family.
They say, 'You must be proud of him.' I tell them, one and all,
That that's why you've got pride of place – the Anzac on the wall.

To the Land I Love
Henry Lawson

Your wife and friends may desert you
And call you a ——— Rat,
All the wide world may reproach you;
But your Country will never do that.

You might lose all your faith in what's human
And hate for the present and past,
You may damn it all: Land, Man, and Woman;
But you'll fight for your country at last!

from . . . Devil-May-Care
JW Gordon (Jim Grahame)

Devil-may-care is on the march, with ever their heads held high;
Theirs is a mighty sacrifice, cheer loud as they're passing by!
Give them a cheer to remember, give them a rousing hand;
Strong and fit, and they'll do their bit, the bravest men in the land.

Shearer's cook and rouseabout, hard-bitten tough of the 'Loo,
Have cobbered up with a parson's son and a freckle-faced jackeroo.
Cream of a nation's manhood, pride of a people's heart,
A Devil-may-care battalion eager to play their part.

Son of a city banker, son of a city slum,
Son of the boundless bushland, keen and alert they come.
Shoulder to shoulder they're marching, hard as steel and as true,
Devil-may-care and reckless – and ready to die or do.

A rollicking hardcase legion – see how the blighters grin!
Those are the kind that are needed, those are the men who'll win.
Swinging to war like their fathers, wiry and ready and game
The Devil-may-cares are marching – on to their deathless fame.

from . . . Maxims of War

AB Paterson ('The Banjo')

Never be needlessly reckless – he who does this is a dunce –
Stopping a bullet is easy – but you don't stop 'em well more than
    once.

Finally never get jumpy – e'en though the fighting is hot!
Think of how often you're shot at – think of how seldom you're
    shot!

Before Action

Leon Gellert

We always had to do our work at night.
I wondered why we had to be so sly.
I wondered why we couldn't have our fight
Under the open sky.

I wondered why I always felt so cold.
I wondered why the orders seemed so slow,
So slow to come, so whisperingly told,
So whisperingly low.

I wondered if my packing-straps were tight,
And wondered why I wondered. Sound went wild . . .
An order came . . . I ran into the night
Wondering why I smiled.

Song of the Dardanelles

Henry Lawson

The wireless tells and the cable tells
How our boys behaved by the Dardanelles.
Some thought in their hearts, 'Will our boys make good?'
We knew them of old and we knew they would!
Knew they would –
Knew they would;
We were mates of old and we knew they would.

335

They laughed and they larked and they loved likewise,
For blood is warm under southern skies;
They knew not Pharaoh ('tis understood),
And they got into scrapes, as we knew they would.
Knew they would –
Knew they would;
And got into scrapes, as we knew they would.

They chafed in the dust of an old dead land
At the long months' drill in the scorching sand;
But they knew in their hearts it was for their good,
And they saw it through as we knew they would.
Knew they would –
Knew they would;
And they saw it through as we knew they would.

The coo-ee called through the Mena camp,
And an army roared like the ocean's tramp
On a gale-swept beach in her wildest mood,
Till the Pyramids shook as we knew they would.
Knew they would –
Knew they would;
(And the Sphinx woke up as we knew she would.)

They were shipped like sheep when the dawn was grey;
(But their officers knew that no lambs were they),
They squatted and perched where'er they could,
And they 'blanky-ed' for joy as we knew they would.
Knew they would –
Knew they would;
They 'blanky-ed' for joy as we knew they would.

The sea was hell and the shore was hell,
With mine, entanglement, shrapnel and shell,
But they stormed the heights as Australians should,
And they fought and they died as we knew they would.
Knew they would –
Knew they would;
They fought and they died as we knew they would.

From the southern hills and the city lanes,
From the sandwaste lone and the blacksoil plains;
The youngest and strongest of England's brood! –
They'll win for the south as we knew they would.
Knew they would –
Knew they would;
They'll win for the south as we knew they would.

In the Trench
Leon Gellert

Every night I sleep
And every night I dream
That I'm strolling with my sheep
By the old stream.

Every morn I wake,
And every morn I stand
And watch the shrapnel break
On the smashed land.

Some night I'll fall asleep
And will not wake at dawn.
I'll lie and feed my sheep
On a green lawn.

from . . . These Expeditions 1914–1924
JAR McKellar

Ten years ago I climbed a hill,
And there I climbed a tree,
So, through the mist and raining,
watched
The troopships go to sea.
A2 – A6 – the numbered list
Steamed out in plunging chain,
Till, hull down in the closing mist,
I lost them in the rain.

ANZACS

Edgar Wallace

The children unborn shall acclaim
The standard the Anzacs unfurled,
When they made Australasia's fame
The wonder and pride of the world.

Some of you got a V.C.,
Some 'the Gallipoli trot',
Some had a grave by the sea,
And all of you got it damned hot,
And I see you go limping through town
In the faded old hospital blue,
And driving abroad – lying down,
And Lord! but I wish I were you!

I envy you beggars I meet,
From the dirty old hats on your head
To the rusty old boots on your feet –
I envy you living or dead.
A knighthood is fine in its way,
A peerage gives splendour and fame,
But I'd rather have tacked any day
That word to the end of my name.

I'd count it the greatest reward
That ever a man could attain;
I'd sooner be 'Anzac' than 'lord',
I'd sooner be 'Anzac' than 'thane'.
Here's a bar to the medal you'll wear,
There's a word that will glitter and glow,
And an honour a king cannot share
When you're back in the cities you know.

The children unborn shall acclaim
The standard the Anzacs unfurled,
When they made Australasia's fame
The wonder and pride of the world.

The Dinkum Ten
AN Shuttleworth

Ten gallant sappers, marching in line
Along came a whizzbang and then there were nine;
Nine gallant sappers, digging in the mud,
One struck something – must've been a dud;
Eight gallant sappers looking for sport
Came on some ammonal – another sapper short;
Seven gallant sappers, shovels and picks,
Caught in barbed wire, and so there were six;
Six gallant sappers, too much alive,
Played with some 'Mills' bombs, and then there were five;
Five gallant sappers, tired and sore,
Picked up a microbe and so there were four;
Four gallant sappers got up to see
Over the parapet, then there were three;
Three gallant sappers, feeling so blue,
One drank the others' rum, then there were two;
Two gallant sappers, met with a Hun
Who turned out a sniper and so there was one;
One gallant sapper who sought souvenirs,
Found a Bosch mine, and – '*mafeesh Engineers*'.

Killed in Action
Harry McCann

Where the ranges throw their shadows long before the day's
    surrender,
Down a valley where a river used to tumble to the sea,
On a rising patch of level rest the men who dared to tender
Life and all its sweetness for their love o' liberty.

In a thousand miles of ugly scrubby waste and desolation,
Just that little space of level showing open to the sea;
Nothing here to lend it grandeur (sure, it needs no decoration)
Save those rows of wooden crosses keeping silent custody.

There's a band of quiet workers, artless lads who joked and chatted
Just this morning; now they're sullen and they keep their eyes away
From the blanket-hidden body, coat and shirt all blood-bespattered,
Lying motionless and waiting by the new-turned heap of clay.

There are records in the office – date of death and facts pertaining,
Showing name and rank and number and disposal of the kit –
More or less a business matter, and we have no time for feigning
More than momentary pity for the men who have been hit.

There's a patient mother gazing on her hopes so surely shattered
(Hopes and prayers she cherished bravely, seeking strength to hide
    her fear),
Boyhood's dreams and idle memories – things that never really
    mattered –
Lying buried where he's buried 'neath the stars all shining clear.

There's a young wife sorrow-stricken in her bitter first conception
Of that brief conclusive message, harsh fulfilment of her dread;
There are tiny lips repeating, with their childish imperception,
Simple words that bring her mem'ries from the boundaries of the
    dead.

Could the Turk have seen this picture when his trigger-finger
    rounded,
Would his sights have blurred a little had he heard that mother's
    prayer?
Could he know some things that she knew, might his hate have
    been confounded?
But he only saw his duty, and he did it, fighting fair.

Just a barren little surface where the grave mounds rise ungainly,
Monuments and tributes to the men who've done their share.
Pain and death, the fruits of battle, and the crosses tell it plainly,
Short and quick and silent suffering; would to God it ended there.

On Water Fatigue
George H Smith

I'd like to get the Hun who sends the little bits of shell
Which buzz around as wearily I top that blooming hill.
He only does his duty, but my only shirt I'd sell
For half a chance to give the cuss a non-return to Hell!

A Little Sprig of Wattle
AH Scott

My mother's letter came to-day,
And now my thoughts are far away,
For in between its pages lay
A little sprig of wattle.

'The old home now looks at its best,'
The message ran; 'the country's dressed
In spring's gay cloak, and I have pressed
A little sprig of wattle.'

I almost see that glimpse of spring:
The very air here seems to ring
With joyful notes of birds that sing
Among the sprigs of wattle.

The old home snug amidst the pines,
The trickling creek that twists and twines
Round tall gum roots and undermines,
Is all ablaze with wattle.

Search and Destroy
A Park

Whilst seated one day in my dug-out, weary and ill at ease,
I saw a gunner carefully scanning his sun-burnt knees;
I asked why he was searching and what he was looking for,
His only reply was a long-drawn sigh as he quietly killed one more.

from . . . Thoughts of Home

Rowley Clark

'Tis springtime now in the Goulburn Valley
And the wheat grows high in the distant Mallee,
And at Widgewa 'tis the lambing tally
And we're not there.

On the Clarence banks they're cutting the cane
On the Bowen Downs, time for milking again,
And the weights are out for the Spring campaign
And we're not there.

On the Diamantina the cattle are lowing,
At Narrabeen now the waratah's growing
Out on the Lachlan the billabong's flowing
And we're not there.

from . . . Arcadia

HE Shell

I've dwelt in many a town and shire from Cairns to Wangaratta;
I've dropped into the Brisbane Show and Bundaberg Regatta,
But now I've struck the ideal spot where pleasure never cloys,
Just list' to the advantages this choice retreat enjoys –

The scenery is glorious, the sunsets are cyclonic;
The atmoshpere's so full of iron, it acts as quite a tonic!
No parsons ever preach the Word or take up a collection;
While politicians don't exist, nor any by-election.

No scandal ever hovers here to sear our simple lives;
And married men are *always* true to absent, loving wives.
And should you doubt if there can be a spot which so excels,
Let me whisper – it is ANZAC! Anzac by the Dardanelles.

After the War

Sapper Cumine ('Kew')

When I am done with this blasted war I will go where the bul-bul
    sings,
And be at my ease under suitable trees discoursing on scandalous
    things.
I will buy me a mug that will hold a quart and fill it with foaming
    ale,
Which I'll frequently quaff while I loudly scoff at any heroic tale.

For men will tell how 'Abdul' ran and how our blood ran red,
But I will relate, in a thoughtful state, of how the general fed,
Of various tins I saw on the beach, asparagus, chicken and tongue;
How around his head in his beautiful bed immaculate net-work
    hung.

Oh, I will tell of the portly men in their dug-outs with soft settees,
Of bottles and corks I found on my walks by the graves of our
    brave O.C.s.
And I will laugh at their tales of war as I leer at my tankard's brim,
For my soul will find peace when the babblings cease and the
    clamour of war grows dim.

The Tenth

Charles Souter ('Dr Nil')

No drums were beat, no trumpets blared, the day they marched
    away;
Their wives and sweethearts watched them go, and none would bid
    them stay!
They heard their country calling them, and asked no second call,
The sacred voice of duty spoke; they answered, one and all.
Hats off to The Tenth!

Untried they faced the deadly hail of shrapnel, shot and shell!
Untried they stormed the fire-swept ridge where earth was
   changed to hell!
Was there a man whose courage failed, a boy who thought to
   flinch;
Did any soldier of The Tenth give ground a single inch?
Hats off to The Tenth!

Some of The Tenth are buried deep on ANZAC's lonely shore,
The womankind who watched them go will look on them no
   more.
But when you see the colours of the famous 'double-blue',
You know you're looking on a Man who served his country true!
Hats off to The Tenth!

In Picardy

Sgt Major Geddes

Have you seen them march to battle
In Picardy?
Heedless of the rifles' rattle,
In Picardy.
Have you seen them leaping, crashing,
(Muscles taut and good steel flashing)
Through the leaden Hell, and dashing
'Gainst the foe in Picardy?

Have you heard the great guns crashing
In Picardy?
Shrapnel hail the air a-lashing
In Picardy?
Have you seen the aircraft winging
Through the sky, and swiftly flinging
Devil's playthings, ever bringing
Hell and death in Picardy?

Have you heard the south wind calling,
In Picardy?
Have you seen the red leaves falling,
In Picardy?
Have you heard the elm trees sighing
Requiem for dead and dying
On the cold white earth low lying,
Anzacs slain in Picardy?

Have you seen the poppies waving
In Picardy?
Blood red poppies dew a'laving
In Picardy?
Have you seen them at the dawning
Droop their heads to make an awning
Guarding 'gainst the mists of morning
Anzac graves in Picardy?

Our Old Tin Hat

'Pip'

There's a helmet made of steel,
That they issue for our nut,
It is used from Picardy
To the fields of far-off Kut.

And its uses they are many;
It will cook some fine burgoo,
Or it makes a bonza dixie
For some soup or bully stew.

It's a bosker washin' basin –
If you put it on the fire,
Do not let the C.O. see you,
It will raise his bally ire.

As for doughnuts it is splendid
If you're cooking for a sub.
I've used it fill'd with whale oil
To give my feet a rub.

Oh, its uses will continue
When this bally war is o'er
You will see me with the kiddies
On the step behind the door,

Pointing out an old fern basket
With its rusted sides of red,
As Mum tells 'em – 'In the great fight
Daddy wore it on his head!'

Palestine and Poets

'Twenty Two'

Where the tracks are hard and dreary, the tracks are long and dry,
The tropic sun is beating down from out a cloudless sky;
There's naught to see but sand and now and then you'll see a
    clump
Of palm trees . . . it's no wonder that the camel's got the hump.

Never-ending sands that stretch to where the sky and land
Meet in a line of blue and brown . . . and poets say it's grand!
But poets stay at home in ease and travel not afar,
To where the way is lighted by a 'pale unwavering star'.

Poets never rise at dawn and feed a blinking horse,
And poets never eat our grub, plain bully-beef, of course.
They never scorch or swelter, at the desert never swear,
The reason why's not hard to find; they never have been there!

Now, when you hear the poet rave of 'vast encircling sands
Whose magnitude is circumscribed by cloudless azure bands
Of Heaven's vault', his poesy's imagination grows;
Just think of all these scorching sands . . . and bash him on the
    nose!

Battling Burberry Dinis
'Koolawarra'

He's not a noble-looking beast, though stout of hide and heart;
It's only fair to say at least he plays a gallant part.
He's never ill, ignores a hill, he trips the roughest roads,
And, strong of will, he carries still his mighty useful loads.

He's just a quiet quadruped we commandeered one day;
Once caught we soon disguised him from his tail unto his bray.
He's found where e're war's din is, so he's not for ridicule:
He's 'Battling Burberry Dinis' – our ammunition mule.

Memories
'Pip'

I am standing in the trenches with the mud up to my knees,
And I'm thinking of the bushland far away;
Where we used to gallop madly through the gum and wattle trees;
And the horse I used to ride – the dapple grey;
And the girl with eyes a-gleaming, way along the winding track,
And the stillness and the lonely mopoke's cry;
Oh, I'm longing for the bushland, and the sun, and my old shack,
And the girl I left behind in Gundagai.

Moving On
AB Paterson ('The Banjo')

In this war we're always moving, moving on;
When we make a friend another friend has gone;
Should a woman's kindly face
Make us welcome for a space,
Then it's boot and saddle boys, we're moving on.

In the hospitals they're moving, moving on;
They're here today, tomorrow they are gone;
When the bravest and the best
Of the boys you know 'go west',
Then you're choking down your tears and moving on.

The Reward
Anon

In after days some child with careless whim
Will gather flowers where now the dead are piled.
He will not know, this careless little child,
What thing it was made bright those flowers for him.

Future Conversation
Rowley Clark

'What did you do in the wartime Dad,
Before the big battle was won?'
'I suffered the greatest privation my lad,
I ate spuds in their jackets, my son!'

11.11.1918
JAR McKellar

They're bones in full battalions now,
The army underground,
And why should we cry out upon
The dwelling they have found?
Good company it is that they are keeping:
Rich earth below, and grass above them, creeping,
The soldiers, sleeping.

They fought, and luck was with them,
When a life was worth the giving.
Day follows day, till one shall find
Them younger than all living.
Good company it is that they are keeping:
I do not think that they would have you weeping,
The soldiers, sleeping.

Lost Youth

Bruce Simpson ('Lancewood')

Medals wink in the sunshine,
Ribbons weep in the rain,
The pipes and the drums are playing
A march from an old campaign,
While we moulder, the lost battalions
Of youth, where we long have lain.

We answered when England called us,
From the ends of the earth we came,
From the Empire's furthest outposts
Like moths to the candle's flame,
Grist for the war god's mill wheels,
Live pawns in a monstrous game.

We answered the call light hearted,
Our idyll was all too brief,
Death stormed our days like a tempest –
Death stalked our nights like a thief;
And our broken, bloodied faces
Stared blindly in disbelief.

We lie in the sands of Sinai,
Where we fought for the age old wells,
We stormed up the cliffs at Anzac
To die by the Dardanelles.
We fell in the mud at Flanders –
The worst of the manmade hells.

Like broken dolls on the wire,
We died by the Somme's dark flood,
As the guns ploughed the 'fields of glory'
To a matrix of man and mud –
Where each yard of the front was purchased
By madness and human blood.

Attrition the generals called it;
We learnt what attrition meant,
As down to the grave dark with us
Our dreams of the future went –
We had marched to hell in our boyhood
To die with our youth unspent.

We died for an English monarch,
For the sake of our 'British birth',
We perished that war might vanish
From the face of the tortured earth.
Then the 'war to end war' was over,
And the war gods rocked with mirth.

Medals wink in the sunshine,
Ribbons weep in the rain,
The pipes and the drums are playing
A march from an old campaign,
But we moulder, the lost battalions
Of youth, where we died in vain.

Song of a Sock

Anon

Found in a pair of socks sent to troops in France

Knitted in the tram-car,
Knitted in the street,
Knitted by the fireside,
Knitted in the heat;
Knitted in Australia
Where the wattle grows,
Sent to you in France dear,
Just to warm your toes.

Knitted by the seaside,
Knitted in the train,
Knitted in the sunshine,
Knitted in the rain.
Knitted here and knitted there
With the glad refrain,
'May the one who wears them
Come back to us again'.

The Return
Henry Lawson

And I watch the track on the red soil plain
To the east when the day is late,
For one who shall surely come back again,
In summer's heat or in winter's rain,
Limping under his swag in pain –
For a wounded Anzac mate.

The Digger Hat
Tip Kelaher

I've seen some lids in days gone by
From Bris to Dunedoo;
Top hats that strive to reach the sky,
And cloth caps round the 'Loo;
The sombrero and the stockman
That shade from Queensland suns,
The topi that is favourite
On many outback runs.

I have seen in busy roadways
All the fashions cities know –
The bowler and the pork-pie
With its crown so very low.
I have seen the swagman's relic,
The turban and the fez,
And all the hats that cut a style
From Sydney to Suez.

But there's a hat I'm wearing,
And I think it beats them all
From the Cape to San Francisco,
From Melbourne to Whitehall;
For it's been in many countries
And in each it did its share,
From the mud and slush of Flanders
To Sinai's heat and glare.

So I'm proud to wear my rabbit's fur
Although she's creased and worn,
And not so slick as polished caps
The Tommies' heads adorn;
For it has an air of Aussie,
Of 'Come and have a drink?'
The good old easy style that leads
To glory or 'the clink'.

It exudes the smell of gum leaves
From crown to sweaty band,
And often makes me homesick
In this Palestinian sand;
But it stands for right and manhood –
And who'd want more than that?
That's why, one day in '40,
I took the Digger hat!

Take Me Back to Dear Australia

Anon

Take me back to dear Australia,
Put me on the Melbourne train.
Take me over there, drop me anywhere:
Sydney, Brisbane, Adelaide, I don't care.
I wanna see my girl again,
Cuddle up with her again,
Aussie is the place to be.
Blighty is a failure, take me to Australia,
Aussie is the place for me.

from . . . Poor Bloody Private

Tip Kelaher

When you've humped a Vickers tripod
till it weighs a half a ton,
And your knees begin to buckle
and your sweat begins to run,
When you've carried belts of ammo
till you've paid for all your sins,
And you've stumbled in the darkness,
fallen down and barked your shins,
'Tis then, my lad, you know that you're a private!

When you've swept and scrubbed the cookhouse,
washed the dixies one by one,
Cut up bread and peeled potatoes
from the dawn till set of sun,
When your luck at two-up's lousy
and you view your meagre pay –
Well you don't get drunk too often
on that two-and-six a day!
Then you often wish you weren't a hard-up private!

Perhaps I shouldn't grizzle,
so I'll stop and dry my eyes,
For I've got some dinkum cobbers
who will always sympathise;
And the war can't last forever,
the tide has turned 'tis said;
When it's won we'll tell the C.S.M.
to go and bag his head,
And be glad that we were only bloody privates!

I Jus' Wanna Go Home
Anon

I jus' wanna go home, I jus' wanna go home,
Machine guns they rattle, Jack Johnsons they roar,
I don't wanna fight in this war anymore.
Take me over the sea, where the Fritzes cannot shoot at me,
Oh my, I don't wanna die, I jus' wanna go home.

One Big Ball
Anon

Hitler . . . has only one big ball,
Goering . . . has two but they are small,
Himmler . . . has something sim'lar,
But poor old Goebbels has no balls at all!

World War II Marching Song
Anon

There once was a farmer who lived by a school;
A simple young fellow who played with his
Toys in the shed with the lady next door
Which wasn't surprising 'cos she was a
Haughty kind of person; she'd sew and she'd knit,
While the boys in the farmyard were shovelling
Shavings and sawdust and bailing the herds
And carefully picking up freshly-dropped
Turtle dove eggs which they found on the grass
And gave to the lady to put in her
Artichoke tin which she kept on the shelf
Right next to the bench where she fingered her
Self-raising flour while making a crust
Till the young farmer came in and he licked her
Bowl and her spoons till it made him quite sick
And the lady got worried and she grabbed his
Dirty old coat which was covered in muck

And sent him back home without even a
Feed just in case his poor tummy got sore . . .
And that is the end 'cos there isn't no more.

Thirst in Exile

Tip Kelaher

I miss the Sydney bright lights, the city's friendly din,
I miss the Sydney beaches where the southern seas come in,
I miss the Sydney lasses, the parties and the rest,
The cricket and the football in the land I love the best.

I miss the western sunsets, the summer morning haze.
I miss the station horses and the old back country ways.
I miss the brindle cattle pup. I miss the poddy lamb.
I miss galahs all screeching just at sundown on the dam.

I miss the chestnut filly, I thought she'd have some pace,
And when the 'Picnics' came again be fit to win a race.
I miss the stony creek-beds, with water running clear,
But most of all in Egypt I miss Australian beer!

Thanks for the Letter, Captain

Jim Haynes

I've just read a captain's letter, written sixty years ago,
About a young bloke dying, a bloke I feel I know.
I know him from his writing, though he's years beyond my reach,
I know he loved the places I love – Randwick, Coogee Beach.
He was taught where later I'd be taught, played where I would play –
Rugby, on fields where boys play rugby still today.

Like me, he loved the Aussie poets, Banjo and the rest,
Like me, he loved the 'horsey' ones, like Ogilvie, the best,
He knew the north-west country, a place where I lived too,
So, I really feel I know him, and captain, thanks to you,
There's a moving record of his death, a brave attempt to try
To make sense of his sacrifice, in Egypt, one July.

'Tip Kelaher', your letter said, was 'popular with the chaps',
They 'idolised him' for his verse, you liked him too, perhaps.
'By the railway line at Tel el Eisa', enemy closing fast,
'He stayed by his gun and kept it in action till the last.'
'With no thought for himself . . . an inspiration,' so you said,
'A great loss to "A" company.' Tip Kelaher was dead.

I sometimes think about Tip, at Coogee in the sun,
I think about the things he did . . . and what he might have done,
Perhaps at Randwick racecourse, as the horses take the track,
Or when I read the verse he wrote, for that, at least, came back.
And I know I owe Tip something, as his memory grows dim,
For I still enjoy what Tip lost . . . when 'A' Company lost him.

Freighter

Tip Kelaher

Now the days were long and dismal,
Though the wildflowers blossomed bright
And Spring's warm sun made living glad for some.
There was plenty good tobacco,
But we felt the 'drought' at night,
When in our tents we'd smoke and yarn of home.

And the big, bare slopes seemed cheerless
With their camel bush and rocks,
And barley, golden in the morning light;
But a happy rumour's reached us,
Hailing from the Suez docks,
That has somehow changed life's prospects over-night.

For a freighter's berthed in Tewfik,
That has sailed from southern seas,
A-laden to the decks with cargo rare.
And each mulga mail's confirmed it,
Borne in on the southern breeze –
She's beat the Japs and anchored safely there.

No, she's not an ocean liner,
Just a rusty, battered tramp,
With a tired stoker leaning on the rail;
But she's heaved the green seas from her,
And we reckon she's a champ,
For she's brought a load of Aussie beer and *mail*!

The Infanteer

'A Gunner'

He is born to the earth; on the day he enlists
He is sentenced to life on the soil,
To march on it, crawl on it, dig in it, sprawl on it,
Sleep on it after his toil.

Be it sand, rock or ice, gravel, mud or red loam
He will fight on it bravely, will die,
And the crude little cross telling men of his loss
Will cry mutely to some foreign sky.

He's the tired-looking man in the untidy garb,
Weatherbeaten, footsore with fatigue,
But his spirit is strong as he marches along
With his burdens for league upon league.

He attacks in the face of a murderous fire,
Crawling forward, attacking through mud.
When he breaks through the lines, over wire and mines
On the point of his bayonet is blood.

Should you meet him, untidy, begrimed and fatigued,
Don't indulge in unwarranted mirth,
For the brave infanteer deserves more than your sneer,
He is truly the salt of the earth.

Mike – The Malaria Mo-Skeeter
'NX116478'

In tropical regions, there's 'mozzies' in legions
But none causes havoc completer
Than one little devil who's not on the level,
It's Mike, the Malaria Mo-skeeter.

With no foe or ally is Mike ever pally,
His aim is to be a world beater;
For Tojo and Aussie's the same to this mozzie,
To Mike, the Malaria Mo-skeeter.

The world's aviation has yet no creation
Like Mike in his striped single-seater,
Bad trouble is comin' when you hear the hummin'
Of Mike, the Malaria Mo-skeeter.

He sure is a glutton and he won't eat mutton –
No sir – nor is Mike a beefeater.
For Mike likes consumin' the blood of a human,
Does Mike, the Malaria Mo-skeeter.

So please heed my warning, at sundown or dawning,
Altho' you may dwell in a heater,
Just keep yourself covered, lest you be discovered
By Mike, the Malaria Mo-skeeter.

In time's smallest fraction you'll be out of action
If once he injects his saltpetre.
The world's greatest vermin is not Jap or German,
It's Mike, the Malaria Mo-skeeter.

To My Enemy
'N78508'

I cannot see you through the blinding sand,
I only hear your bullets whine and sing.
The day is ending and the night will bring
Us close together here in this strange land.
Each trained to kill and in each nervous hand
Strong tools of death, with striker, fuse and spring:
If we should meet to-night the steel will ring
And we may die before we understand.

But at the end when all our debts are paid,
Should we live on – being too strong to die;
When men grow weary of a lost crusade
And leave their lifeless cities to the sky –
There may be then some place where you and I
Can meet again – unarmed and unafraid.

A Returning Soldier Speaks
'NX9500'

I am coming back with a singing soul through the surge of the
    splendid sea,
Coming back to the land called home, and the love that used to be;
I am coming back through a flash of spray, through a conquered
    tempest's hum,
I am coming back, I am coming back – God! Do I want to come?

I have heard the shriek of the shrapnel speak to the dawn of a
    flaming day,
And a growling gun when the fight was won and the twilight
    flickered grey;
I have seen men die with their chins raised high and a curse that
    was half a prayer;
I have fought alone when a comrade's groan was tense on the
    blinding air.

I have tramped a road when a burning load was strapped to my
 aching back;
Through miles of mud that was streaked with blood, when my
 closing eyes turned black,
I have cried aloud to a heedless crowd of a God that they could
 not know;
And have knelt at night when the way was bright with a rocket's
 sullen glow.

I am going home through the whirling foam – home to her arms
 stretched wide;
I am going back to the beaten track and the sheltered fireside.
With gasping breath, I have sneered at death, and have mocked at a
 shell's swift whirr,
And safe again through the years of pain, I am going back – to her!

I am coming back with a singing soul through the surge of the
 splendid sea;
Coming back – but my singing soul will never quite be free;
For I have killed and my heart has thrilled to the call of the battle
 hum,
I am coming back to the used-to-be, but, God! Do I want to come?

Peace

'P484'

We seem to be sure about winning this war
It's winning the peace that's the worry.
We know that the last was a failure that passed
To die in a chaos of flurry.
When asked by the mites what we did in the fights,
Our boasting and tales never cease;
It's just as well they never face us and say,
'And what did you do in the peace?'
Would we wave it aside as it only applied
To parliaments, mayors and kings?
Or be honest and say, 'My child, in my day
I failed in responsible things.
I never could see that the world was just me

In thousands and thousands of men,
And that peace-terms were born in the things that I'd scorn
As being too trivial then.
What things? Oh, a shake of the hand for the sake
Of straightening quarrels and strikes,
And saying 'I'm wrong' to help things along,
For pride is the source of dislikes.'

When boosting this strife we've made ev'ry life
A servant to national claim,
And now ev'ry man must honestly plan
To make peace his personal aim
By facing his wife, his office, his life
From ill-feeling seeking release;
With an honest delight in setting things right,
Determined to hang on to peace.

Hidden Battlefields
'VX116298'

I came – as yet I knew not battle's roar –
To view the scenes of conflicts gone before,
And thought to find, throughout this rugged land,
Destruction, debris, death, on every hand.
But this I saw –

A climbing, twisting, trailing mass of vine,
Through foliage fresh and branches intertwined,
A living cloak of variegated green,
That covered o'er the sight of what had been,
And one thing more –

For here and there, like sentinels of Mars,
Stood stately palms, beheaded, thick with scars
Of bullet, bomb, and shell, and all the rest
Through which men fought and bled, yet stood the test
Of total war.

And then I pondered how we might repay
The sacrifice of men who passed this way,
And realised if we could somehow bring
To this sick, war-torn world those simple things
They struggled for –

The very right to work, the right to play,
To live and love and hope, the right to pray,
To keep secure the greatest of all joys –
The carefree laughter of their girls and boys;
They asked no more.

If we in times to come forsake our greed,
And grant, to rich and poor, to every creed,
Those rights, then all the toil, the fear, the pain
And death they suffered, shall not be in vain,
And they once more

Will rise in glory, and, like sentinels,
Stand quiet guard, while over hill and dell
The foliage fresh of peace will gently rest,
And men with freedom, love and hope be blest
For evermore.

The Dead Don't Care

Jack Sorensen

Oh sad, bewildered world: you have the reaping
Of that which you have sown throughout the years
And you have garnered all your hellish harvest
Of blood and tears.

There shall be spring clad days of dream contentment,
And halcyon nights that merge with hopeful dawn;
And there will come the solace of sad memories,
To those who mourn.

But you, and you, who gave yourselves to slaughter,
What matters it that other days be fair?
That ships of state, star-guided, find a haven?
The dead don't care.

Hellfire Pass

Jim Brown

I've just come back from Hellfire Pass, I'll never be the same,
Because now, you see, I understand how that place got its name.
A railway cutting hewn from rock, fire making light,
For men like dancing skeletons to toil both day and night.

'Death railway', men have called it, a railway built on blood,
Every sleeper cost a life, laid down in rock and mud.
Then came Dr Edward Dunlop, known as Weary to his men,
He hardly ever closed his eyes – he'd sleep just now and then.

How did you do it, Weary? How did you carry on?
To keep the hopes of men alive when all real hope was gone.
How many diggers did you save? Did you ever stop to ask?
While your weary hands kept working in the flames of Hellfire Pass.

Weary survived Hellfire Pass, and to his final breath,
Believed hate inside a heart was just another form of death.
So he started building bridges, he knew revenge must cease.
'There'll be no victory,' he said, 'without a lasting peace.'

It is no shame for men to cry – we all cry, weak or brave,
And Weary often shed a tear for those he couldn't save.
So he had it written in his will, 'There's just one thing I ask
Please place my ashes with the boys back there at Hellfire Pass.'

Weary – is that the River Kwai? or the Murray flowing fast?
Is that the Southern Cross, or the sparks from Hellfire Pass?
No more nightmares, Weary, now you rest in peace at last,
You're the saint who outshone Satan in the flames of Hellfire Pass.

The Memorial
Enid Derham

Its stones are set on the bleeding heart of sorrow,
The arms of despair about its feet are cast,
Glory and love may wither and be forgotten,
But grief is eternal – this with grief shall last.
When the house of the living is struck as a tent and folded,
When its hearth is buried beneath the dust of the years,
Gold in the sun and grey ghost pale in the starlight
This shall endure, a frozen fountain of tears.

SECTION TEN

Curses and Complaints
You Just Can't Win

Australians are always the first to accuse others of 'whingeing' and complaining. We claim to be easy-going and have an aversion to 'whingeing Poms' and 'whining wowsers'. We've all heard the jokes like, 'How do you know a 747 is full of Poms? The whining doesn't stop when the engines are turned off.' But we are pretty good whingers ourselves.

Of course every nationality likes to complain about others – even if the complaint is that the others complain too much! And 'us Aussies', like most human beings, are not slow to share our complaints and problems as soon as we begin to chat with friends and family. In other words, we all like a good whinge! Luckily, life's little difficulties and annoyances make good material for rhymed verse, so there are quite a few examples of creative complaining in our heritage of verse.

Curses, on the other hand, are perhaps something that Australians are not particularly creative about. Anglo-Celtic verse is full of wonderful creative curses, lovely things such as this one, used on being refused a drink at an inn:

> The whey-faced hag of a she in the inn over there
> Threw me out on my head for asking the loan of a pint of
>   beer.
> May she marry a ghost and bear him a kitten
> And may the high lord of creation permit it to get the
>   mange!

Unfortunately, Australians usually resort very quickly to the vulgar, the blasphemous and the quite blunt. Perhaps the most colourful Aussie curse in verse is the one that occurs at the end of 'The Bastard From The Bush', where the 'Leader of the Push' says to 'The Bastard':

May heaps of black misfortune soon tumble down on you.
May some poxy harlot dose you till your bollocks turn sky
    blue
May you take a swig of horse-piss, mistaking it for beer,
May the next push you impose on kick you out upon your
    ear.
May pangs of windy spasms throughout your bowels dart,
May you shit your bloody trousers every time you try to fart.
May itching piles torment you, may corns grow on your feet,
And crabs as big as spiders attack your balls a treat.
And when you're down-and-outed and a bleedin' bloody
    wreck . . .
May you fall back through your arse-hole and break your
    bloody neck!

While 'The Bastard From The Bush' is, of course, attributed to Henry Lawson, we can't be absolutely sure that the great Henry actually created the curse in that exact colourful form. 'The Bastard From The Bush' has been much adapted and added to in true oral tradition (the adjectives are changed at will for a start!). Still, I like to think that particular curse has a certain touch of class, something that perhaps shows the creativity and true genius of a writer of Lawson's calibre. It is certainly a wonderful example of the art of cursing.

Complaining and cursing are art forms sadly neglected today. Perhaps these examples will inspire a stylish and imaginative resurgence.

You Just Can't Win

Jim Haynes

Life's full of contradictions,
Understand you just can't win.
Go to church and you're a hypocrite,
Don't go . . . you live in sin.
Give to charity . . . you're showing off,
Don't give and you're a miser,
Use your brain and you're a smart-arse,
If you don't . . . you should be wiser.
If you're rich you must be crooked,
If you're poor then you're a loser.
Don't drink and you're a wowser,
If you do . . . a drunken boozer.
You're reserved . . . they call you 'surly',
Gregarious . . . 'a pest';
My advice? Do what comes naturally,
To hell with all the rest!

Why?

WT Goodge ('The Colonel')

The child is born, becomes a man,
Is wise or foolish, rich or poor:
In any case 'tis but a span,
And life is o'er!

Will some philosopher who can
Translate the writing on the wall
Of life, explain to us why man
Is born at all!

A Over Z

Grahame Watt

I'm sick and tired of being last in everything I do,
Sick of standing at the end of every flamin' queue.
For every time a list is made, compiled by each recorder,
It's always flamin' rostered in alphabetical order.

My name begins with 'W', so when a list is read,
The only ones behind me are 'X' and 'Y' and 'Z'.
Us poor coots are always last when we are itemised,
Just because we're 'W's we're being victimised.

Think of all that standing 'round waiting for our turn,
While 'A B C' and 'D E F' are off with time to burn.
Imagine back when time began if Adam had been Zane,
And the Apple a Zucchini – Eve still would wait in vain.

When Noah called the animals to board the Ark I bet
He used that age-old system, he used the Alphabet.
First he called the Aardvark, 'Would you step up the ramp?'
Meanwhile Willy Wombat was getting rather damp.

And if you're feeling sorry for the Wombat and the Yak.
Spare a thought for poor old Zebra, he'd be last, way out the back.
When God was handing brains out he started off with 'A',
He called, 'Aristotle, Archimedes, you get first choice today.'

Finishing the 'A's off God gave Music to the 'B's',
He called, 'Bach, Brahms, Beethoven, move up quickly please.'
By the time he got to 'W' the shelf was getting bare,
All he had was reject stock, there wasn't much to spare.

Good looks were at a premium, intellect bereft.
Us 'W's got all the bits the other blokes had left.
I reckon when my time is up and the final dice is cast,
I'll change my name to Aaron, then I won't be last.

I can hear St Peter saying in a saintly voice so nice,
'Please form a queue and wait awhile to enter Paradise.
I've changed the age old system, got a brand new one instead,
You can walk right through the Pearly Gate if your name begins
   with 'Z'!'

One Morning

Anon

I woke quite early one fine day, the earth lay cool and still.
And suddenly a tiny bird perched on my window sill,
He sang a song so lovely, a greeting to the day,
A song to make our earth-born troubles slip away.
He sang of far-off places, of laughter and of fun,
It seemed his very trilling brought up the morning sun.
I stirred beneath the covers, crept slowly out of bed,
Then gently shut the window and crushed his little head.
Somebody should have told him, given him a warning.
I'm not the kind of person who's real good in the morning . . .

My Mower

Col Wilson ('Blue the Shearer')

I have a motor lawn-mower,
An abortion of a thing,
And my hate for it increases,
With the coming of each spring.
When first I bought my mower,
The written guarantee,
Said that it would start first time,
With just one pull from me.

I fill it up with petrol,
Make sure I've turned the switch,
Move the throttle, check the choke,
And try to start the bitch.
I pull it once, I pull it twice,
I almost pull my guts out:
Success at last, it gives one cough,
A wheeze, and then it cuts out.

You wonder that I don't complain.
What would be the use?
They'd send an expert to the house.
He'd pick me for a goose.
He'd give one pull, and start it.
I'd lose again, you'd see,
In the never-ending battle,
Between machines and me.

My wife can start it – kids can, too.
The old girl down the street.
Everyone can start it,
But the bugger's got me beat.
I'm sure it sees me coming,
And decides to have some fun,
And though I pull, and pull, and pull,
I can't get it to run.

My family quite enjoys the show.
I know the neighbours do.
They like to see my face turn red,
And watch the air turn blue.
I can't reveal the brand name,
Of that wretched pain-inflictor
But here's a clue (you'll never guess)
It rhymes with 'boa constrictor'!

Spring is Here
Neil Carroll ('Hipshot')

Spring is here, the grass is riz,
I wonder where the flowers is
Time for plants, and time for seeds
Time for chippin' flamin' weeds!
Winter long the ground's been fallow
Except for clover and marshmallow.
Spring is here, and she's a goer,
Now try to start the bloody mower!

Housewife's Lament

Suzanne Wilkinson

The sink is piled high full of dishes
The rubbish bin's filled to the top
The basket is full in the laundry
The floor needs much more than a mop

The bread box is empty – ashtrays are full
You could all sign your names in the dust
The bathroom's a mess; the kids have missed school
(Slept in and were late for the bus!)

How can one family do this to a house?
Toys, clothes and papers all through it!
What does a housewife do all day long?
I decided today not to do it!

Hay and Hell and Booligal

AB Paterson ('The Banjo')

'You come and see me, boys,' he said;
'You'll find a welcome and a bed
And whisky any time you call;
Although our township hasn't got
The name of quite a lively spot –
You see, I live in Booligal.

'And people have an awful down
Upon the district and the town –
Which worse than hell itself they call;
In fact, the saying far and wide
Along the Riverina side
Is "Hay and Hell and Booligal".

'No doubt it suits 'em very well
To say it's worse than Hay or Hell,
But don't you heed their talk at all;
Of course, there's heat — no one denies —
And sand and dust and stacks of flies,
And rabbits, too, at Booligal.

'But such a pleasant, quiet place,
You never see a stranger's face —
They hardly ever care to call;
The drovers mostly pass it by;
They reckon that they'd rather die
Than spend a night in Booligal.

'The big mosquitoes frighten some —
You'll lie awake to hear 'em hum —
And snakes about the township crawl;
But shearers, when they get their cheque,
They never come along and wreck
The blessed town of Booligal.

'But down in Hay the shearers come
And fill themselves with fighting rum,
And chase blue devils up the wall,
And fight the snaggers every day,
Until there is the deuce to pay —
There's none of that in Booligal.

'Of course, there isn't much to see —
The billiard table used to be
The great attraction for us all,
Until some careless, drunken curs
Got sleeping on it in their spurs,
And ruined it, in Booligal.

'Just now there is a howling drought
That pretty near has starved us out —
It never seems to rain at all;
But, if there *should* come any rain,
You couldn't cross the black soil plain —
You'd have to stop in Booligal.'

'*We'd have to stop!*' With bated breath
We prayed that both in life and death
Our fate in other lines might fall:
'Oh, send us to our just reward
In Hay or Hell, but gracious Lord,
Deliver us from Booligal!'

Mallee Morning

Wilbur G Howcroft

Bright early in the mornin',
The dawn a-showin' red,
I levers up me eyelids
An' blunders outa bed.

I lights me up a gasper
Then moseys out ter see
What palpitatin' prospects
Fate has in store fer me.

There's maggots in the meat safe,
The rain tank's sprung a leak
An' damn me if the cart horse
Ain't bogged down in the creek.

Me old dog's got the staggers
An' whimpers as in pain,
The wheat crop's slowly dyin'
Through want o' ruddy rain.

The crows are at the chickens,
A water pipe 'as bust
While headin' hell fer leather
I spots a wall o' dust.

The sheep are in the haystack,
The milkin' cow is dead –
I shoves aside the missus
An' climbs back inter bed.

The Whingeing Gold Digger
Anon

'Well, it don't suit me,' said Tim, 'I'm sure;
That crowbar makes my hands too sore.
And miserably soaked, all day I've stood,
Rocking the cradle, knee-deep in mud.
Now mucking at cooking, and slushing all day;
Now delving through dirty rocks and clay.
Gold digger! Bah! It's all my eye,
And that you'll say, lads, by-and-by.
You're welcome to your golden joys,
Your duffs, and Johnny cakes, doughboys,
Your vile lobscouse and milkless teas,
Your endless bacon fry and cheese,
Your dreary nights and weary days,
Your bar'brous, semi-savage ways;
Farewell to all your toil and strife,
And welcome quiet, cleanly life.'

Mutton Toast
Anon

The Lord of Love look from above
Upon this leg of mutton,
It once was sweet and fit to eat.
But now, by God, it's rotten!

Make a Sporting Gesture
Max Fatchen

Before you leap in with a claim or complaint
You well might consider a little restraint,
Don't bully your colleagues or discord bequeath
But show some restraint or I'll kick in your teeth.

To picket's not cricket. Don't seek a new wage.
No stunting, confronting. Don't fly in a rage.
Don't storm or perform but depart with a shrug.
Don't grumble, don't fumble, and kick it, ya mug.

Watch feeding with breeding and check appetite.
Don't borrow tomorrow, the climate's not right.
No tension, dissention, it's such a disgrace.
These views don't abuse or I'll smash in your face.

Negotiate nothing, I'll counter your claims.
Your dreams and your schemes I will shoot down in flames.
I'll bounce you, denounce you until you grow faint
For all that we need is a bit of restraint!

Swagman's Prayer

'Veritas'

O Lord thou knowest but too well
The swagman's life is one long hell,
The rain thou dost from Heaven send
Has flooded every river bend,
The fish won't take the bait at all,
They eat their comrades if they're small.
My boots are heavy with blue clay,
I've knocked off quite a ton today.

I've got no work or even bread!
I've got no place to lay my head,
There are no empty huts around
Where lice and fleas and ticks abound.
I've got no 'bacca, Lord – or soap,
To wash my shirt there is no hope.
Though Thy son in a manger lay
He's better off than me, today.

Grass-seeds prick me in the leg,
As through the swampy ground I peg.
My matches they are soaking wet –
Another box I cannot get –
My drinking water's full of weeds,
My shirt a new tail sadly needs,
My limbs are stiff from humping bluey,
And one of them's a wee bit skewey.

These are but a few trials of mine,
To which, O Lord, thy ear incline.
Oh God! I trust I'll get a job
Or some poor devil I shall rob.
So stop the rain and stop the flood –
(Mosquitoes too, who suck my blood),
Lord, please hear a swagman's prayer
And make a note of it – up there.

Bachelor Blue
Wilbur G Howcroft

This washing up I must declare
Would even cause a saint to swear;
This endless wash of forks and knives
Could easily bring one out in hives.
Each time I wash and dry up too
My language makes the air turn blue.
Oh lackaday, Oh dreadful fate,
Good cripes I've smashed another plate!
This wash-up trough must surely be
A sink of deep iniquity!
The lowest job a man can do
Is clean a frying pan of stew.
All ye who never scoured a pot
Should surely not bemoan your lot;
You've never felt the sting of fate
Until you're forced to scrape a plate.
Instead of this parade of woes
I'd sooner break stones with my nose;

Or if you like, in place of that,
I'd much prefer to shear a cat.
Although the claim may sound bizarre,
I'd rather manicure a bear;
Or better still in lieu of these
I'd choose to work at robbing bees.
Day in, day out, there is no hope,
Good grief, I've lost the blanky soap!
This is the end, there is no doubt –
The ruddy plug has just come out!

The Shape I'm In

Anon

There's really nothing the matter with me,
I'm as healthy as I can be.
Tho' my pulse is weak, and my blood is thin,
I'm awfully well for the shape I'm in.

Sleep is denied me every night,
But every morning I'm quite all right.
I often get dizzy, my head seems to spin,
But I'm awfully well for the shape I'm in.

Here's the moral that should be told –
For you and me who are growing old,
It's better to say 'I'm fine,' and grin,
Than to let folk know the shape we're in.

A Stranger from Somewhere

Jack Moses

Did you ever strike a one-horse town,
A Stranger from Somewhere,
And note them quiz you up and down
As if you'd no right there?
You can read their thoughts, just like a book,
All written in their stare;
'Hullo!' they say, 'here's something crook,
A Stranger from Somewhere.'

I don't object to be on view,
But I tell you when I jaw –
If I find a blind with noses through
Or 'peep-oh' round the door.
They're justified in what they do.
I suppose they think it fair
To use their eyes to riddle you,
A Stranger from Somewhere.

The other day I struck a place
And found a barber's chair;
I told the man to shave my face
And slightly trim my hair.
'A stranger?' said the barber chap,
'I am,' I did declare.
Now that is how they start to tap
The Stranger from Somewhere.

'Do you plan a lengthy stay?'
I said I thought I would
Stay there until I went away,
If I didn't stop for good.
'D'you come for air or just for biz? –
Excuse me asking, sir.'
It's an awkward thing to be, it is,
A Stranger from Somewhere.

I did not care to here reveal
If I wanted 'biz' or air,
But on he went to pare and peel
Till identity was bare.
The barber's shop's a witness-box
(They ply the acid there)
They know the sort of sox are on
The Stranger from Somewhere.

Now, the women folks must feel it most,
They have more than eyes to meet.
There's slander at the corner-post,
And whispers on the street;

But the chump who brands you at a look –
I wonder would he care
If St Peter said, 'You must be crook,
You're a Stranger from Somewhere.'

On the Outer Barcoo
Anon

On the outer Barcoo they eat only nardoo
Jumbuck giblets and pigweed stew.
Fever, ague and scurvy plague you
But worst of the lot are the Barcoo rot
And the Bellyando spew!

Said Hanrahan
PJ Hartigan (John O'Brien)

'We'll all be rooned,' said Hanrahan,
In accents most forlorn,
Outside the church, ere Mass began,
One frosty Sunday morn.

The congregation stood about,
Coat-collars to the ears,
And talked of stock, and crops and drought,
As it had done for years,

'It's lookin' crook,' said Daniel Croke;
'Bedad, it's crook, me lad,
For never since the banks went broke
Has seasons been so bad.'

'It's dry, all right,' said young O'Neil,
With which astute remark
He squatted down upon his heel
And chewed a piece of bark.

And so around the chorus ran
'It's keepin' dry, no doubt.'
'We'll all be rooned,' said Hanrahan,
'Before the year is out.

'The crops are done; ye'll have your work
To save one bag of grain;
From here way out to Back-o'-Bourke
They're singin' out for rain.

'They're singin' out for rain,' he said,
'And all the tanks are dry.'
The congregation scratched its head,
And gazed around the sky.

'There won't be grass, in any case,
Enough to feed an ass;
There's not a blade on Casey's place
As I came down to Mass.'

'If rain don't come this month,' said Dan,
And cleared his throat to speak –
'We'll all be rooned,' said Hanrahan,
'If rain don't come this week.'

A heavy silence seemed to steal
On all at this remark;
And each man squatted on his heel,
And chewed a piece of bark.

'We want a inch of rain, we do,'
O'Neil observed at last;
But Croke maintained we wanted two
To put the danger past.

'If we don't get three inches, man,
Or four to break this drought,
We'll all be rooned,' said Hanrahan,
'Before the year is out.'

In God's good time down came the rain;
And all the afternoon
On iron roof and window-pane
It drummed a homely tune.

And through the night it pattered still,
And lightsome, gladsome elves
On dripping spout and window-sill
Kept talking to themselves.

It pelted, pelted all day long,
A-singing at its work,
Till every heart took up the song
Way out to Back-o'-Bourke.

And every creek a banker ran,
And dams filled overtop;
'We'll all be rooned,' said Hanrahan,
'If this rain doesn't stop.'

And stop it did, in God's good time;
And spring came in to fold
A mantle o'er the hills sublime
Of green and pink and gold.

And days went by on dancing feet,
With harvest-hopes immense,
And laughing eyes beheld the wheat
Nid-nodding o'er the fence.

And, oh, the smiles on every face,
As happy lad and lass
Through grass knee-deep on Casey's place
Went riding down to Mass.

While round the church in clothes genteel
Discoursed the men of mark,
And each man squatted on his heel,
And chewed his piece of bark.

'There'll be bush-fires for sure, me man,
There will, without a doubt;
We'll all be rooned,' said Hanrahan,
'Before the year is out.'

Please Refrain

Anon

Passengers should please refrain
From using toilets while the train
Is standing at the station for a while;
We encourage constipation
While the train is at the station
Or we'll have a nasty little pile!

Australian Bards and Bush Reviewers

Henry Lawson

While you use your best endeavour to immortalise in verse
The gambling and the drink which are your country's greatest
   curse,
While you glorify the bully and take the spieler's part –
You're a clever southern writer, scarce inferior to Bret Harte.

If you sing of waving grasses when the plains are dry as bricks,
And discover shining rivers where there's only mud and sticks;
If you picture 'mighty forests' where the mulga spoils the view –
You're superior to Kendall, and ahead of Gordon too.

If you swear there's not a country like the land that gave you birth,
And its sons are just the noblest and most glorious chaps on earth;
If in every girl a Venus your poetic eye discerns,
You are gracefully referred to as the 'young Australian Burns'.

But if you should find that bushmen – spite of all the poets say –
Are just common brother-sinners, and you're quite as good as they –
You're a drunkard, and a liar, and a cynic, and a sneak,
Your grammar's simply awful and your intellect is weak.

To the Provincial Reviewer Who Hated My Last Book

Jim Haynes

Rode some hobby-horses, didn't you,
In that nasty, negative review?
And missed the point of my collection,
'Twas not a scholarly selection.
Just good old doggerel to amuse,
The sort an average bloke might choose.

You'd have known that if . . . how shall I put it?
. . . You'd read the intro and understood it.
Why couldn't you just say, 'Look,
I wanted to read a different book.
For my pretentious tastes I need,
Books no one else would want to read.'

It's succesful, none eschewed it,
Four reprints after you reviewed it.
Please hate my next collection too!
I'd love to get thumbs down from you.
Don't hold back criticism . . . state it,
It'll be a hit if you'll just hate it.

The Waiter

George Wallace

'What'll you have?' asked the waiter,
Reflectively picking his nose.
'Two boiled eggs, you bastard,
You can't stick your fingers in those!'

from . . . The Wail of the Waiter

Marcus Clarke

'Toast and butter!' Eggs and coffee!'
'Waiter, mutton chops for four!'
'Flathead!' 'Ham!' 'Beef!' 'Where's the mustard?'
'Steak and onions!' 'Shut the door!'

'Bloater-paste!' 'Some *tender* steak, sir?'
'Here, confound you, where's my chop?'
'Waiter?' 'Yessir?' '*Waiter?*' 'Yessir?'
(Running till I'm fit to drop.)

'Irish stew!' 'Some pickled cabbage!'
'What, no beans?' 'Bring me some pork!'
'Soup, sir?' 'Yes, you grinning idiot!
Can I eat it with a fork?'

'Take care, waiter!' 'Beg your pardon.'
'Curse you, have you two left legs?'
'I asked for bread an hour ago, sir!'
'Now then, have you laid those eggs?'

'Sherry?' 'No, I called for *beer*!
Of all the fools I ever saw!'
'Waiter?' 'Yessir?' '*Waiter?*' 'Here sir!'
'Damn you, sir, this steak is *raw*!'

The Wicked, Wilful Wog

Wilbur G Howcroft

A much dreaded event which all bushfolk resent
Is that terrible scourge called the Wog.
This pernicious disease can quite suddenly seize
With a grip like a rabbiter's dog.

A tough drover out west was attacked by the pest
As he sat by his campfire one day.
On his quartpot he wrote this pathetic last note:
'I bin struck down – an' ain't drawn me pay!'

A poor cocky, it's said, was confined to his bed
When the pestilent bane laid him low.
For a fortnight or more he hung close to death's door,
As he sweated and tossed to and fro.

A kind neighbour, one day, who rode over the way
Was informed by their young son aged ten:
'Dad's much better, thank you, an' we think he'll pull through
'Cos he's startin' to swear once agen!'

An aged bagman outback was struck down on the track
And collapsed by his swag, like a log.
When discovered he sighed, and then plaintively cried:
'Gimme rum – I've bin bit by the Wog!'

An expatriate Greek was once swimming a creek
When the deadly germs started to gnaw,
With a heart-rending moan he sank like a stone –
But the virus all swam to the shore.

A prospector named Ned was discovered half-dead
From a fall in a high mountain chain.
He was taken, perforce, firmly tied on a horse,
To a hospital down on the plain.

For three weeks or so it was just touch and go
'Til his fevered mind burst through the fog.
Then he boastfully said to the nurse by his bed:
'This ain't nothin' – *I once 'ad the Wog!*'

from . . . Invalid

Frank Wilmot (Furnley Maurice)

Raid, raid, go away,
Dote cub back udtil I say.
That wote be for beddy a day.

Ad what's the good of sudlight dow,
When I ab kept id bed,
Ad rubbed and poulticed for to cure
The cold that's id by head?

Oh, what a log, log day it is!
I'be tired of blocks and books;
I'be cowted all the ceilig lides.
I've thought of sheep ad chooks.

Ad when is father cubbig obe?
He'd dot be log he said.
If this is just a cold it bust
Be awful to be dead!

Ad what's the good of sudlight dow,
Ad what's the good of raid,
Ad what's the good of eddythig,
When all your head's a paid?

Raid, raid, go away,
Ad dote cub back udtil I say.
Ad that wote be for beddy a day.

Tully

Anon

It rained and it rained and it rained and it rained,
The average fall was well maintained,
And, when the tracks were simply bogs,
It started raining cats and dogs.

Then, after a drought of almost an hour,
We had a most refreshing shower,
After which (the most curious thing of all)
A gentle rain began to fall.

The Tragedy

Henry Lawson

This was an advertisement for Heenzo cough syrup which Lawson wrote during World War I – it shows how good he was even when he wasn't trying.

Oh, I never felt so wretched, and things never looked so blue
Since the days I gulped the physic that my Granny used to brew;
For a friend in whom I trusted, entering my room last night,
Stole a bottleful of Heenzo from the desk whereon I write.

I am certain sure he did it (though he never would let on),
For all last week he had a cold and to-day his cough is gone;
Now I'm sick and sore and sorry, and I'm sad for friendship's sake
(It was better than the cough-cure that our Granny used to make).

Oh, he might have pinched my whisky, and he might have pinched
    my beer,
Or all the fame or money that I make while writing here –
Oh, he might have shook the blankets and I'd not have made a row,
If he'd only left my Heenzo . . . till the morning, anyhow.

So I've lost my faith in mateship, which was all I had to lose
Since I lost my faith in Russia and myself and got the blues;
And so trust turns to suspicion, and so friendship turns to hate,
Even Kaiser Bill would never pinch his Heenzo from a mate.

Wow, Sir!

Bartlett Adamson

The wowser is a mean pervert,
He has an evil eye.
He keeps his brain-pan full of dirt,
And murmurs, 'Let us pry.'

387

I'm a Tolerant Man

Anon

I don't mind blokes who digs or stokes,
Who fettle or work on derricks;
I can even stand a German band,
But I draw the line at clerics.

Why, strike me pink, I'd sooner drink
With a cove sent up for arson
Than a rain-beseeching, teaching, preaching,
Blanky, cranky parson.

Give me a blaspheming, scheming, screaming,
Barracking football garcon –
In preference to reverend gents,
Or a blithering, blathering parson!

Reflections

Glenny Palmer

I want another mirror,
The one I've got is broke.
I looked in it and what I saw,
Fair dinkum, was a joke.
I said, 'I'd be embarrassed
If I looked like her, because,
She's old and fat,' and when
I put my glasses on . . . I was!

Dilemma

John Bray

I have inherited eight chairs,
Straight-backed Victorian affairs,
Leather, stuffed with equine hairs,
Plucked from the manes of Arab mares,
In days of bustles, chignons, squares,
Disraeli bought the Suez shares,
Ladies in carriages and pairs
Drove to inspect the tradesmen's wares,
My grandmother purchased chairs.
Now they are slashed with rents and tears,
The springs stick out like Gorgons' hairs,
They are turned into risks and snares
To trap the sitters' derrieres
And hurl them groundwards unawares.
The cost to make needful repairs
Would, the upholsterer declares,
Suffice to pave the Golden Stairs,
Then last for sixty years, he swears.
Should I submit? What poet cares
To waste good money on old chairs
To pad the arses of his heirs?

No More Pencils

Anon

No more pencils no more books
No more teachers' dirty looks.
When I grow up I'll be a fool,
But at least that's better than going to school!

Foney It'd Rain
Jim Haynes

Foney it'd rain, foney it'd rain
We could stop hand-feedin', get some seed in,
Foney it'd rain.

Foney it'd rain, foney it'd rain
We could do some sowing, get things growin',
Foney it'd rain.

Foney it'd rain, foney it'd rain
We'd get a crop in, do some shoppin',
Foney it'd rain.

Bonfire
Anon

Build a great big bonfire with headmaster on the top,
Put the teachers underneath and burn the bloody lot!

The Baby
WT Goodge ('The Colonel')

When the baby's asleep there is calm,
When the baby's asleep!
And a peaceful unspeakable charm
Which is soothing and deep.
And the air has a beautiful balm,
Soft and sweet as the chant of a psalm,
When the baby's asleep there is calm,
When the baby's asleep!

When the baby's awake there's a storm,
When the baby's awake!
And he carries about in his form
A perennial ache!
And the smothered-up adjectives swarm
And the air is decidedly warm,
When the baby's awake there's a storm,
When the baby's awake!

Gippsland Farmer

Wilbur G Howcroft

Over the paddocks the wet wind blows,
I've bugs in me hair and a cold in me nose,
The rain comes spattering out of the sky;
I'm a Gippsland farmer – God knows why!

The cattle, hunched with their heads hung low
And tails tight-turned to the sleet and snow,
Sink steadily down as the days go by;
I'm a Gippsland farmer – God knows why!

The creek's gone mad and has spread so wide
I'll soon have to swim to go outside,
The dog's gone cranky and the cow's gone dry;
I'm a Gippsland farmer – God knows why!

The damp spreads over each stark grey stone,
Me wife's cleared out so I sleep alone.
Up with the bottle, 'Here's mud in your eye!'
I'm a Gippsland farmer – God knows why!

Tobacco

Anon

Tobacco is a noxious weed
'Twas the devil sowed the seed
It rots your teeth and stinks your clothes
And makes a chimney of your nose.

The Dog Poo Hits the Fan

Neil McArthur

When I walked out in my backyard, every single morn,
There'd be piles of dog poo, all around the lawn.
Why is it that a man like me, who doesn't own a dog,
Draws in all the neighbours' dogs to come and have a bog?
So, out there with the shovel, I'd scoop up all the crap,
And throw it over my back fence for the other chap,
The neighbour at the back who owns a big black labrador.
I figured that his dog must crap, he wouldn't mind some more.

This ritual went on for months, it seemed to make good sense,
Just scoop up all the dog poo and throw it 'cross the fence,
Every kind of dog poo, from poodle poop to logs,
Different kinds of different turds from different kinds of dogs.

Then one day while out walking I met my neighbour from the
    back,
We met out on the footpath and stopped to have a yack.
I asked him 'bout the family and how his garden grew,
I even asked about his dog, how it was going too.

'Funny thing you mention that,' he said, and glared at me,
(As if his mind was clicking to a probability)
'Our dog's been dead for several weeks and we all took it hard,
But his ghost still comes in every night and craps in our backyard!'

I'll Have Chips!

Jim Haynes

A sinister invasion has been going on for years,
A cultural takeover that's driving me to tears.
Australia's disappearin' beneath those neon signs,
And TV shows from overseas, let's draw the battle lines.

Do you wonder where you're livin' when you turn on your TV?
Do you wonder if they spell 'rap' music with a silent 'C'?
Do you wonder why Australia's less Australian every day?
Well, when they ask, 'Would you like fries?' Do you know what to say?

I'll have chips! . . . I'll have chips!
C'mon Aussies everywhere, retrain your minds and lips!
It's still Australia mate – not an American state!
When they ask if you want *'fries'*, say, 'No mate, *I'll have chips!*'

Australia's multicultural. as anyone can see,
But we didn't import this culture, they sent it COD
So if you'd rather be somebody's 'mate' than anybody's 'dude'.
Stand up for the right to name your own flamin' food.

I'll have chips, just say, 'I don't want fries today.'
C'mon Aussies everywhere, retrain your minds and lips!
It's still Australia, mate – not an American state!
When they ask if you want *'fries'*, say, 'No mate, *I'll have chips!*'

Throw that baseball cap away, c'mon, take a punt.
Wear an Aussie one, be daring, put your pointy bit out front.
Don't support a foreign team, support an Aussie one!
Show the world you know which way your bloody head fits on.

I'll have chips, of course, with good old tomato sauce!
Foreign stuff called 'ketchup' will never pass my lips!
It's still Australia mate – not an American state!
When they ask if you want *'fries'*, say 'No mate, *I'll have chips!*'

Smoke Gets in Your Eyes
Robert Webb

I was introduced to nicotine while still a boy at school,
Like other kids around my age I thought a drag was cool.
But I couldn't see through all the smoke the thing I'd most regret,
Being sucked in like the nicotine in that blasted cigarette
Now my breath it stinks, what's left of it, my lungs are browned off
    too,
But to keep a fag between my lips I'd spend my last razoo
I kid myself that all is well with the logic of a joker
But when I weigh nine stone how can I be a heavy smoker?

Council Worker's Lament
Val Read

We've got the worst job in the world and cop a lot of flack.
We work in sun and rain and hail yet people call us slack.
They say we stand around all day just leanin' on a pick,
What do they know? We earn our dough. They make me flamin'
    sick!
If it wasn't for us council blokes the roads'd be a mess,
We bear the scorn, the tooted horn, it's hell under duress.
We dig big holes and fill 'em up and put in roundabouts,
And when the planners change their mind we dig the darn things
    out.
They keep us in a state of stress and sorely underpaid,
That's why we have to meditate while leaning on our spade!

Tomato Sauce
Anon

No matter how you shake the bottle
First none'll come and then a lot'll.

One Day Cricket

Peter Fenton

Endless matches
Classic catches
Ring this number
Fight that slumber.

Coaches hyping
Cross bat swiping
Journos typing
Critics griping.

Streakers baring
All that's daring
Umpire glaring
No one caring.

Bored announcers
No more bouncers
This is cricket?
Take my ticket.

SECTION ELEVEN

Musings and Memories
The Old Tin Trunk

We all love to get out 'the old tin trunk' from time to time and explore our memories. It's a very common human activity and poetry in all cultures is largely occupied with memories, musings and reminiscences.

The subjects reflected upon in this section vary from the deeply philosophical to the banal. The titles range from such eloquent and 'poetic' phrases as 'Death Is But Death' to the prosaic 'When Your Pants Begin To Go'.

Some of the verse in here is poetry of the highest order, complex, poignant and challenging; touching on life's 'big' questions. Other verse here, like my sixties poem, is simply tongue-in-cheek nostalgic doggerel!

Some of the memories in the old tin trunk are fun, others are painful; some are light-hearted while others are heart-breaking. Some of the subjects are especially Australian, while others are universal. After all, our memorabilia often stretches back far beyond our 'Australianness' to other lands, other times and other lives.

The old tin trunk in the attic or basement is always a lucky dip. You never know what memories or emotions you may discover and stir into life when you lift the lid on the old tin trunk.

The Old Tin Trunk

JW Gordon (Jim Grahame)

'Twas deep in an old tin trunk we found them,
Things stacked away when our blood was red
(No silken ribbon it was that bound them,
But a twisted double of woolpack thread).
Old droving records and stock-route sketches;
The tanks were marked with a star beside;
Broad arrows pointed the long dry stretches
Where the unfenced pastures were wild and wide.

Relics of days that are gone forever;
Victoria's head on a gumless stamp;
A tattered map of the Never-Never
Brought memories racing of track and camp;
Of bright campfires with the billy swinging,
When our worldly wealth was the clothes we wore;
Of tracks we tramped when our hearts were singing
And light the burden of care we wore.

They took us back to old shanty dances
With girls who never had glimpsed the sea;
But there was guile in the luring glances
They flung at the men who were spending free.
We saw in fancy their flounces swinging
As the fiddle wailed like a thing in pain;
While doubtful story and tuneless singing
Came echoing out of the past again.

Beneath the litter we found a letter,
Its words and phrases long out of date –
The last lone link of a broken fetter –
That helped to steer us and keep us straight;
Mellow with age, it was rent and tattered –
We had carried it round for thirty years –
The ink was pale and the pages spattered
By water was it – or the splash of tears?

Prelude

AB Paterson ('The Banjo')

I have gathered these stories afar, in the wind and the rain,
In the land where the cattle camps are, on the edge of the plain.
On the overland routes to the west, when the watches were long,
I have fashioned in earnest and jest these fragments of song.

They are just the rude stories one hears in sadness and mirth,
The records of wandering years, and scant is their worth.
Though their merits indeed are but slight, I shall not repine,
If they give you one moment's delight, old comrades of mine.

The Muse of Australia

Henry Kendall

Where the pines with the eagles are nestled in rifts,
And the torrent leaps down to the surges,
I have followed her, clambering over the clifts,
By the chasms and moon-haunted verges.
I know she is fair as the angels are fair,
For have I not caught a faint glimpse of her there;
A glimpse of her face and her glittering hair,
And a hand with the Harp of Australia?
I never can reach you, to hear the sweet voice
So full with the music of fountains!
Oh! When will you meet with that soul of your choice,
Who will lead you down here from the mountains?
A lyre-bird lit on a shimmering space;
It dazzled mine eyes, and I turned from the place,
And wept in the dark for a glorious face,
And a hand with the Harp of Australia!

There Was a Song

Henry Lawson

There was a song – there was a song –
We seemed to hear it all day long:
I do not know the right or wrong –
But I know this: there was a song
In those old days when men were strong!

The Something that Never Comes

Henry Lawson

Away in the world of battle,
Or at home in our quiet homes,
We all grow weary of waiting
For something that never comes.

We find that fame is barren,
And that fortune weighs like lead,
That the faith we trusted is broken,
And the love we craved for dead.

Till we feel as we grow older,
And we long and suffer thus,
That in Heaven and not in this world
The something is waiting for us.

When the Seasons Come Again

Jack Moses

The west is looking green and grand,
The country's smiling sweet;
The cocky's stirring up the soil,
And showering in the wheat.
The squatter has his wool in,
God send the country rain! –
You can give us any government
When the seasons come again!

from . . . Song of the Future

AB Paterson ('The Banjo')

'Tis strange that in a land so strong.
So strong and bold in mighty youth,
We have no poet's voice of truth
To sing for us a wondrous song.

So may it be, and he who sings
In accents hopeful, clear, and strong,
The glories that the future brings,
Shall sing, indeed, a wondrous song.

from . . . After Many Years

Henry Kendall

The song that once I dreamed about, the tender, touching thing,
As radiant as the rose without the love of wind and wing –
The perfect verses to the tune of woodland music set,
As beautiful as afternoon, remain unwritten yet.

It is too late to write them now; the ancient fire is cold;
No ardent lights illume the brow as in the days of old.
I cannot dream the dream again; but, when the happy birds
Are singing in the sunny rain, I think I hear its words.

I think I hear the echo still of long forgotten tones,
When evening winds are on the hill and sunset fires the cones.
But only in the hours supreme with songs of land and sea,
The lyrics of the leaf and stream, this echo comes to me.

There is a river in the range I love to think about:
Perhaps the searching feet of change have never found it out.
Ah! oftentimes I used to look upon its banks and long
To steal the beauty of that brook and put it in a song.

Ah! let me hope that in that place the old familiar things,
To which I turn a wistful face, have never taken wings.
Let me retain the fancy still that, past the lordly range,
There always shines, in folds of hill, one spot secure from change!

No longer doth the earth reveal her gracious green and gold:
I sit where youth was once and feel that I am growing old.
The lustre from the face of things is wearing all away:
Like one who halts with tired wings, I rest and muse today.

But in the night, and when the rain the troubled torrent fills,
I often think I see again the river in the hills.
And when the day is very near, and birds are on the wing,
My spirit fancies it can hear the song I cannot sing.

Something Better

Henry Lawson

Tho' the workers' bitter struggle for a better state of things
May not touch the man in reach of all the joys that money brings.
There are times, and very often, when such joys begin to pall,
And his better nature rises in revolt against it all,
Stirring up the nobler manhood that is in him even now,
Like the hand of some pure woman on a dying blackguard's brow.

'Tis the hope of something better than the present or the past –
'Tis the wish for something better strong within us to the last –
Stronger still in dissipation – 'tis the longing to ascend –
'Tis the hope of something better that will save us in the end.

Give a man all earthly treasures – give him genuine love and pelf –
Yet at times he'll get disgusted with the world and with himself;
And at times there comes a vision to his conscience-stricken
    nights,
Of a land where 'Vice' is cleanly, of a land of pure delights;
And the better state of living which we sneer at as 'ideal',
Seems before him in the distance – very far, but very real.

'Tis the hope of something better than the present or the past –
'Tis the wish for something better – strong within us to the last.
'Tis the longing for redemption as our ruined souls descend;
'Tis the hope of something better that will save us in the end.

Native Names

John Dunmore Lang

I like the native names, as Parramatta,
And Illawarra, and Woolloomoloo;
Nandowra, Woogarora, Bulkomatta,
Tomah, Toongabbie, Mittagong, Meroo;
Buckobble, Cumleroy, and Coolangatta,
The Warragumby, Bargo, Burradoo;
Cookbundoon, Carrabaiga, Wingecarribee,
The Wollondilly, Yurumbon, Bungarribee.

I hate your Goulburn Downs and Goulburn Plains,
And Goulburn River and Goulburn Range,
And Mount Goulburn and Gouburn Vale! One's brains
Are turned with Goulburns! Vile scorbutic mange
For immortality! Had I the reins
Of government a fortnight, I would change
These Downing Street appellatives, and give
The country names that should deserve to live.

Stockman's September

Tip Kelaher

The horses' hooves will thunder on the cool, crisp morning air,
As they canter up towards the yard across the claypan bare,
And the kelpie's bark and clamour at the early day's delight
Will wake the laggard stockman and dispel the gloom of night.

There'll be yellow daisies blowing on the sand ridge once again;
There'll be wattle on the hillside and blue crow-foot on the plain;
And the river gums all mottled, with the sunlight streaming
    through,
And the high, rank, river grasses gleaming golden with the dew.

With the ringbarked flats all drowsy, sleeping through the warm,
    still noon,
Dame Time slips by unnoticed on her noiseless, velvet shoon,
Till the sheep come in to water, filing down the dusty track,
And the creeping shade gives notice that it's time for making back.

The flat below the homestead where the station horses pass,
Slowly feeding while the big bells tinkle music in the grass,
Is now dotted with the 'hoppers' who have lately found the need
To come in from the scrub to flog the frontage of its feed.

There are fleecy white clouds drifting behind the belts of pine
And the ragged mulga ridges in a land that once was mine,
And fired with gold and crimson are the topmost boughs aglow
With the last rays of the setting sun that seems so loth to go.

So, the warmth of olden friendship in the blaze of campfire light
Is reaching out across the seas to touch my heart tonight;
And ere the paper daisies spread two carpets on the plain
God grant I'll spur the old bay horse to wheel the lead again!

Stars in the Sea

Roderic Quinn

I took a boat on a starry night
And went for a row on the water,
And she danced like a child on a wake of light
And bowed where the ripples caught her.

I vowed, as I rowed on the velvet blue
Through the night and the starry splendour,
To woo and sue a maiden I knew
Till she bent to my pleadings tender.

My painted boat she was light and glad
And gladder my heart with wishing,
And I came in time to a little lad
Who stood on the rocks a-fishing.

I said 'Ahoy!' and he said 'Ahoy!'
And I asked how the fish were biting;
'And what are you trying to catch, my boy,
Bream, silver and red – or whiting?'

'Neither,' he answered, 'the seaweed mars
My line, and the sharp shells sunder:
I am trying my luck with those great big stars
Down there in the round skies under.'

'Good-bye!' from him, and 'Good-bye!' from me,
And never a laugh came after;
So many go fishing for stars in the sea
That it's hardly a subject for laughter.

When the Visitors Go
Henry Lawson

When the house is full – and it holds a score –
And you've known them all for a week or more;
And the last day comes and they crowd the hall,
With babies and baskets and rugs and all.

When the time is close, and the train is near,
And startlingly shrill the whistle you hear,
When 'good–byes' are said and handkerchiefs wave,
The house is as dead as a bushman's grave.

With a sinking feeling you can't resist
You go outside and see in the mist
Through something nearly akin to tears –
The hurrying ghosts of the vanished years.

Friends
JAR McKellar

O! I'll not want to be alive
When all my friends are dead,
For a man's heart dies the day they die,
Kneels at his own death bed.
None to receive – that's the end of giving.
No one to come at call.
O! I'm not wanting to be living
With the last one under wall.

A-Roving

Victor Daley ('Creeve Roe')

When the sap runs up the tree,
And the vine runs o'er the wall,
When the blossom draws the bee,
From the forest comes a call,
Wild, and clear, and sweet, and strange,
Many-tongued and murmuring
Like the river in the range –
'Tis the joyous voice of Spring!

On the boles of grey, old trees,
See the flying sunbeams play
Mystic, soundless melodies –
A fantastic march and gay;
But the young leaves hear them – hark
How they rustle, every one! –
And the sap beneath the bark
Hearing, leaps to meet the sun.

Oh, the world is wondrous fair
When the tide of life's at flood!
There is magic in the air,
There is music in the blood;
And a glamour draws us on
To the distance, rainbow-spanned,
And the road we tread upon
Is the road to Fairyland.

Lo! the elders hear the sweet
Voice, and know the wondrous song;
And their ancient pulses beat
To a tune forgotten long;
And they talk in whispers low,
With a smile and with a sigh,
Of the years of long ago,
And the roving days gone by.

Wattle

Jack Moses

The wattle is our native gem;
I love its flower, leaf and stem.
If bird and bee sip honey there
Why should I not the wattle wear?

It is the emblem of our land;
The seed was sown by God's own hand.
He put the scent and sunshine there;
Why should you not the wattle wear?

Joy is with us every hour
When spring brings forth our golden flower,
Sent to drive away our care,
Sent for you and me to wear.

from . . . A Dedication

Adam Lindsay Gordon

They are rhymes rudely strung with intent less of sound than of
    words,
In lands where bright blossoms are scentless and songless bright
    birds;
In the spring, when the wattle gold trembles 'twixt shadow and
    shine,
Where each dew-laden air draught resembles a long draught of
    wine;
When the sky-line's blue burnished resistance
Makes deeper the dreamiest distance,
Some song in all hearts hath existence – such songs have been
    mine.

A Refutation

Henry Lawson

Of course we've all heard the relentless,
And British-born words:
'The land where bright flowers are scentless,
And songless bright birds.'
But there ne'er was enclosed in a bottle
Of cut glass, nor sung to a king,
A scent like the scent of the wattle,
Or a song like the bellbird can sing.

Mullock Gold

Quendryth Young

There might be gold in that mullock heap,
But then – you never know!
They had wielded their picks as their limbs grew sore
They then dug the dirt till their hands rubbed raw
For their hopes were pinned on that golden ore
But they scarcely got a show.

There might be treasure the eye can't see
But then – you never know!
There's an old man lives in a crevice deep,
And his skin is cracked and his clothes are cheap,
And he makes me think of a mullock heap
For his heart is gold below.

What wealth may lie in that crumbled shack
But then – you never know!
It was at rest in a cooling day
After gruelling hours with the barren clay
As a well-fed man with his woman lay
In a joyful afterglow.

An ugly sight is the old iron tank,
But then – you never know
How the family prized every precious drop
As they drank or washed or they planted crop;
Then the rain arrived and it didn't stop
Until filled to overflow.

A hollow ring from the fruitless shaft,
But then – you never know;
For the open shaft by the mullock hill
Has a tragic past and there's danger still,
But its gold once paid off a massive bill
So a dynasty could grow.

There might be gold in that mullock heap
Though it's left a trail of woe.
It has broken dreams, it has broken backs,
It has broken homes in those lonely shacks
Till the heart breaks too and the spirit cracks.
But then – you never know.

I Danced Before I Had Two Feet

Max Dunn

I danced before I had two feet
And sang before I had a tongue;
I laughed before I had two eyes
And loved before my heart was young.

I swam before I had two hands
And held the distance in my toes
Before I heard the stars or knew
The wild compulsion of the rose.

I bore the fruit of many lives
Before I came into this day;
I knew before my grave was made
The worms eat only death away.

Succession

Mary Fullerton ('E')

Winter must march, the almanac
Had ordered her begone,
And so to go a step with her
I put my stout shoes on.
I mittened well my chilly hands –
Not then so very chill,
But she would take them both in hers
At parting on the hill.

Lo! as we went a soft blue breeze
With wings of yellow silk,
Ran kissing all the ground, and left
A scent of mead and milk,
And set a million hands a-wave
To her that must begone,
With whom to walk a little way
I'd put my stout shoes on.

I turned to cry my large delight,
But she was vanishing
Upon the distant hill, and I
Was deep involved in spring.

We Came – The Pioneers

George Wright

We came – the pioneers. Fence after fence
Narrow'd the limits of the black man's home.
He saw all vain would be his best defence;
And, scowling, watch'd the living tide roll on.
The Anglo-Saxon wave that drove him back
Mile after mile, till on the foeman's track
He found – a grave – ('tis all we left the black).

The Road to Old Man's Town

AB Paterson ('The Banjo')

The fields of youth are filled with flowers,
The wine of youth is strong:
What need have we to count the hours?
The summer days are long.

But soon we find to our dismay
That we are drifting down
The barren slopes that fall away
Towards the foothills grim and grey
That lead to Old Man's Town.

And marching with us on the track
Full many friends we find:
We see them looking sadly back
For those that dropped behind.

But God forbid a fate so dread –
Alone to travel down
The dreary road we all must tread,
With faltering steps and whitening head,
The road to Old Man's Town.

Get-Up-and-Go

Anon

Many a time has the poet sung
That youth is wasted on the young.
How did I know that my youth was spent?
Well, my 'get-up-and-go' got up and went.
But I really don't mind when I think with a grin,
Of the places my 'get-up-and-go' has bin.

Old age is golden I've heard it said,
But sometimes I wonder as I go to bed,
With my ears in the drawer, my teeth in a cup,
And my eyes on the table until I wake up.
As sleep overtakes me, I ask myself,
'Is there anything else I can leave on the shelf?'

I have arthritis in both my knees,
When I walk or talk, I puff and wheeze.
Still, I get up each morning, dust off my wits,
Pick up the paper and read the Obits,
If my name isn't there I know I'm not dead,
So I have a good breakfast and go back to bed.

The Greying of My Hair

Henry Lawson

Oh! the world is very shifty
In every land and clime –
We were dark-haired men of fifty
In my father's father's time;
And in vain I seek to borrow
Comfort – for they too had care;
I can only gaze in sorrow
At the greying of my hair.

I have not been over naughty,
And I've not been over good,
But a grey-haired man of forty
My tribe never understood.
I took no heed of the morrow,
I was brave to do and dare –
So I gaze in pride and sorrow
At the greying of my hair.

Growing Old
JW Gordon (Jim Grahame)

I think the world seems kinder since I've laid aside ambition
And have given over following old hopes that were in vain.
Now peace and calm and comfort seem the natural condition
As I rise to greet the morning without thought of loss or gain.
It's grand to have that feeling that there is no need to hurry,
As I watch keen youth and vigour chasing name and fame or gold,
When I'm sure their phantom ideals are unworthy of the worry,
While I take the way that's easy and I'm glad I'm growing old.

When my garden plots are blooming comes to me great
    satisfaction,
As I dawdle through the forenoon where the standard roses grow,
And a thriving row of cabbages nowadays has more attraction
Than did seats of high and mighty more than thirty years ago.
As I count that clutch of chickens over yonder by the wicket
Each fluffy cheeping morsel brings to me a thrill of joy.
I will spend an hour of leisure where my peas spread like a thicket,
And while hoeing young tomatoes I feel youthful as a boy.

If it's raining in the morning I may lie abed and listen
To the rhythmic splash of water as it trickles from the eaves,
And later, see the raindrops in the sunlight, all aglisten
Where the spiders have been spreading filmy nets amongst the
    leaves.
String may replace a shoelace or a nail a broken button,
I am not ashamed of patches or a threadbare jacket rent.
Give me white bread, good tea with juicy Riverina mutton
And I will be as happy as a king, and more content.

Picking Lemons
Graham Fredriksen

I rode my bike down to the creek
To pick some lemons for my Dad.
It's just like playing hide-and-seek
When there are lemons to be had.

They hide up in the lemon tree –
With thorny branches everywhere.
They are too hard to get for me –
I think that I will leave them there.

I'll tell my Dad if he should seek
To have some lemons on his shelf,
Then he should go down to the creek
To pick the lemons for himself.

The Little Ship

Charles Souter ('Dr Nil')

I sent a little dream-ship a-sailing on the sea.
Her canvas was of mousselline, her hull of ivory,
And all her gilded masts and spars,
And jewelled blocks like tiny stars,
Were flying in the sunset with pennons flying free.

Her rigging was of silk-twist, her decks of polished shell,
And high upon her fo'c'sle head there hung a silver bell.
Her gallant skipper's name was 'Hope',
And every cable, chain and rope,
Was handled by a seaman bold who knew his duty well!

Ambition was the cargo that filled her ample hold;
And as I watched her from the shore, into the west she rolled.
A snow-white wave about her breast,
Into the ribboned sun-lit west,
And vanished in a molten glow of purple, green and gold!

But that was fifty years back; and none know what befell,
Or where now lies my ship of dreams, or sounds her fo'c'sle bell.
My ship and captain, freight and crew,
Have long and long been overdue,
And, haply, gone to 'Davy Jones'? For no man can me tell!

A Vision of Captain Cook

Kenneth Slessor

James Cook tested two chronometers for the Admiralty on his round-the-world voyage; the one made by Arnold gained time while the one made by Kendal lost time.

Two chronometers the captain had,
One by Arnold that ran like mad,
One by Kendal in a walnut case,
Poor devoted creature with a hangdog face.

Arnold always hurried with a crazed click-click
Dancing over Greenwich like a lunatic,
Kendal panted faithfully his watch-dog beat,
Climbing out of Yesterday with sticky little feet.

Arnold choked with appetite to wolf up time,
Madly round the numerals his hands would climb,
His cogs rushed over and his wheels ran miles,
Dragging Captain Cook to the Sandwich Isles.

But Kendal dawdled in the tombstoned past,
With a sentimental prejudice to going fast,
And he thought very often of a haberdasher's door
And a yellow-haired boy who would knock no more.

All through the night-time, clock talked to clock,
In the captain's cabin, tock-tock-tock,
One ticked fast and one ticked slow,
And Time went over them a hundred years ago.

Drinking from My Saucer

Anon

I've never made a fortune and it's probably too late now.
I don't worry about that too much 'cos I'm happy anyhow.
I go along life's highway reaping better than I sowed.
I'm drinking from my saucer, 'cos my cup has overflowed.

Haven't got a lot of money, sometimes the going's tough.
But I've loving ones around me and that makes me rich enough.
So I thank God for his blessings, the mercies He's bestowed.
I'm drinking from my saucer, 'cos my cup has overflowed.

If I have strength and courage when the way grows steep and
　　rough,
I'll not ask for other blessings, I'm already blessed enough.
May I never be too busy to help others bear their load.
And I'll keep drinking from my saucer, 'cos my cup has
　　overflowed.

Blackwattle Bay

JAR McKellar

A timber ship unloaded
Her cargo in the bay,
Log linked to fellow convict log
A floating forest lay.
As idly I looked on them,
The thought occurred to me
That one of these, in course of Time,
My coffin well might be.

I Remember

Anon

I remember the milk from the billy,
With all the rich cream on the top,
When dinner came hot from the oven,
Not from the fridge in the shop.
When kids used their imagination,
And didn't need money for kicks,
And we'd walk to the tram, or the station
To go to the Saturday flicks.
I remember the shop on the corner
Where a penn'orth of lollies was sold,
Were we really so much more contented?
Or is it that I'm getting old?

Grandma's Laundry

Archie Bigg

I remember Grandma's laundry
With a basket made of cane
And lines that stretched from wall to wall
To hang things when it rained.

There used to be a copper
Out where Grandma used to toil
And a stick to lift the clothes out
When the water reached the boil.

There were twin tubs made of concrete
With a wringer in between
A wringer in a laundry now
Is hardly ever seen.

Upon a shelf a little box
Of starch called Silver Star,
Kero tins for buckets –
Remember back that far?

A dipper with a handle
To help our Grandma cope
And a little wire basket
With a piece of Sunlight soap.

She used to have a washboard
For scrubbing out the clothes
You must be getting on in years
If you used one of those.

A saucer on the window sill
With bags of Reckitt's Blue
To make the white clothes whiter still
And good for beestings too.

Some sand soap and a scrub brush
For scrubbing every floor,
Some firewood for the copper
In a box behind the door.

A tin roof and some guttering
With a funny sort of sag
And a heap of wooden dolly pegs
In a homemade hessian bag.

And out the back, a clothes line,
Not the kind that spins around
And a clothes prop held the clothes up
Stopped 'em dragging on the ground.

I wonder what would Grandma say
If only she could see
That wash-a-matic marvel
Where the copper used to be.

The dryer in the corner
The tubs of stainless steel
Hot water pouring from the taps,
I wonder how she'd feel.

I think that Grandma would approve
The changes made, and yet
There were things in Grandma's laundry
That I simply can't forget!

Corroboree
Yungha-dhu (Beryl Philp-Carmichael)

Corroboree, corroboree, which way he goes?
Not like a disco, everybody knows,
Corroboree, corroboree, how can we tell?
With everybody shouting, 'Get to hell!'
Corroboree, corroboree, I must know,
Some tell me quick, others tell me slow,
Do you jump up and down – or bend low?
Round and round in circles – too bloody slow!
I like to shake a leg in a proper way –
Not go to classes – too much to pay,
Corroboree, corroboree, making dust fly,
Shuffle feet aplenty, nearly make you cry;
Corroboree's a story for young and old,
Keep the dance going – don't let it go cold,
Corroboree, corroboree, into the night,
Kicking up the dust till nearly daylight!

Menzies
Jim Haynes

I remember the era, don't you,
When voters to Menzies were true.
Gee, things were stable,
And Australia was able
To doze for a decade or two.

from . . . Same As You
EJ Brady

You may never back the winner, you may never win the maid;
You may never find a nugget, make a fortune out of trade;
But you'll always find your manhood, if you keep the fact in view,
That some other chaps are trying to be honest – same as you.

The Roaring Days

Henry Lawson

The night too quickly passes
And we are growing old,
So let us fill our glasses
And toast the Days of Gold;
When finds of wondrous treasure
Set all the South ablaze,
And you and I were faithful mates
All through the roaring days!

Then stately ships came sailing
From every harbour's mouth,
And sought the land of promise
That beaconed in the South;
Then southward streamed their streamers
And swelled their canvas full
To speed the wildest dreamers
E'er borne in vessel's hull.

Their shining Eldorado,
Beneath the southern skies,
Was day and night for ever
Before their eager eyes.
The brooding bush, awakened,
Was stirred in wild unrest,
And all the year a human stream
Went pouring to the West.

The rough bush roads re-echoed
The bar-room's noisy din,
When troops of stalwart horsemen
Dismounted at the inn.
And oft the hearty greetings
And hearty clasp of hands
Would tell of sudden meetings
Of friends from other lands;
When, puzzled long, the new-chum
Would recognise at last,
Behind a bronzed and bearded skin,
A comrade of the past.

And when the cheery camp-fire
Explored the bush with gleams,
The camping-grounds were crowded
With caravans of teams;
Then home the jests were driven,
And good old songs were sung,
And choruses were given
The strength of heart and lung.
Oh, they were lion-hearted
Who gave our country birth!
Oh, they were of the stoutest sons
From all the lands on earth!

Oft when the camps were dreaming,
And fires began to pale,
Through rugged ranges gleaming
Would come the Royal Mail.
Behind six foaming horses,
And lit by flashing lamps,
Old 'Cobb & Co's', in royal state,
Went dashing past the camps.

Oh, who would paint the goldfield,
And limn the picture right,
As we have often seen it
In early morning's light;
The yellow mounds of mullock
With spots of red and white,
The scattered quartz that glistened
Like diamonds in light;
The azure line of ridges,
The bush of darkest green,
The little homes of calico
That dotted all the scene.

I hear the fall of timber
From distant flats and fells,
The pealing of the anvils
As clear as little bells,
The rattle of the cradle,
The clack of windlass-boles,
The flutter of the crimson flags
Above the golden holes.

Ah, then their hearts were bolder,
And if Dame Fortune frowned
Our swags we'd lightly shoulder
And tramp to other ground.
But golden days are vanished,
And altered is the scene;
The diggings are deserted,
The camping-grounds are green;
The flaunting flag of progress
In the West unfurled,
The mighty bush with iron rails
Is tethered to the world.

The Sixties

Jim Haynes

Let's celebrate the Sixties, the way it was back then.
When surfboards were all twelve foot long – and only owned by
   men.
How do you remember it? Was it all fab and frenzied?
Or did it just seem so much fun 'cos we'd all been Bob Menzied?

The thing about the Sixties, here my memory is strong,
Is that here in Australasia, they lasted so darn long!
In Sydney the Sixties were groovy, they were heavenly.
But they didn't have the Sixties down in Melbourne till the
   seventies.

So you could move around Australia and stay in the Sixties, wow!
(And the Sixties should be in New Zealand any minute now.)
Some people have lived in the Sixties every single day
For forty years, honest . . . they all live near Byron Bay.

Living in the Sixties could be pretty dangerous stuff,
If you managed to survive ten years, that was good enough.
We had love-ins, we had protests, we had concerts in the park,
And we all looked like we'd been dressed by Vinnies – in the dark!

We had Moonwalks, we had James Bond – it all seemed so much
    fun,
We had The Beatles and The Rolling Stones . . . we had the
    Singing Nun.
Were you really groovy? Were you really hip?
Or was a weekend at Katoomba more your kind of Sixties 'trip'?

Well, just in case you missed it, there are re-runs on TV,
Of all those groovy movies we just had to go to see.
And it's funny when you watch them now, and I have watched a
    lot,
'Cos they all seem really boring, some don't even have a plot.

They don't seem innovative now, they don't seem really deep,
I turn on the TV, I tune in, I go to sleep.
They don't seem like the movies that I couldn't wait to see,
Maybe 'cos the thing that's in the sixties now . . . is me.

Summer Sunday

JAR McKellar

When I go down to swimming,
Across the drowsy blue
The swallows will be skimming
Just as they used to do.

And in the paddocks, Cricket
Will make of Church the sin
While lads can build a wicket
Of any rusty tin.

Or marbles, in due season
Make geometric schools,
While those too young for reason
Go puddling in pools.

Tops will be out of fashion
Before they're fairly in –
A week outwore our passion
For button, string, and spin . . .

As I swing down and under
The crest of Randwick's hill,
I'll stop and watch and wonder
If Time is standing still,

And since my thought takes measure
From that first tale of Troy,
The ways lads took their pleasure
When Hector was a boy.

And wish blind Homer told us,
Instead of naming fleets,
How many boys lugged puppies,
Protesting, through the streets.

The Days of Sweet October

John Bernard O'Hara

The days of sweet October
With song and bloom are here,
With forest bowers
Aflame with flowers,
The sweetest of the year;
With low winds lisping in the leaves,
With laughing woodland ways,
With sundowns bright'ning on the eaves
Of sweet October days.

The days of sweet October,
How pleasantly they pass!
Through yellow shrines
The violet twines,
O'er slopes of waving grass;
With dipping oars and vacant mirth
On willowy waterways,
With sundawns bright'ning on the birth
Of sweet October days.

The days of sweet October
Are come with leaf and bird,
With golden wings,
With winnowings
Of woods by wind-waifs stirred,
With winding streams by white moons kissed
To silver waterways,
With sundowns widening tow'rds the West
In sweet October days.

The days of sweet October
Have brought the wild red rose
To fairy falls,
Where echo calls
The sweetest wind that blows;
With elfin lutes in leaves enshrined
By soft, green waterways;
With spirits of the wave and wind,
In sweet October days.

O, days of sweet October!
When blows November's breath,
The forest grieves
With dropping leaves
For Spring's too early death;
Yet, when the shining days have died,
In mourning woodland ways
We miss the march of glad springtide,
The sweet October days.

Sound

Helen Simpson

A length of gut whereon the horsehairs whine,
The tapping of a hammer on a string,
A reed vibrating; these things, more than wine,
Or drugs, or even sleep itself, will bring
Dreams into life, and tears, salter than bitter brine.

Such visions, drawn in sorrow or in mirth
Out of these common, unconsidered toys,
– By breath or finger swiftly brought to birth –
Are proof, in their too evanescent joys,
Of the divinity that dwells in things of earth.

Death Is But Death
Will Dyson

There is no soft beatitude in Death:
Death is but Death;
Nor can I find
Him pale and kind
Who set that endless silence on her breath.
Death is but Death!

There is no hidden comeliness in Grief:
Grief is but Grief;
Nor for thy ill
Canst thou distil
An unguent from the laurel's bitter leaf.
Grief is but Grief!

There is no potent anodyne in tears:
Tears are but Tears;
Nor can the woe
Of green wounds grow
Less green for their salt kindness through the years.
Tears are but Tears!

Encounter
JAR McKellar

When I go out to meet my death
(I would not meet him blind)
I hope that even comes my breath
And that my lips are kind
Lest they by any chance impart
The terror that is in my heart.

Flesh
Mary Fullerton ('E')

I have seen a gum-tree
Scarred by the blaze
Of the pioneer axe,
Mend after long days;
Lip to lip shut
Of the separate bark,
Till the gape of the wound
Was a vanishing mark.

I have seen in the hunt
The pulse of rent flesh;
Seen the fingers of Time
Unite it afresh.
I have heard a man's cry
As the teeth of the mill
Bit marrow and bone –
To hurt, not to kill.

Oh, strong is the flesh
To cure and defend:
'Tis but the stopt heart
That Time cannot mend.

Morla el Do
Archie Bigg

'Morla el Do', in Archie's native Pitcairn/Norfolk tongue, translates as 'tomorrow will do'.

The lawn it needs mowing
But the mower won't start.
The garden's not growing,
It's breaking my heart.
This summer's been dry
But what can I do?
I should fix the mower
But *morla el do*.

The man from the bank
Has been trying to call
But the phone has gone blank
Since it fell off the wall.
My account's in the red
As he tries to get through.
I'd call in today
But *morla el do*.

My car wouldn't start
But there's no need to panic
It needs a new part
'Cos I asked the mechanic.
He said he could fix it,
It's easy to do.
First thing in the morning,
Yeah, *morla el do*.

Sometimes I dream
Of a big lottery win
I'd plan and I'd scheme
With the cash rolling in.
When would I like it?
Well, I'm telling you
I'd like it today
But *morla el do*.

So if you feel tired
And you've still lots to do
And a great lazy feeling
Overtakes you
Why worry today
You'll still get through
Go have a good rest
'Cos *morla el do*.

It's taken a while
But I've learned through the years
Life's full of smiles
And sometimes there's tears.
Here's one simple rule
That will help you get through
What you can't do today
I'm sure *morla el do*.

One Certainty
Bartlett Adamson

Let's live our life in a hearty way,
And taste what joys the fates have sent,
For death is sure to come one day,
And death is so damn permanent . . .

Christmas Eve
Tip Kelaher

The crowds will throng the pavements of the city's streets that
    night.
With the loaded trams a-rattle and the shops a blaze of light.
There'll be merry greetings echoed through the smoke haze in the
    bars;
There'll be frolic and flirtation beneath the summer stars.

And there'll be hoofbeats drumming along the river road,
With perhaps a bright moon swinging through the myalls as a
    goad;
For there isn't time to loiter, Cupid's arrow's on the breeze,
And a little lady waiting down beneath the pepper trees.

I've spent Christmas in the city, I've spent Christmas in the bush,
I've spent it on the beaches with all the surf-club 'push',
And though the climate's chilly and we're pretty short of beer,
You can bet I'll be a starter to enjoy a Christmas here!

But no matter where it finds me I shall think of southern climes,
Of the happiness and laughter of those other Christmas times.
Despite Adolf and Musso we shall see such times once more
When we all come sailing homeward – but first we'll win the war!

If I Could Put the Clock Back

Jack Moses

If I could put the clock back
A score of years or so
I'd seek again my old bush tracks
And pals I used to know.
I'd light once more the yarran sticks
And smoke and yarn with mates
Where the finger-posts are planted
Beyond the city gates.

When Your Pants Begin to Go

Henry Lawson

When you wear a cloudy collar and a shirt that isn't white,
And you cannot sleep for thinking how you'll reach to-morrow
    night,
You may be a man of sorrows, and on speaking terms with Care,
But as yet you're unacquainted with the Demon of Despair;
For I rather think that nothing heaps the trouble on your mind
Like the knowledge that your trousers badly need a patch behind.

I have noticed, when misfortune strikes the hero of the play,
That his clothes are worn and tattered in a most unlikely way;
And the gods applaud and cheer him while he whines and loafs
    around,
And they never seem to notice that his pants are mostly sound;
But, of course, he cannot help it, for our mirth would mock his
    care,
If the ceiling of his trousers showed the patches of repair.

You are none the less a hero if you elevate your chin
When you feel the pavement wearing through the leather, sock,
   and skin;
You are rather more heroic than are ordinary folk
If you scorn to fish for pity under cover of a joke;
You will face the doubtful glances of the people that you know;
But – of course, you're bound to face them when your pants begin
   to go.

If, when flush, you took your pleasure – failed to make a god of
   Pelf,
Some will say that for your troubles you can only thank yourself –
Some will swear you'll die a beggar, but you only laugh at that
While your garments hang together and you wear a decent hat;
You may laugh at their predictions while your soles are wearing low,
But – a man's an awful coward when his pants begin to go.

Though the present and the future may be anything but bright,
It is best to tell the fellows that you're getting on all right.
And a man prefers to say it – 'tis a manly lie to tell,
For the folks may be persuaded that you're doing very well;
But it's hard to be a hero, and it's hard to wear a grin,
When your most important garment is in places very thin.

Get some sympathy and comfort from the chum who knows you
   best,
That your sorrows won't run over the presence of the rest;
There's a chum that you can go to when you feel inclined to whine,
He'll declare your coat is tidy, and he'll say: 'Just look at mine!'
Though you may be patched all over he will say it doesn't show,
And he'll swear it can't be noticed when your pants begin to go.

Brother mine, and of misfortune! times are hard, but do not fret,
Keep your courage up and struggle, and we'll laugh at these things
   yet.
Though there is no corn in Egypt, surely Africa has some –
Keep you smile in working order for the better days to come!
We will often laugh together at the hard times that we know,
And get measured by the tailor when our pants begin to go.

Now the lady of refinement, in the lap of comfort rocked,
Chancing on these rugged verses, will pretend that she is shocked.
Leave her to her smelling-bottle, 'tis the wealthy who decide
That the world should hide its patches 'neath the cruel cloak of
    pride;
And I think there's something noble, and I'll swear there's nothing
    low,
In the pride of Human Nature when its pants begin to go.

Beware the Cuckoo

Ernest G Moll

Beware the cuckoo, though she bring
Authentic tidings of the spring.
And though her voice among the trees
Transport you to the Hebrides!

I saw her come one sunny day,
And pause awhile and fly away,
And I knew where she took her rest
There was a honeyeater's nest.

Later I came again and found
Three dead fledglings on the ground,
And red ants busy in a throng
At throats that had been made for song.

But in the low nest in the tree
The cuckoo chick sat cosily,
And seemed to my unhappy sight
A grey and monstrous appetite.

Beware the cuckoo! By what name
You call her, she is still the same.
And, if you must admire her art,
Keep a wing over your heart.

Wide Spaces

Henry Lawson

When my last long-beer has vanished and the truth is left unsaid;
When each sordid care is banished from my chair and from my bed,
And my common people sadly murmur: ''Arry Lawson dead,'

When the man I was denounces all the things that I was not,
When the true souls stand like granite, while the souls of liars not –
When the quids I gave are counted, and the trays I cadged forgot;

Shall my spirit see the country that it wrote for once again?
Shall it see the old selections, and the common street and lane?
Shall it pass across the Black Soil and across the Red Soil Plain?

Shall it see the gaunt Bushwoman 'slave until she's fit to drop',
For the distant trip to Sydney, all depending on the crop?
Or the twinkling legs of kiddies, running to the lolly-shop?

Shall my spirit see the failures battling west and fighting here?
Shall it see the darkened shanty, or the bar-room dull and drear?
Shall it whisper to the landlord to give Bummer Smith a beer?

Will they let me out of Heaven, or Valhalla, on my own –
Or the Social Halls of Hades (where I shall not be alone) –
Just to bring a breath of comfort to the hells that I have known?

Luck

Dorothea Mackellar

I wasn't born (said the Seventh Son)
Sucking a silver spoon,
But I saw black swans the other night
Flying across the moon,
At dusk, on a rising moon.

I haven't been lucky in love (he said)
Nor picked up a sixpence yet,
But I found the place where the seagulls sleep,
After the sun is set;
White drifts when the sun is set.

Though I missed some concerts and comedies
And balls in the usual way,
I've come on a mother platypus
With her babies out at play,
Velvety twins at play.

I wasn't born (said the Seventh Son)
With a silver spoon to suck,
Nor bowled to church in a limousine,
But my christening brought me luck.
There are several sorts of luck.

Keep the Billy Boiling

Jack Moses

We've cracked our jokes and had our fun
And done our share of toiling:
We hope those mates who follow on
Will keep the billy boiling.

INDEX OF AUTHORS

INDEX OF TITLES

INDEX OF FIRST LINES